VISUAL QUICKSTART GUIDE

iMOVIE 3

FOR MAC OS X

Jeff Carlson

Peachpit Press

Visual QuickStart Guide

iMovie 3 for Mac OS X

Jeff Carlson

Peachpit Press
1249 Eighth Street
Berkeley, CA 94710
(800) 283-9444
(510) 524-2178
(510) 524-2221 (fax)

Find us on the World Wide Web at: www.peachpit.com
To report errors, please send a note to errata@peachpit.com
Peachpit Press is a division of Pearson Education

Editor: Nancy Davis
Production Coordinator: Lisa Brazieal
Composition: Jeff Carlson, Jeff Tolbert
Illustrations: Jeff Tolbert, Jeff Carlson
Cover Design: The Visual Group
Cover Production: Nathalie Valette
Indexer: Caroline Parks

ISBN: 0-321-19397-0

9 8 7 6 5 4 3 2 1

Printed and bound in the United States of America

Dedication:

To Leonard, whose one-month film class at Whitworth instilled in me an appreciation of movies beyond mere popcorn entertainment.

Special Thanks to:

Nancy Davis, for knowing when to ask, "How are you doing?" and making the author's end of producing a book much easier.

Brooke Wheeler, who thought she could escape me this time by moving to England, only to realize that the time difference meant that I wrote while she slept, and she copyedited while I slept.

Caroline Parks, for producing the index in such a way that I didn't have to ask about it or worry about its status. As with the other indexes she's created for me, it just appeared like magic, fully formed and ready to go.

Lisa Brazieal, for helping me get through production challenges, and for riding the motorcycles that I'd probably hurt myself on.

Jeff Tolbert, for updating my embarassing line drawings of computer and video equipment, for creating the lighting renderings in Chapter 4, and for picking up the compositing slack (and watching my back).

Don Sellers, for getting me up to speed with shooting, lighting, sound, composition, and providing a real-world reference.

Michael Uy, Lara Vacante, and **Keri Walker** at Apple, and **Suraya Akbarzad** at Edelman, for answering my questions and providing resources when I needed them.

Glenn Fleishman, David Blatner, Steve Roth, and **Laurence Chen (plus the various long-distance inhabitants) at the Greenwood compound** for being the best reasons to go to the office every day (well, nearly every day). They're good inspiration and reassurance that this freelance thing actually works.

Nancy Aldrich-Ruenzel, Connie Jeung-Mills, Gary-Paul Prince, and even some non-hyphenated folks like **Kim Lombardi, Kate Reber, Marjorie Baer, Mimi Heft, Rebecca Ross,** and **Paula Baker** at Peachpit Press.

And, of course, **Kim Carlson,** who never hesitates to ask, "How can I help?" and keeps me inspired to do what I do each day (and who wrangles a garden into beautiful submission better than anyone I know).

Table of Contents

INTRODUCTION

When I first heard that Apple was planning to extend video editing to "the rest of us," I was dubious. Despite comparisons with desktop publishing, which brought the world of professional printing to even the most inexperienced publisher, video editing was an entirely different beast. Video has traditionally entailed motion, audio, lighting, and special effects, not to mention the costs of buying or renting a good camera, storing the massive video files on tape or on disk, and then outputting them to a handful of other possible formats. Video editing is a skill that people spend years mastering in specialized schools.

But then Apple introduced iMovie, and seeing it in person at a Macworld Expo was a bonafied "a-ha" moment for me and most of the people in attendance. *Of course* this was going to work. When Steve Jobs presented a short video of two children playing, I knew the days of long, choppy, unedited videotape recordings was coming to a close. Not only can you easily—let me repeat that: *easily*—capture video footage and transfer it to your computer, you can now edit out all the bad shots, the awkward moments, and those times when the camera was inadvertently left recording while dangling at your side.

Who Should Read This Book

iMovie 3 for Mac OS X: Visual QuickStart Guide is aimed at the beginning or intermediate videographer who wants to know how to quickly and easily edit movies in iMovie. Perhaps you've just purchased your first camcorder and want to turn your home movies into little masterpieces, but don't have the time or money to invest in a professional video-editing-application. Or maybe you're an old hand at shooting video but new to editing the footage on a computer. Then again, maybe you're a budding Spielberg with scripts in your head and a passion for telling stories on film—the movie business is a tough one to crack, but it's entirely possible that your iMovie-edited film could be the springboard for a career in Hollywood. Or you could also be the owner of a new Macintosh, and want to know why Apple is going to the trouble of giving you a powerful video editing application *for free*.

Since iMovie's introduction, we've seen a boom in digital video editing. Sure, it was possible before, using much more complicated and expensive programs such as Adobe Premiere or After Effects (and you can still take that route). But with iMovie, *anyone* can make a movie. That sounds like the type of hype found in advertisements, I know, but I mean it.

What's New in this Edition

The big news with iMovie 3 is how it integrates with the rest of the iLife suite (iTunes, iPhoto, and iDVD), which is detailed in these pages, plus tips for smoothing the process.

I've also broken out the process of editing still pictures into its own chapter (see Chapter 9), and covered the very welcome changes to editing audio within clips. And, a new Troubleshooting appendix rounds out this cut of the book.

What You Should Know

Every endeavor requires at least some prior knowledge, so I've made some assumptions about your knowledge while writing this book.

- **Macintosh fundamentals.** You need to be able to operate your Mac, which includes launching applications, accessing menus, using the mouse, etc. If you're a complete beginner to the Mac, don't worry: play around on the computer for a little while to get a sense of how things work. You'll pick it up quickly and won't break anything.
- **How to use your camcorder.** Although I'll cover some of the basics, this isn't a book about camcorders. You should know how to record, stop, and review what you've recorded.
- **How to bounce back after screwing up.** It's inevitable that something won't go the way you wanted it to: a clip got deleted, the wrong transition was applied, you spelled your kids' names wrong in the movie title...you know what I'm talking about. The great thing about iMovie is that you can go back and fix or re-create scenes that didn't turn out as you expected. Have fun with it. I insist.

An iMovie Toolbox

A full-size movie crew can be unbelievably large and take up a city block. You probably won't require that much gear, but a few items are necessary to use iMovie.

- **Mac OS X 10.2.** iMovie 3 runs under Apple's now and future operating system, Mac OS X, version 10.2 (Jaguar) or later. You also need a Mac with a PowerPC G3 or G4 processor running at 300 MHz or faster. Apple also says your Mac needs to be equipped with FireWire, but that's not technically true. iMovie will work on a Mac without it, but you lose the capability to directly import footage from your camera.
- **iMovie 3.** If you've purchased a Mac sometime after January 2003, you probably have iMovie 3 already—look in the folder named *Applications*. iMovie 3 is also available as part of the $50 iLife package, which includes iTunes 4, iDVD 3, and iPhoto 2. And, you can download iMovie 3 for free from Apple; see Chapter 6 for more information.
- **A digital camcorder.** This handy and compact device records the raw footage that you will edit in iMovie. If you own a camcorder that's not digital, you can still import video into iMovie using a third-party analog-to-digital converter. That said, I can't stress how much easier it is to work when you have a digital camcorder. See Chapter 7 for details.
- **Lots of hard disk space.** Storage is getting cheaper by the day, which is a good thing. You'll need lots. I don't mean a few hundred megabytes tucked away in a corner of your drive. Realistically, if you don't have at least 10 GB (gigabytes) of storage to use for iMovie, shop for a bigger hard drive. See Chapter 7.

The Moviemaking Process

Creating a movie can be a huge spectrum of experience, but for our purposes I'm going to distill it as follows.

1. **Preproduction.** If you're filming a scripted movie (with actors, sets, dialogue, etc.), be sure you hire the actors, build the sets, write the script, and otherwise prepare to shoot a film. See Appendix B for some resources on where to learn more about the process of getting a movie before the cameras. On the other hand, if you're shooting an event or vacation, preproduction may entail making sure you have a camcorder (see Chapter 1), its batteries are charged, and that you have enough tape available.
2. **Capture footage.** With preproduction out of the way, it's time to actually film your movie. The shooting part is when this book starts to come in handy. Chapters 2 through 5 discuss methods of composing your shots, lighting the scenes, and capturing audio.
3. **Import footage into iMovie.** Your tape is full of raw video waiting to be sculpted by your keen eye and innate sense of drama. The next step is importing it onto your computer and into iMovie. See Chapter 7.
4. **Edit your footage in iMovie.** Before iMovie, average folks had no simple way to edit their footage. The result was endless hours of suffering as relatives were forced to watch every outtake, flubbed shot, and those 10 minutes of walking when you thought the camera was turned off. iMovie changes all that. See Chapters 8 through 13 to see how to edit your video and audio, plus add elements such as transitions, titles, and special effects.

5. **Export video.** The movie is complete, and it's a gem. Now you need to share it with the world. Using the information found in Chapters 14, 15, and 16, you can export the movie onto a videotape, as a QuickTime movie for downloading from the Web, or onto a DVD (using Apple's iDVD software).

What You Can Accomplish by the End of this Book

To say, "Prepare your acceptance speech" would be overextending it a bit, but the truth is that you can theoretically use iMovie to create a feature film, award-winning documentary, or even just the best darn vacation video you've ever seen. As you delve deeper into digital video and nonlinear editing (NLE), you'll realize that more options and more control can be had with more sophisticated (and pricey) systems, such as Final Cut Express and Final Cut Pro. But nothing says you can't do what you want with iMovie.

Stepping out of the clouds, you should easily (there's that word again) be able to shoot, edit, and distribute your movie. In the process, you'll find a new respect for film and video—you can't help it. After using iMovie for a few hours, you'll start watching television with a new eye that picks up aspects like pacing, framing, transitions, and audio that you never may have noticed before.

That's been my experience, and now look at me: I've written two editions of a book about iMovie. And assembled some of the best darn vacation movies you've ever seen.

Part 1
Shooting

1

The Digital Camcorder

My copy of iMovie sat neglected on my hard drive for months because I had no easy way to import video footage. Sure, I could have used an analog-to-digital converter to bring in the contents of some old videotapes I had lying around (see Chapter 7), but it would have been a hassle. What I needed was a digital camcorder.

Digital camcorders weren't much more than proof-of-concept devices only a few years ago, but the rapid advance of technology has made them plentiful today. Although digital camcorders cost more than analog models, you can still get a good quality one these days for less than $800. You can also easily spend $5,000 or more, with plenty of models falling between those ranges.

For the money, you also get a host of features—and gimmicks. If you've not yet purchased a digital camcorder (and I highly recommend you get one to use with iMovie), this chapter will help you decide which combination of features is right for you. Note that I'll give some examples, but won't be recommending any particular model because (like all technology) the field can change pretty quickly. If you already own a camcorder, give this chapter a quick skim to see which features are important and which you should leave turned off.

Buying a Camcorder

If you don't yet own a digital video (DV) camcorder, you need one. Here's a look at the important characteristics of these devices.

Camcorder size

Ah, camcorder envy. You're carrying a new, tiny handheld camcorder, but then you spy someone whose camcorder is even more compact. For those of us who've had to lug shoulder-mounted VHS cameras, the miniaturization of camcorder technology is amazing. Although the majority of digital camcorders aren't super small, they're remarkable nonetheless—many fit into a large pants pocket or small purse (**Figure 1.1**).

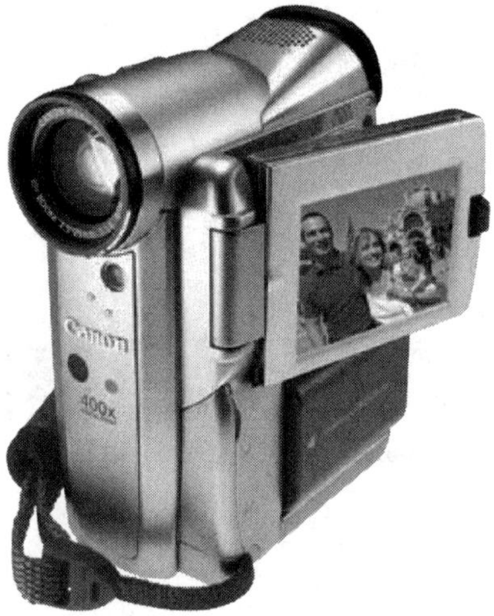

Figure 1.1 Today's digital camcorders are small enough to fit in your palm.

The small sizes are ultra convenient, but have two drawbacks. You're paying a premium for compactness, so expect to shell out more money for a smaller device. Also, a small camcorder that doesn't weigh much can be harder to keep steady when shooting. If you're looking for something portable to use for grabbing footage anywhere and anytime, go as small as you can afford. If you anticipate more staged shots, where a camera can sit on a tripod for hours, size becomes less of an issue.

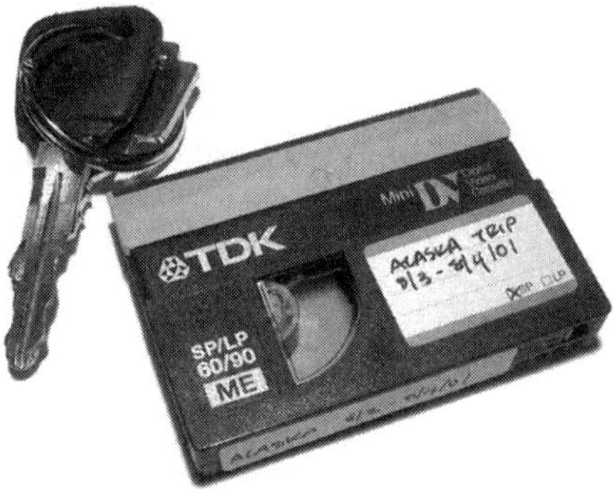

Figure 1.2 As part of the miniaturization of digital camcorders, the tape media is smaller too. But despite the size, MiniDV tapes store roughly one hour of high-quality video.

MiniDV tape format

One of the more daunting tasks related to buying a camcorder is sorting through the different tape formats available, but I'm going to make things easy and say: get a camcorder that uses the MiniDV format. MiniDV tapes are compact, store 100 percent digital information, and record between 60 minutes (at standard playing, or SP, speed) or 90 minutes (at long playing, or LP, speed) of footage (**Figure 1.2**). They're not particularly cheap, but they aren't too expensive either: An online search can find them in bulk for around $5 to $7 per cassette.

Avoid MicroMV Camcorders

It sounds like a great idea: a digital camcorder that really can fit into the palm of your hand, or even into a shirt pocket without stretching the seams. These camcorders are on the market now, but stay away from them for the time being.

What's the catch? Instead of using MiniDV tapes, these new camcorders from Sony and others use *MicroMV* tapes, which are amazingly small. To get a decent amount of data on such small tapes, the MicroMV format uses MPEG compression to shrink the image data, resulting in image quality that isn't as good as MiniDV. And due to the way MicroMV data is stored, whenever you stop recording, the camera takes the last frame and creates a still photo that occupies a few seconds of tape.

Wait, it gets worse. Currently MicroMV only works under Microsoft Windows, and only using special software. So as an iMovie-using Mac owner, there's no easy way to import your footage and edit it.

Is MicroMV a colossal blunder? Not exactly. The format was designed for people who aren't likely to edit their footage on a computer, who want a compact video recorder that can grab a few minutes of action for reviewing later. Some cameras include built-in wireless networking options, so you can shoot a scene, then zap it to a friend using a compatible cellular phone.

Definitely nifty stuff, but in the context of iMovie, it's quite useless. For now, skip MicroMV camcorders.

MiniDV can store roughly 500 horizontal lines of resolution, which means you're capturing more information than other formats (televisions display about 330 lines). It can also record 16-bit audio at 48 kHz, which is slightly better than CD-quality. What's more, MiniDV tapes retain that quality when you record over them, or make copies from other MiniDV tapes. The same can't be said for VHS tapes, which degrade in quality each time you make a copy.

✔ Tips

- Wait...*tape*? Isn't a digital camera supposed to avoid tape altogether? Yes and no. Although the camcorder is capturing footage and storing it digitally, tape is still the dominant—and relatively cheap—medium for storing large quantities of data. In the future, camcorders will probably include small high-density hard disks (like the tiny 30 GB drive used by Apple's current high-end iPod), but for now tape is the best solution. The data is still stored as a series of ones and zeros, resulting in better image quality than other tape formats.
- You can also buy 80-minute MiniDV tapes (which record 80 or 120 minutes of footage), but from what I've read, they can be unreliable due to how thin the tape is (which is what makes it possible to put more tape in the same cartridge size). If the tape breaks while filming, you could be looking at an unwelcome repair bill to clean out the camera's recording heads. Frankly, I haven't wanted to risk damaging my camcorder to find out if 80-minute tapes are worth it.
- If you're going on a trip, stock up on MiniDV tapes. It depends where you're vacationing, but I've found MiniDV tapes hard to come by in most stores. Bring more than you think you'll need.

FireWire/i.Link

As you'll soon discover, digital video data is massive—approximately 3.6 MB *per second* (see Chapter 7). Even a short movie would take forever to transfer from your camcorder to your Mac if it wasn't for the FireWire connection between the two. Also known on Sony camcorders as i.Link, FireWire is necessary to import movies into iMovie (**Figure 1.3**). If the camcorder doesn't include a FireWire port, find another that does.

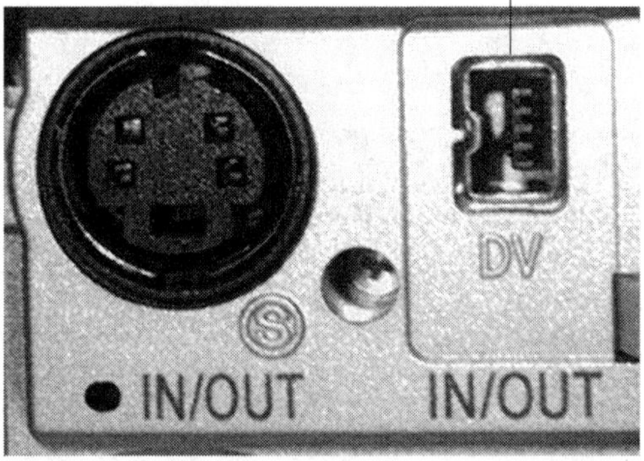

Figure 1.3 The FireWire port on a digital camcorder is smaller than the one on your Mac.

✔ Tip

- Most digital camcorders don't come with a FireWire cable, even though they include a FireWire port. So when you purchase a camera, be sure to also buy a cable that will bridge the two devices (**Figure 1.4**). It will likely be labeled as an IEEE 1394 (the standard on which FireWire is based) cable, and has a smaller plug on one end. Expect to pay around $30 for this essential add-on. (But before you buy, check the packaging that came with your Mac—Apple includes this cable with some models.)

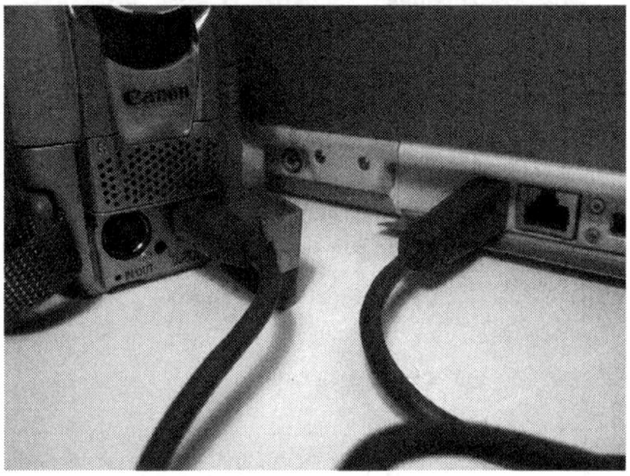

Figure 1.4 Use a high-speed FireWire connection to import your footage into iMovie on your Mac. You may need to purchase a cable like this one, which has both sizes of FireWire plugs.

Number of CCDs

A traditional movie camera records light onto a strip of film as it passes through the lens. In a digital camcorder, the light comes through the lens and is recorded by a charge-coupled device (CCD), containing arrays of thousands or millions of tiny sensors that note what color of light is striking them. When you put the sensors all together, they create the image you see on video. The higher the number of CCDs, the better your image quality is going to be—but it will cost you a pretty penny. Top-of-the-line cameras feature up to three CCDs, while consumer-level devices typically only have one.

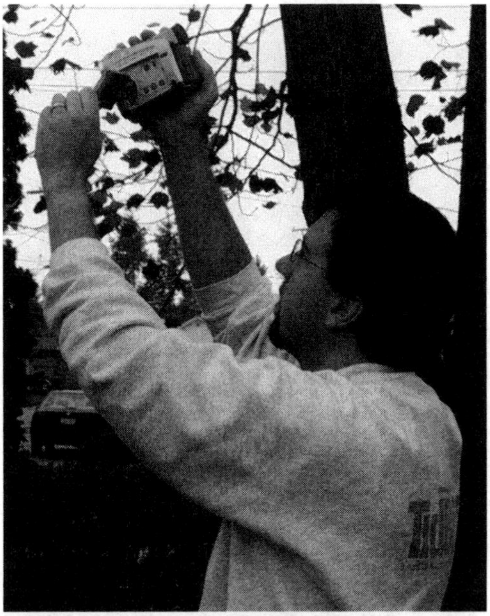

Figure 1.5 An LCD viewfinder gives you the ability to shoot at odd angles by rotating the screen.

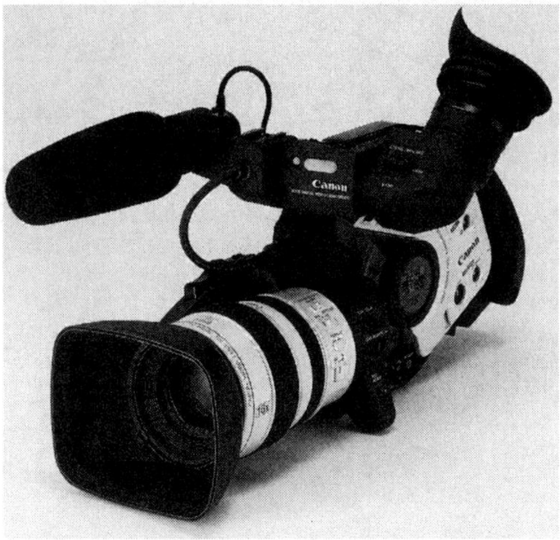

Figure 1.6 Canon's XL1-S is a MiniDV camera with all the trimmings. The microphone is mounted above the unit to record what you're shooting, not the sound of the camera itself.

LCD viewfinder

Most digital camcorders include a liquid crystal display (LCD) viewfinder that pops out from the side of the camera and shows you what the lens sees. LCDs vary in size, from 2.5 inches (diagonal) on up. You can use it in place of the built-in viewfinder, which is often advantageous when you need to hold the camera above your head or near your feet (**Figure 1.5**), or if you're filming yourself and want to make sure your head hasn't slipped out of frame.

The LCD is especially useful when you want to review the footage you've taken, or show some video to a few people looking over your shoulder. And you'll find it invaluable for fast-forwarding to the end of your footage to make sure you don't accidentally shoot over your existing video.

✔ Tip

- Remember that it takes power to light up the LCD's pixels and backlighting. Using it often will drain your camera's batteries faster than using the built-in viewfinder.

Microphone

Every digital camcorder has a microphone, usually built into the body of the camera, but sometimes mounted to the top or front of the camera (**Figure 1.6**). One thing to watch out for is where the microphone is housed: if it's too close to the camcorder's motors, it could pick up the sound of the camera operating (including things like zoom control). Whenever possible, experiment with a few different camcorder models to see what their audio output is like. You can also attach an external microphone to the camera. See Chapter 5 for more information.

Electronic image stabilization

It's likely that I'll spend this entire book saying, "You know what else is great about digital?" So I'll help you get used to it now. Another great thing about a modern digital camcorder is that the software running it can help you stabilize your image and prevent the shaky footage associated with small handheld cameras. To do this, the camcorder uses an outer portion of the total image as reference, then compares movement of objects within the field of view to the outer area (**Figure 1.7**). If most of the image moves together, the software assumes that the whole camera is moving instead of just the objects, and compensates by shifting the active image.

Electronic image stabilization is helpful, but certainly has its drawbacks. It doesn't record the entire screen, so in some cases you may find that objects on the periphery don't wind up in the final footage. It's also not good if you're intentionally moving the camera, such as when you pan or zoom, because the software has to figure out that your motion is deliberate; the end result is sometimes blurry motion that would otherwise be clearer. Still, compared to footage that looks like it was shot during an earthquake, these trade-offs become more acceptable.

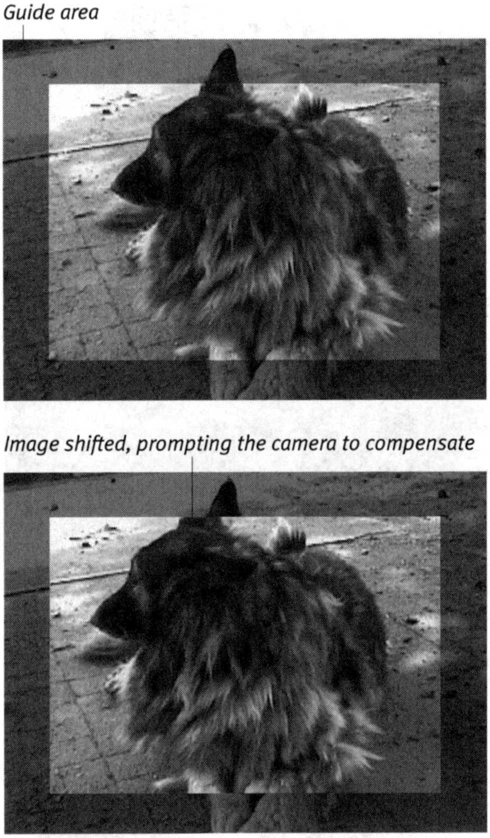

Figure 1.7 In this *massively* simplified diagram, the original image (top) is shifted to the left (bottom) by the camera operator's nervousness around such an obviously vicious animal. The camera compares the image to the pixels in the unrecorded guide area and compensates by shifting the main image to match. (In reality, it doesn't use such a huge guide area—it divides the image into several quadrants and continually compares the guide area to the image area.)

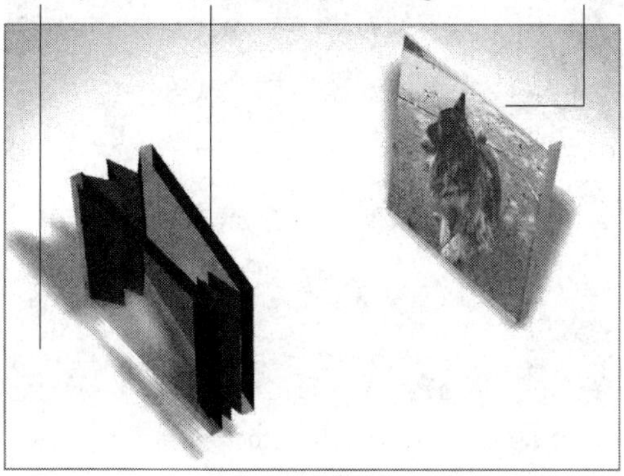

Figure 1.8 An optical image stabilization system uses two lenses to detect light refraction.

Optical image stabilization

Another option for stabilizing your video is to buy a camera with optical image stabilization. Unlike the digital method, optical stabilization uses a prism composed of two lenses with silicon fluid between them. The prism determines whether the light coming into the lens is refracted (think of how a stick poking halfway out of water appears to bend below the water's surface). If it is, the camcorder adjusts the lenses to remove the refraction (**Figure 1.8**). An optical stabilizer can work a bit slower than electronic stabilization—since it's performing mechanical, not digital, adjustments—but tends to be a bit smoother overall.

Lens optics

The camera's lens is your eye to the footage you'll shoot, so optical quality is an important consideration. The lenses in the majority of cameras are of good quality, but more-expensive models tend to feature better optics.

Remote control

It's not like you don't have enough remote controls lying around the house. I thought having a remote control for a camera was a dumb idea until I realized its two main purposes: playing back video when the camera is attached to a television or monitor, and controlling recording when you can't be near the camera (such as when you're in the frame). The remote ended up being more important than I thought.

Features Worth Noting

Electronics manufacturers love to make bulleted lists of features. Some you may never need or want, while others can help you improve the footage you shoot.

Focus

It's a safe bet that you want the subjects in your video to be in focus—but which subjects, and when? Camcorders feature automatic focus control, which is great when you're shooting footage on the fly. Who wants to try to manually focus when following animals in the wild (**Figure 1.9**)?

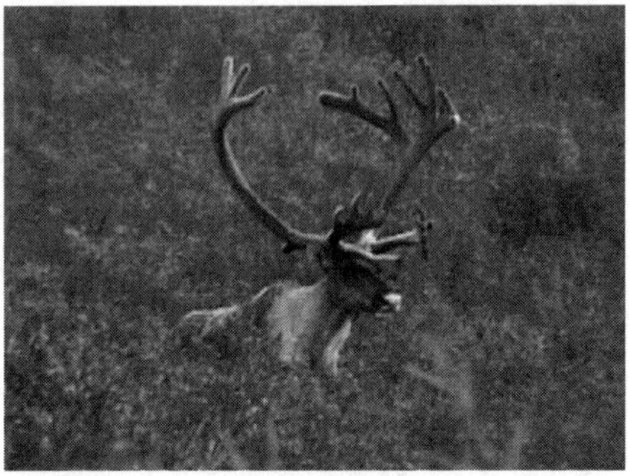

Figure 1.9 Gratuitous vacation footage inserted here. But really, when you're shooting video on the run, trying to manually focus at the same time would have meant losing the shot. You can view this movie clip at this book's companion Web site (`www.necoffee.com/imovievqs`).

However, sometimes the automatic focus can be too good, bringing most objects in a scene into focus—which is why camcorders include an option for manually focusing the lens. (Higher-end models include a focus ring built around the lens, like on a 35mm still camera. Most smaller camcorders sport small dials or scroll wheels to control manual focus.) Manual focus is essential for some situations, such as interviews, when you're not moving the camera (see Chapter 2).

Shutter speed

The term "shutter speed" is a bit misleading here, since a digital camcorder doesn't technically have a shutter (a door or iris that opens quickly to allow light to enter the lens). However, it's possible to duplicate the effects of different shutter speeds by changing the setting on the camera. This is good for filming action with movement that would otherwise appear blurry (such as sporting events). Shutter speed is measured in fractions of a second, so a setting of 1/60 is slower than 1/8000 (see Chapter 2).

Normal

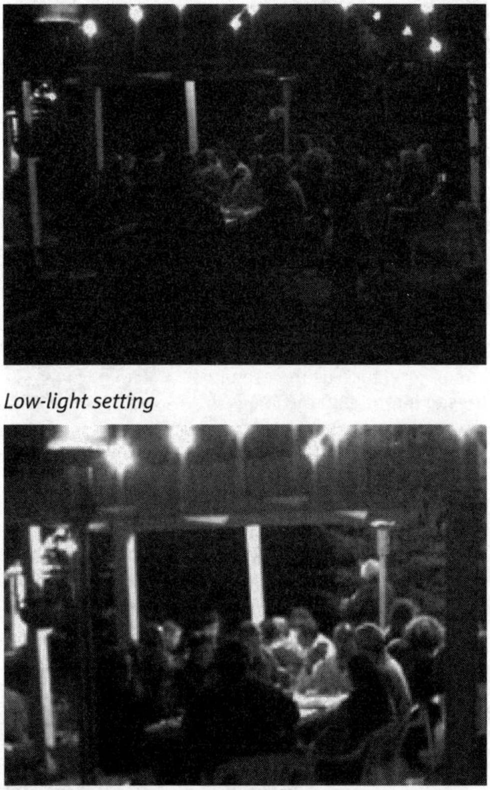

Low-light setting

Figure 1.10 Some camcorders feature a low-light setting, which boosts the effectiveness of the available light.

S-Video port

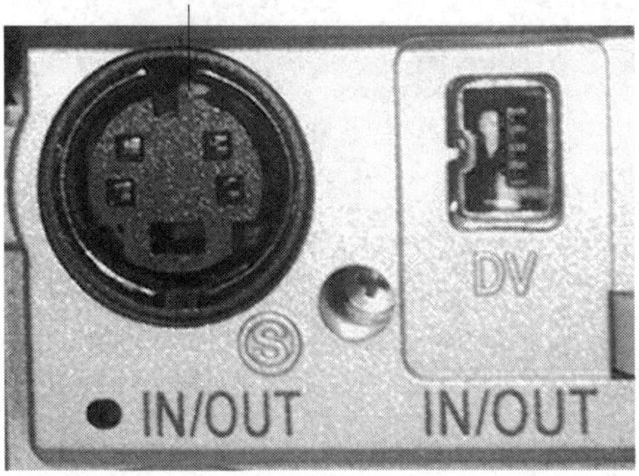

Figure 1.11 An S-Video port offers higher-quality image playback on televisions and monitors.

Night vision/low light

You have a few options for filming in low-light conditions. You could always carry around a full lighting setup, but that's not realistic. To compensate, some cameras include a night-vision mode that picks up heat from objects near the camera and displays a greenish representation of the scene.

Other cameras may include a low-light setting, which boosts the amount of available light that's picked up by the camera's image sensors (**Figure 1.10**). It's surprisingly effective, though the playback can be stuttered or blurry if there's a lot of movement in the scene.

S-Video port

All camcorders offer some type of output port so you can hook up a television or monitor to play back your footage. Usually, RCA-style plugs are included, but some models also offer an S-Video port (**Figure 1.11**). Hooking up your camera to a TV with an S-Video cable gives a clearer picture than with other AV cables. Use it if you've got it.

Features to Ignore/Avoid

Just as there are features you should pay attention to, some features should be ignored or outright avoided. Most of these are included for buyers who don't have the means to edit their movies after shooting. But iMovie does all of the following better than a camera. Most importantly, these effects permanently alter your footage, which you can't correct later in iMovie.

- **Digital zoom.** One of the first features you'll see on a camera is that it has a 200X (or higher) digital zoom. The technical interpretation is that the computer inside the camera digitally enlarges the image it's seeing and appears as if the camera is zoomed beyond its optical capabilities (**Figure 1.12**). The real-world interpretation, at least for now, is that some marketer somewhere is smiling and thinking about the wisdom of P.T. Barnum. Digital zoom isn't pure hokum, but it's also not a mature enough technology to be used in your movies. I expect that as cameras become more powerful and the image processing chips and software speed up (as they inevitably will), digital zoom will become a powerful tool. But not yet.

- **Special effects.** Before iMovie, you couldn't apply "sophisticated" techniques such as fade-in or fade-out without using an expensive professional editing system. So, camcorder makers added the capability to apply fades, wipes, and image distortions such as sepia tones or solarization (**Figure 1.13**). Well, forget special effects entirely—you can do them better in iMovie, with more control, and without degrading your footage.

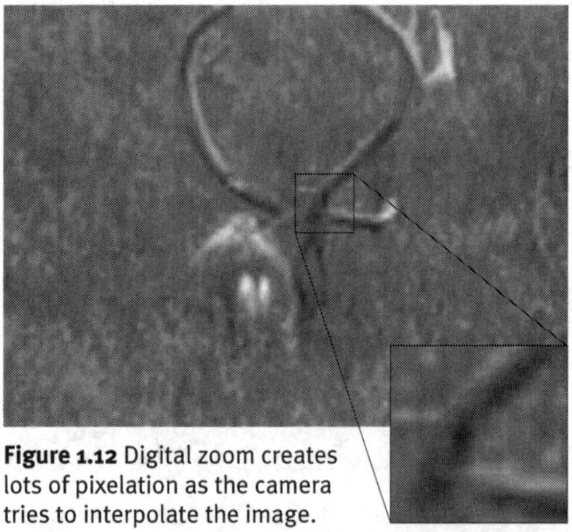

Figure 1.12 Digital zoom creates lots of pixelation as the camera tries to interpolate the image.

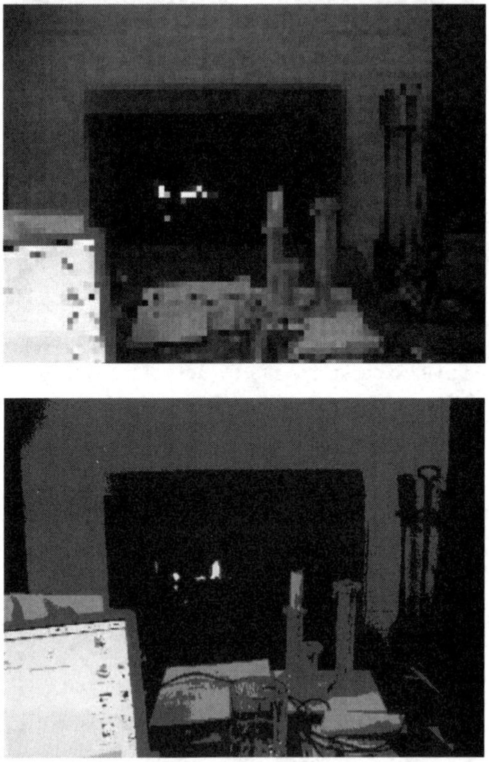

Figure 1.13 In-camera special effects are really only good for ruining otherwise good footage. And not to sound mean, but the Mosaic (top) and Art (bottom) effects shown here aren't even that interesting. Let iMovie handle your effects (see Chapter 13).

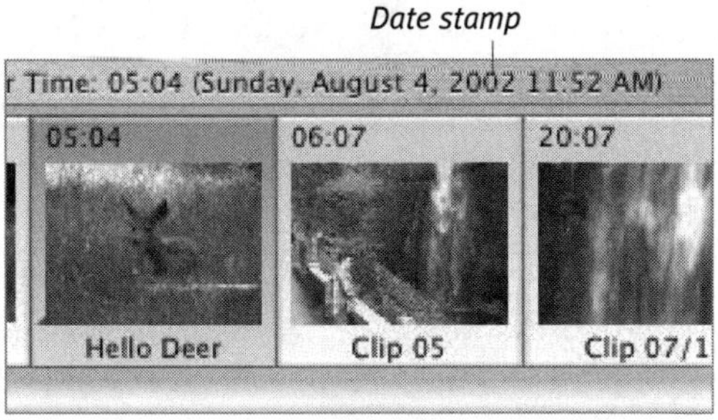

Figure 1.14 iMovie displays the date and time a clip was shot, so you don't need to use a date stamp feature that permanently adds it to the footage.

- **Date stamp.** You can optionally display the date and time on your footage, which would appear to be helpful if not for the fact that the information remains on the tape. Even with this feature disabled, your camcorder is recording (but not displaying) this information, which shows up in iMovie when you select a clip (**Figure 1.14**). Similarly, avoid built-in options for adding titles.
- **Still photo.** Some entry-level camcorders advertise the capability to take still photos, but it's a bit of a ruse. In reality, the camera is taking a still picture and writing it to about five seconds of tape (since it's still recording during that time, you'll get five seconds of audio, even when the image is unchanged). Again, iMovie can do this better without wasting tape by creating a still clip from a single frame of video (see Chapter 8). But another problem is that the photos are stored at video resolution, which is 72 dots per inch (dpi) and interlaced (every other line is displayed on a television screen).

  Check your camera for details. Some cameras now include the capability to capture progressive-scan images—which means every pixel is grabbed—and then save them to a separate memory card (such as MultiMedia Card or Sony Memory Stick cards). These result in better images—about 1 megapixel in quality—but still not as good as what you'd get from a low-end digital still camera. Also, iMovie can't import those still pictures, so you'll end up using something like iPhoto to save them to disk anyway.

2

Composition and Coverage

Camcorder in hand, it's time to start shooting. Where to start? The easiest route is to point the lens at something and start recording. You're bound to get some good footage. However, by learning how to improve your video as you shoot it, you'll end up with better source footage when it's time to edit.

The material in this chapter (and the rest of the chapters in this section of the book) isn't rocket science. If you've grown up watching television or movies (as we all have, to varying degrees), some of it may be too obvious to warrant mentioning. And yet, when it comes time to shoot, it's all too easy to forget the basics and just let the camcorder run—again, perfectly acceptable, but you might kick yourself when you start working with your footage in iMovie. Remember, with iMovie you can edit your clips into a professional-looking movie, but it can't help you improve mediocre source material.

In this chapter, I'll touch upon the basics of getting a shot, and introduce you to some techniques for framing your scenes and shooting plenty of coverage to work with later. Depending on what you're shooting, some or all of this material may apply—you may have control over aspects such as lighting and how the subjects act, or you may be on safari trying to videotape elephants while avoiding getting eaten by lions.

Preproduction

In general, the term *preproduction* refers to everything done before the camera starts rolling. I think it's safe to assume that you know how to operate your camcorder, and you probably know roughly what you want to shoot. The following steps—except for the first one, which I consider essential—are optional, depending on the type of movie you're shooting. (For example, feel free to storyboard your baby's first steps, but she'll ultimately be the one to decide how that scene plays out.)

- **Imagine the End Result.** Before you even turn on your camcorder's power, start with an idea of what type of video you'll end up with. Will it be viewed on a television, movie screen, computer monitor, or maybe a combination of them all? This decision will help you when shooting. For example, if your movie will only appear on the Web, you may want to shoot more close-ups of people, to make sure they're identifiable in a 320 by 160-pixel window on your computer screen. If it's going to be shown on a big-screen television, on the other hand, you could frame your shots with wider vistas or complex background action in the shot.
- **Write the script.** If you're shooting a fictional story, with scenes, sets, actors, and the like, you're going to need a script. Sure, the bigwigs in Hollywood don't always start movies with a script, but you've no doubt seen one of those stinkers and wondered if entire sections of Los Angeles underwent covert lobotomies. A good movie starts with a good script, without exception. Even in the low-budget world of digital video filmmaking, a good script can often overcome bland direction, lighting, staging, acting, sound, etc.

An Afternoon, A Life

Shortly after starting work on this book, I spent an afternoon with a colleague of mine, who also happens to be an Emmy-winning filmmaker, to pick his brain about filmmaking. "Anything in particular?" he asked me.

"Shooting, lighting, sound...," I replied.

He laughed. "Some people spend their entire lives learning just one of those skills."

Filmmaking is an evolutionary art, and involves far more than I can include in this book. I'll cover the basics, but I highly recommend consulting Appendix B for resources on where to learn more about shooting.

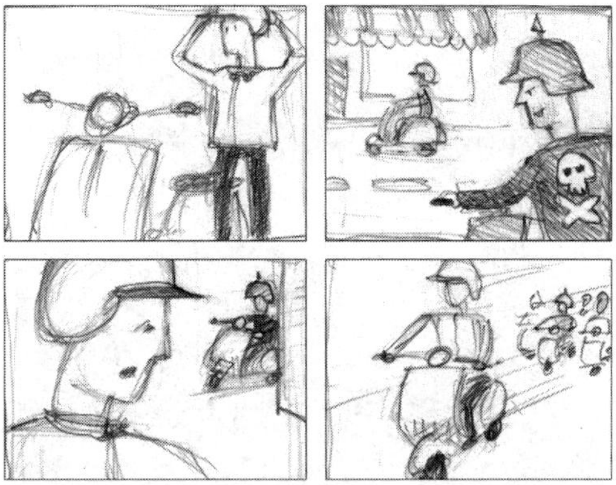

Figure 2.1 Drawing up a storyboard will help you visualize your shots and save time. If you're shooting casually or on the go, create a list of shots you want to try to get.

- **Create storyboards.** Another step in producing a good fictional movie is creating storyboards: shot-by-shot sketches of what you want to shoot (**Figure 2.1**). In fact, you can use storyboards for documentary-style shooting, too. The point of storyboarding is to formulate your idea of what to shoot before you actually shoot; this process will save you time and help ensure that you're capturing all the visuals you want. At the very least, make a list of things you want to shoot, even if you're grabbing vacation video.
- **Prepare your equipment.** Do you have plenty of MiniDV cassettes? Spare batteries (and are they charged)? Lens cleaning cloth? Tripod? "Going to shoot video" can simply mean bringing your body and camcorder; or, it can involve hauling truckloads of equipment. In either case, make sure you have what you'll need to accomplish the job.

Understanding Timecode

As you shoot, you're recording video to the MiniDV tape. If you ever want to find that footage again, you need to understand timecode, the method all camcorders use to label and keep track of footage. You'll use timecode constantly in iMovie, to the point where it becomes as natural as breathing.

As the tape advances, the camcorder notes where footage is being recorded and displays it in the viewfinder or on the LCD screen (**Figure 2.2**). A full timecode notation looks like this:

```
01:42:38:12
```

The interpretation of those numbers is a lot like telling time on a digital clock, except for the last two digits:

```
Hours:Minutes:Seconds:Frames
```

So, our timecode number above is read as 1 hour, 42 minutes, 38 seconds, and 12 frames. Digital video records at 30 frames per second, so the last number starts at :00 and ends at :29.

When you're recording, you typically won't see all of those numbers. More common is something like 0:03:31 (zero hours, 3 minutes, and 31 seconds), because the camera doesn't split out partial seconds (so no frame numbers are shown). In iMovie, however, you can split clips between frames, not just between seconds, so the full number becomes important (see Chapter 8).

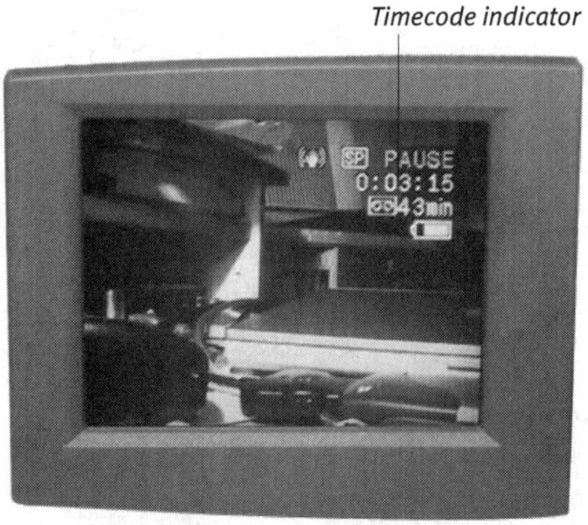

Figure 2.2 The camera assigns a timecode to each frame of film, which is used to manage your footage later in iMovie.

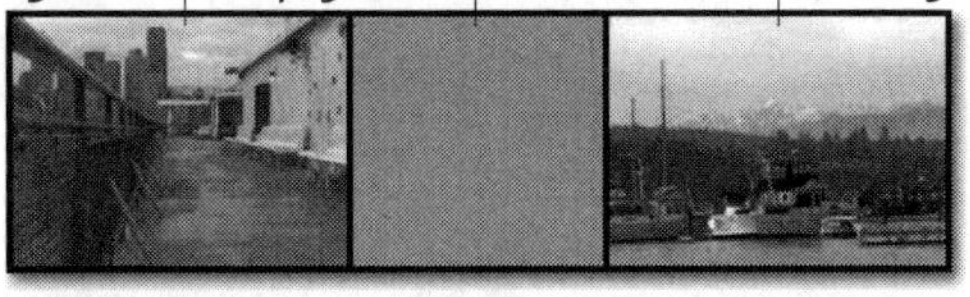

Figure 2.3 Broken timecode occurs when blank tape exists between sections of footage. The camcorder uses the last known timecode marker (in this example, 04:15) to compute the time for later frames. However, the portion of blank tape before the new footage has reset the timecode back to zero (00:00).

I Broke It. So What?

It's not essential that you maintain unbroken timecode throughout your video. Such breaks aren't going to damage your footage, or even confuse iMovie. They will make it more difficult for you to go back and locate specific scenes that you've shot, however. It's far easier to insert your tape and advance to 0:27:18 than to remember that your scene is at 0:02:24 somewhere in the middle of the tape.

Keeping timecode intact

The camcorder's timecode indicator ticks away as you shoot, so in theory you can reach the end of a 60-minute tape with a timecode value of 59:59:29 (or thereabouts; I don't think I've ever actually wrapped up a tape that was exactly 60 minutes in length).

However, depending on how you've been shooting, you may notice that the timecode has started over at zero at some point. If this happens, your timecode is broken.

Before you complain to the manufacturer, look at how you were shooting. If you rewound the tape to review some footage, then started again a few seconds after the end of that clip, you inadvertently broke the timecode. The camera counts forward based on the last timecode recorded. If you move into an area of tape that hasn't been marked with a timecode, the camera doesn't know where to begin counting, and starts over at zero (**Figure 2.3**). Fortunately, there's a way to fix broken timecode as you're shooting—but you'll record over any video recorded after the breaking point.

To fix broken timecode:

1. With your camera in Play (VCR) mode, rewind the tape until you see the last footage with unbroken timecode.
2. Advance the tape until you're about two seconds from the end of that footage.
3. Switch the camcorder to Camera mode and begin recording from that point.

continues on next page

✔ Tips

- iMovie doesn't use timecode to work with the tape in your camera. Most high-end video editing packages let you specify a timecode value and then the program advances or rewinds the tape to that point. In iMovie, that task is up to you. If you have unbroken timecode on your tape, it's a lot easier for you to find the footage you're looking for without having to review every minute.
- Maintaining unbroken timecode means less wear and tear on your camera. When you search by reviewing your footage, the tape is in contact with the playhead inside the camera. A camcorder's life span is based on the number of hours the playhead is used, so repeatedly scanning the video using the fast-forward and rewind features while it's playing contributes to the wear of the playhead. Instead, forward or rewind the cassette without playing it, when the tape is not in contact with the playhead. This doesn't mean you're going to kill the camera by viewing your footage, just that you are helping to speed the process a little.

iMovie Timecode versus Real-World Timecode

Video purists may bristle when I talk about timecode in iMovie, because the concept of timecode in iMovie is a bit different from the timecode used in the industry at large.

For the sake of simplicity, say you import a 5-minute clip into iMovie that appeared halfway through your MiniDV tape, or roughly 00:30:00:00 (zero hours, 30 minutes). When you select that clip in the Shelf, its timecode begins at 00:00:00:00 and ends at 00:05:00:00 (I'm using full-length timecode notation for this example; in iMovie, it appears as 05:00).

In professional editing programs like Final Cut Pro, the timecode for that clip would begin at 00:30:00:00 and end at 00:35:00:00 to reflect precisely where on the tape the clip originates. This is important if the editor needs to recapture an exact section of footage.

However, iMovie was designed for people who don't necessarily need to know exact timecode, which is why iMovie timecode remains relative to the length of the clip.

Take Notes

When you're shooting, you may think you'll remember that the panda bears were located at roughly the 24-minute mark of the tan Panasonic tape, but in reality you'll find yourself scanning through the footage and wishing you'd taken the time to take notes. Get a simple binder and make columns for the tape, timecode, and notes. Then as you're shooting, jot down what you've just filmed. It doesn't have to be complicated, as long as it offers a quick reference to where your scenes occur. Taking notes is also essential when you need to keep track of locations and the names of people who appear in your video.

✔ Tips

- Label your tapes. They add up quickly, tend to look alike, and are guaranteed to fall off your desk in a cluttered heap just before you need to grab the right one in a hurry.
- I hate taking notes, too. With digital video, however, you have an advantage: before or after a shot, simply keep the camera running and speak your details. It won't help you find a clip in the middle of a tape, but it will give you the important details of what was recorded.

Shooting Video Without Disruption

I'm always a little self-conscious when I'm shooting, because often I have to make myself conspicuous in order to get the shot I want. On vacation, this isn't always a problem (my little camcorder is much less intrusive than that other guy's honkin' 35mm lens), but some occasions—for example, weddings—call for discretion. There are a few different approaches to shooting without disruption.

For one, you don't have to shoot with the camera in front of your face. You can rotate the LCD screen and film from your hip (or even shoot behind you). If it's inevitable that your camera is going to be noticeable, don't be rude about it. People will understand if you need to step softly into view for a few seconds to get a shot, then retreat to a neutral location. Depending on the circumstances, try to ingratiate yourself into the scene so the people involved will trust that you won't be obnoxious.

Or, you could take the route of a professional still photographer who was on a recent vacation I took: not only was he taking great pictures, he offered to sell the resulting photos to fellow vacationers. People (at least the ones whom I assume bought the album) no longer seemed to mind so much if he blocked their view.

Composing Your Shots

If you really want to, you can hold the camcorder up in the air and hit record—with your eyes closed. But by putting a small amount of thought into the composition of your shots, you can give them a much more professional look.

Shoot large

I had the opportunity to see a 70mm print of *Lawrence of Arabia* a few years ago on the massive screen at Seattle's Cinerama theater. The movie is filled with sweeping desert vistas where you can see miles in every direction, taking full advantage of a large-screen experience.

Most likely, your video will instead play on a television screen or as a QuickTime movie on a Web page (**Figure 2.4**). For that reason, try to "shoot large"—make sure the subject is large enough in the frame that it's instantly recognizable even on a small screen. Getting closer also reveals more detail than can be seen from a distance.

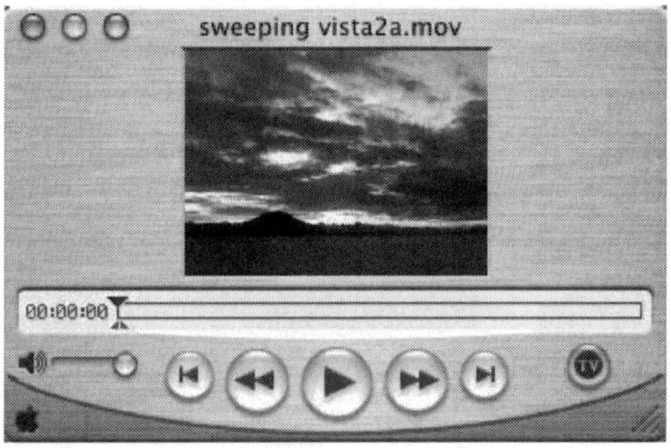

Figure 2.4 Sweeping vistas don't always work in small movie windows, so try to shoot large when you can. Don't abandon wide shots, however. Tape is relatively cheap, so grab the shot when it's available; you can intercut the wider shots later when you're editing in iMovie. See "Coverage" later in this chapter.

Maintain an axis

Most people are fluent enough in the language of film that they aren't thrown by sudden cuts or changes in a scene. But visually crossing an axis tends to freak them out. The idea is this: if you have two people in a scene, and you're switching between close-ups of each one, they should both remain on their own sides of the screen (**Figure 2.5**). If character A is on the left side of the table, but then you move the camera so that he appears on the right side of the *screen*, the viewer is left wondering how he moved so quickly. At the very least, she'll notice that something odd has happened, which distracts her from the movie's content.

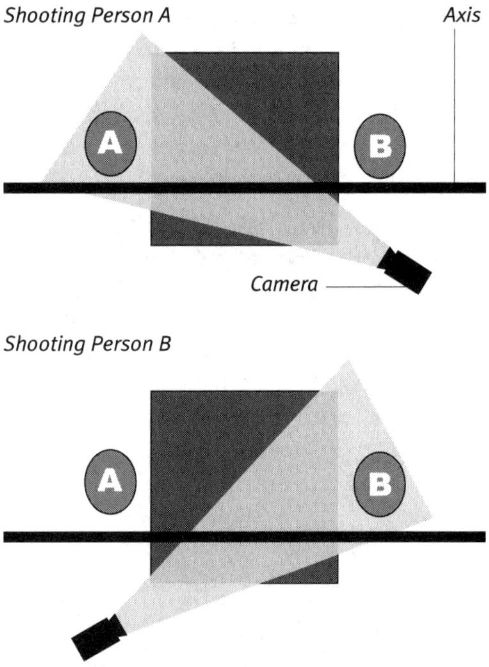

Figure 2.5 Keeping the camera on the same side of your axis line helps the viewer maintain a mental geography of the scene.

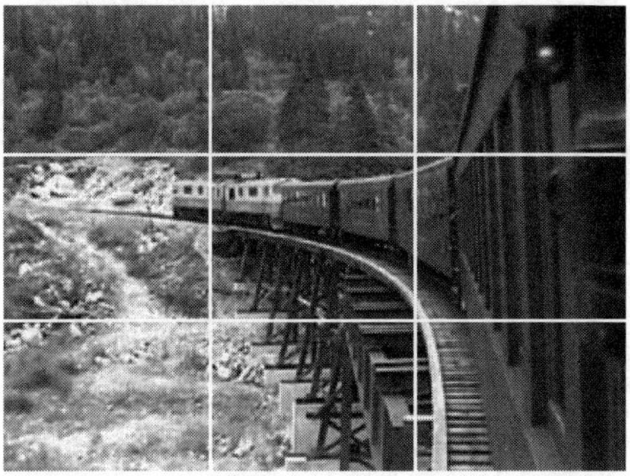

Figure 2.6 The train's engine appears in the first third vertical portion of this shot.

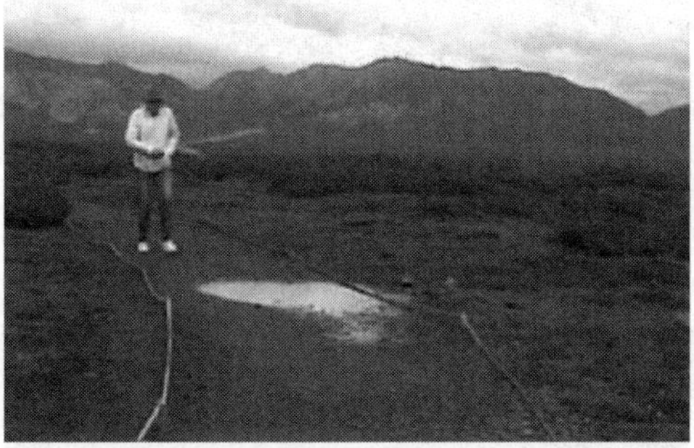

Figure 2.7 When your subject faces toward the middle of the frame, he remains engaged with the rest of the shot, rather than looking outside the frame at something else (which is then where your viewers will want to look).

Balance your shots

As I look through still photos I've taken over the years, I notice an annoying consistency: everything is centered. People, monuments, sunsets—all evenly positioned between the edges of the frame. Perhaps it's just our nature to center objects, but it's a good habit to break. Go watch a movie or television and you'll see that almost nothing is centered.

Positioning elements slightly askew of center makes them more interesting. Another take on this positioning is called the rule of thirds: the focus of your composition should appear one third of the way from the edge of the frame (**Figure 2.6**). Also make sure that the subject is facing into the frame, not toward the outside (**Figure 2.7**).

✔ Tips

- As you're shooting, be aware of everything in your field of view—don't just focus your attention on the subject. If something else is distracting or disturbing elsewhere in the frame, viewers will likely gravitate toward that, and away from your subject.
- Similarly, take your environment into consideration when possible. Because video is interlaced (every other horizontal line on the television screen is displayed), some objects such as window blinds may create distracting patterns onscreen.
- Many cameras today have the capability to shoot in a 16:9 aspect ratio, also known as widescreen mode. On the camera, it looks as if the image has been squished in from the sides, but some video editing programs can interpret the ratio correctly. Unfortunately, iMovie is not one of them. Video shot in 16:9 remains squished in iMovie. Some iMovie plug-in developers offer 16:9 converters, though (see Appendix B).

Focus

Pity the poor UFO watchers of days gone by, with their bulky cameras and—most distressingly—manual focus. It's hard enough to spot a saucer in the sky, but to also keep it in clear focus was a daunting task.

I suspect that today's sky-watchers are thrilled with modern camcorders, if for no other reason than the inclusion of *automatic focus control.* Thanks to millions of calculations processed while shooting, a camcorder can do an amazing job of keeping objects in focus. Sometimes, however, the camera performs its job too well.

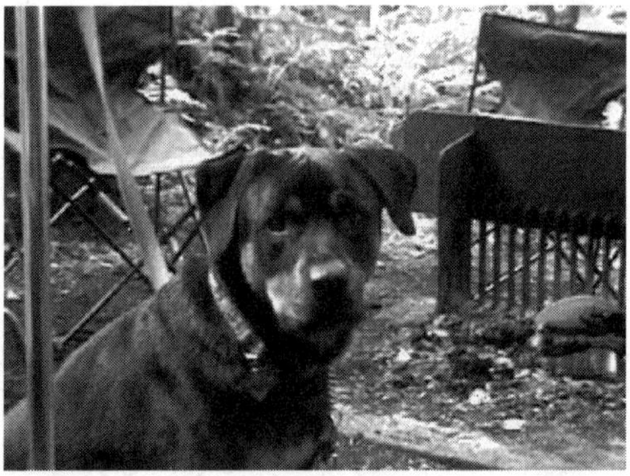

Figure 2.8 Camcorders do a good job of focusing—sometimes too good. In this shot, Greta is competing with the chair and the firepit in the background for the viewer's attention.

Automatic focus versus manual focus

Digital camcorders use automatic focus by default. Although they include some sort of manual focus control (which is often a small dial that's hard to adjust in the middle of shooting), most likely it's not the type of focus ring found on your 35mm still camera. Nonetheless, don't be tempted to let automatic focus dominate your shots.

Auto focus tends to focus everything in view, causing footage to appear hyper-real at times (**Figure 2.8**). Your eyes don't bring everything into focus as you look around, so video that is predominantly focused can be distracting.

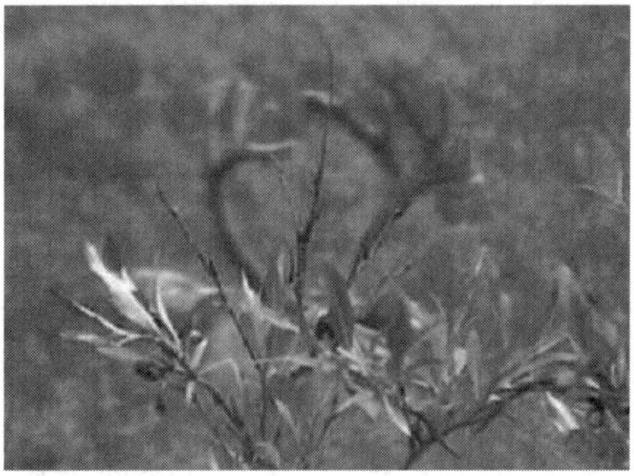

Figure 2.9 Objects in the foreground can throw off your camcorder's automatic focus.

In an ironic twist, automatic focus can actually contribute to blurry images. The camera generally attempts to focus the objects in the foreground (which may appear on the periphery of the image and not be immediately visible to you), but that can throw off the focus in the rest of the shot and leave your subjects blurry (**Figure 2.9**).

If your camera is mostly stationary, experiment with manual focus to make sure the objects you want to be in focus remain in focus.

Figure 2.10 The background is out of focus and lit dimly compared to the foreground, helping to visually separate the two.

Depth of Field

We usually want to keep things in focus, but when everything appears sharp, most scenes begin to look flat. Instead, highlight objects in the foreground by keeping them in focus, and separate them from the background by keeping it soft. When you increase this depth of field, you're more effectively simulating how a viewer's vision works, and subtly influencing what they should see. This works particularly well during interviews or scenes where a character is occupying the frame.

To increase depth of field:

1. Position the camera as far away from your subject as possible.
2. Use the camcorder's zooming controls to zoom in close to the subject.
3. Set the manual focus so that the subject is clear (**Figure 2.10**).

✔ Tip

- If you're shooting a fixed object where the camera won't move (such as a person being interviewed), use manual focus. Sometimes the motion of the person talking (if they move forward slightly when making a point, for example) will trigger the camera to adjust its focus, causing other elements in the frame to "bounce."

Coverage

With some basics under your belt about framing your shots, we come to a bigger question: what shots are needed to create a movie? If you're shooting a family event, you may think the question doesn't apply to you; after all, you shoot whatever happens, right?

Well, shooting the event itself is a good start, but you need more than that. And you need to make sure you have enough *coverage*, the footage that will give you plenty of room to work when you're editing in iMovie.

Shoot to edit

At the beginning of this chapter, I advised you to imagine the end result of your movie before you begin shooting. A similar notion is shooting to edit. In the days before anyone with a Mac could edit their movies, amateur filmmakers shot "in the camera," meaning they structured their shot process so that scenes fell sequentially in the order they would appear when the tape was played—"editing" was done in advance by planning what to shoot.

Now, you're shooting with the knowledge that your raw footage is going to be edited in iMovie. You don't have to shoot things in order, limit yourself to the main subject, or even use footage from the same session.

By way of example, suppose you're filming a family reunion. Immediately following the pick-up basketball game (where Uncle Barney surprised everyone with 32 points and a slam dunk), you shoot a few minutes of a woodpecker perched on a nearby tree. Then you return to the festivities. The woodpecker has nothing to do with the family reunion, so you may not even use it in your final video—or perhaps you'll pop a few seconds of it into the beginning to show what a beautiful, nature-filled location everyone enjoyed.

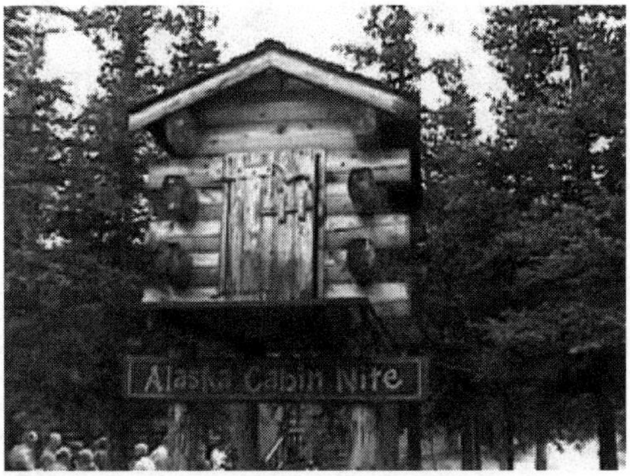

Figure 2.11 An establishing shot gives the viewer a sense of where the scene is beginning, such as this shot of the entrance to a location where the next scenes will occur.

As another example, to round out your movie you want to show the sunset and then fade to black. Unfortunately, the sunset footage you shot wasn't as memorable as you remembered, so instead you grab 20 seconds of sunset footage you took on another location and insert that into your movie. Unless it's painfully obvious that the two locations are different (the presence of a sandy beach where before you were in the middle of a forest, for example), no one will know the difference, and your movie will end stronger. In each example, you had extra footage at your disposal because you were shooting to edit.

Types of coverage

When shooting a feature-length motion picture, a director will use multiple camera setups to shoot as much coverage as possible. So in one scene, the camera may shoot both actors in the frame, each actor from one or more different positions, and various combinations of points of view. The goal is to present a scene in the edited movie where the camera position is integral to the scene's mood or content.

- **Establishing shot.** This is usually an overview shot that's wide enough to let the viewer know the setting and which characters inhabit the scene (**Figure 2.11**). It can be a sign reading "Welcome to Twin Falls," a shot of someone's house, or a shot of a room. The important thing is that the establishing shot provides a physical geography of where objects appear. (This technique is used to great effect in dozens of movies and television shows: you see an establishing shot of the Chicago skyline and assume that the action takes place there, even though the actual filming took place in Vancouver.)

continues on next page

- **Medium shot.** Most shots end up as variations of medium shots. Generally, this shot is large enough to frame two or three people's torsos, although it can vary between a shot of a single person or half of a room (**Figure 2.12**).

- **Close-up.** The screen is filled with part of a person or object (**Figure 2.13**). Close-ups usually show a person's head and shoulders, but can also push in closer (known as an extreme close-up) so you see only the person's eyes. Other examples of close-ups include shots of a person's hands, or any object that occupies the entire frame.

- **Cut-away shots.** Sometimes referred to as B-roll footage, cut-aways are shots of associated objects or scenes that aren't necessarily part of the central action in a scene. An example would be the view from a ship traveling through a passage, which cuts away to a shot of the darkening sky, then returns to the ship safely emerging from the passage. The woodpecker footage mentioned in the family reunion example earlier could easily be used as a cut-away shot.

- **In points and out points.** If possible, give yourself some shots that can be used to enter or exit a scene, sometimes known as in points and out points. For example, if you're shooting an interview and your subject has just declared his intention to walk on Mars, don't immediately stop recording. Hold the camera on him as he finishes speaking, then perhaps pan down to his desk where a model of his rocket ship is mounted.

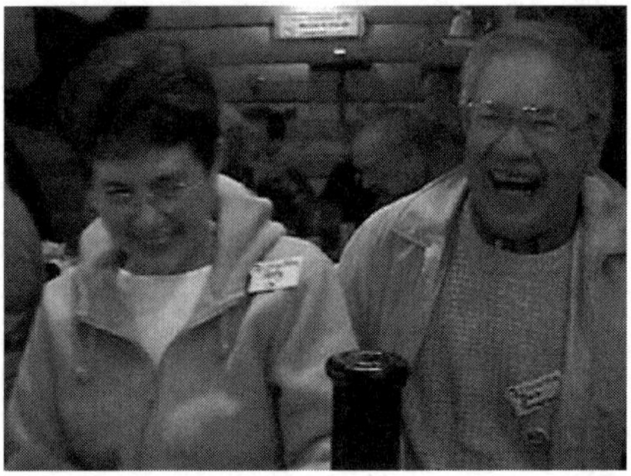

Figure 2.12 A medium shot is typically close enough to include two or three people.

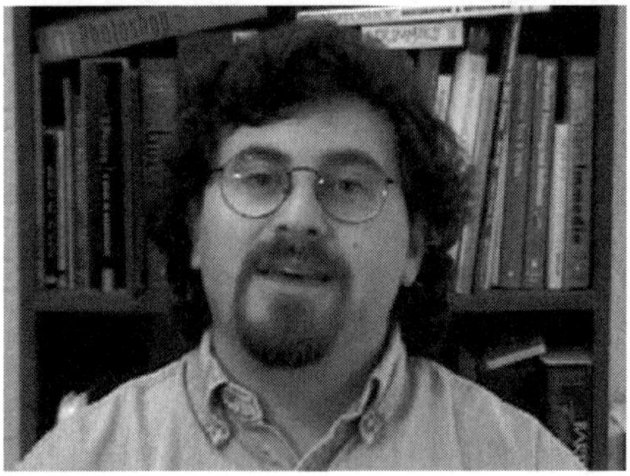

Figure 2.13 A close-up focuses on one person or object that occupies most of the frame.

✔ Tips

- Linger on shots when you can. It's far easier to cut footage out than to add it back in later (especially if it's vacation footage or something similar...unless you *really* need to rationalize a trip back!).
- How long should you hold on to a shot? First of all, don't automatically shut off the camcorder right when the action has stopped. Linger for a few seconds or minutes to let the emotion of a scene dissipate. This is true when you're doing interviews or shooting wildlife. You can always trim it later in iMovie.
- Here's a tip I came across while on a soggy camping trip. When shooting in poor weather, you'll need to protect your gear. You can buy hoods and covers and other accessories, which are fine but add bulk. Instead, I have a fleece vest that I use to cover the camera: the lens points through one arm hole, protecting it from the rain but still giving enough room to operate the camera.

The Camera in Motion

3

My digital camcorder is small enough that I can take it almost anywhere. While we're driving to work, my wife will occasionally grab the camera out of my bag and start shooting anything that catches her eye: a brilliant sunrise, the way Seattle's skyline materializes on a foggy morning, rows of orange-tipped trees alongside the freeway in the Fall. Although we initially bought the camera to take with us on vacation, it has turned into an unofficial chronicler of our lives.

One of the advantages of a small camera is that it easily moves with you. However, when you're shooting, motion can become a character in its own right. Slowly moving across a scene imparts a different feeling than quickly scanning your surroundings, for example. This chapter addresses the most common ways of moving the camera to add motion to your movie, including the number one rule: don't move.

Don't Move

It's time to go watch TV again (hey, this moviemaking stuff is easy!). Turn to a scripted dramatic show and note how often the camera moves. I don't mean how often the *camera is moved*, which provides different angles of the same scene, but how often the camera is actually moving—not much. When it does move, such as when following a character through a set (*The West Wing* often uses this technique when transitioning between scenes), the movement is smooth and measured.

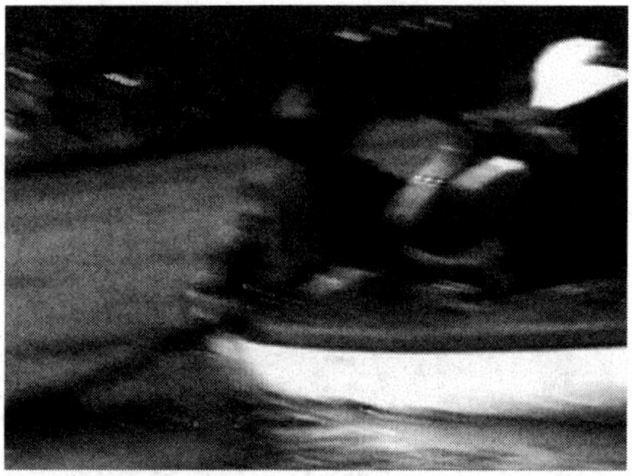

Figure 3.1 Sudden camera moves introduce blurriness to your footage. Try to keep the camera stationary for most of your shots, if possible.

As much as possible, limit your camera's movement. You want action that emotionally affects the viewer, which is more likely to happen when the camera is stationary and focused on the contents of a scene. A shot that's bouncing, zooming, or otherwise sloshing about like a drunk at happy hour is a scene where the movement is distracting from the action. Of course, there are times when motion is called for: can you imagine reality-television shows like *COPS* or *ER* using stationary cameras? I imagine it's difficult enough to chase a suspected criminal down a dark alley and over a chain-link fence without asking him to pause for a few minutes while the crew sets up its lights and tripods.

Staying still has another practical benefit: excess movement causes blurring in your images (**Figure 3.1**). Our eyes do a good job of pulling detail out of motion blur, but there's a limit to how often they can tolerate fuzzy swabs of color streaking across the screen.

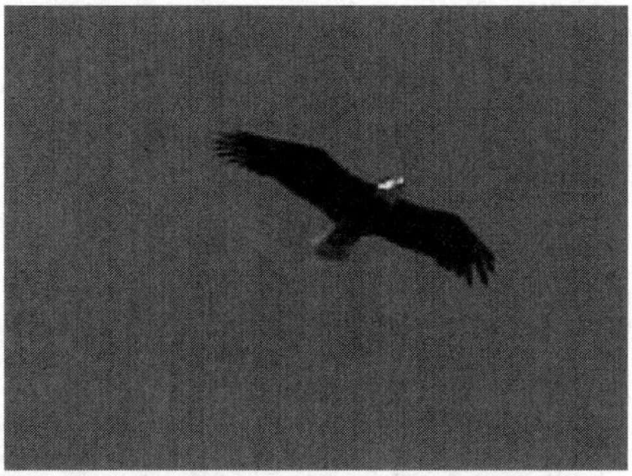

Figure 3.2 Optical zoom and automatic focus can be a great combination when you're shooting something from far away.

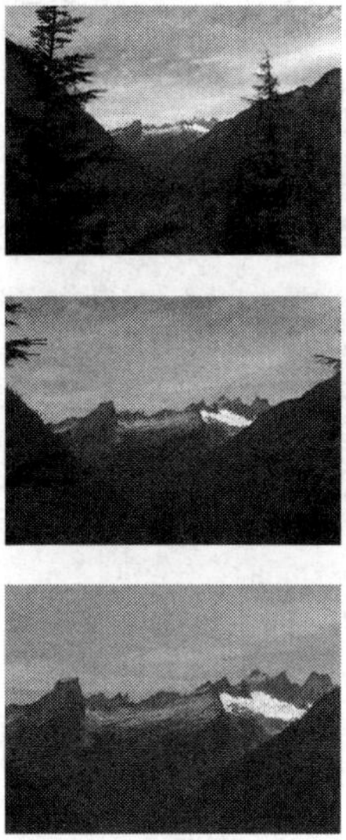

Start with the camera zoomed out...

...and slowly zoom in...

...then hold on the zoomed-in image before slowly zooming back out.

Figure 3.3 Quick zooms in and out are effective ways to instill headaches in your viewers. Instead, slowly zoom in, hold, then slowly zoom out. This technique gives you good, clear footage at several distances.

Zooming

Now that I've lectured on the evils of moving your camera, let's get into the realities of the types of motion you'll encounter. To start, let's look at one of the most common trouble-makers, the zoom control.

When you bought your camera, the first thing you probably did was play with the zoom control. It's usually a rocker switch that moves between W (wide) and T (telephoto), and enables you to view distant objects. Combined with a camera's automatic focus feature, especially when shooting in the field, zooming can get you closer to your subject (**Figure 3.2**).

However, the control can be sensitive, leading to abrupt or too-quick zooms in and out. A better approach is to smoothly zoom in on your subject, hold for a bit, then slowly zoom out (**Figure 3.3**). Practice with the control to get a feel for how much pressure is needed, and try to run through the shot a few times before you actually record it.

✔ Tips

- If you missed the memo in Chapter 1: turn off the digital zoom feature of your camera. The camera tries to enlarge the pixels, thereby appearing to zoom beyond its optical limit. All you really end up with is large blocky pixels.
- Sometimes you want an abrupt zoom, either because it enhances the action or because you don't have time to shoot, stop recording, zoom in, then begin recording again. In the latter case, zoom quickly and hold onto the shot—you can edit out the actual zoom later in iMovie.
- A good zoom is handy when you're not recording. If you're not toting a pair of binoculars, your camcorder will help you see objects in the distance.

Dollying

Dollying is similar to zooming, in that the camera moves in toward (or away from) a subject. However, a dolly shot doesn't use the zoom control at all. In feature film shoots, a dolly is a platform that holds the camera and rides on rails similar to railroad tracks. When filming, one or more people (known as grips) push the dolly, resulting in a smooth shot.

When you zoom, the camcorder's lens is simulating the appearance of moving closer to your subject. When dollying, you're actually moving the camera closer. The difference is especially pronounced in the background, which appears different depending on the method you use (**Figure 3.4**).

✔ Tips

- As with zooming, you want to ease in and out of a dolly shot. Grips aren't just people who push equipment around. A good grip can accelerate and decelerate smoothly and, often more importantly, *consistently* during multiple takes.
- A dolly shot is a professional-looking camera move, but it's likely you don't have a dolly setup or want to spend the money to rent one. But you can use a number of alternative dollies. Wheelchairs are great (and comfortable!), and skateboards also work in a pinch. It doesn't matter so much how you get the shot, only that the shot turns out the way you want it.

Zoomed in

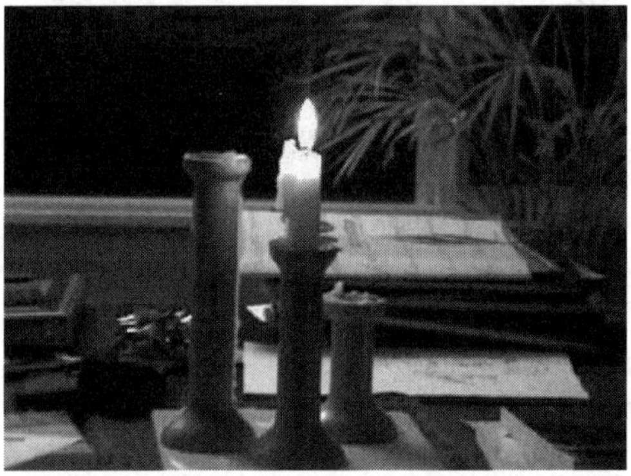

Pushed in on dolly, no zoom

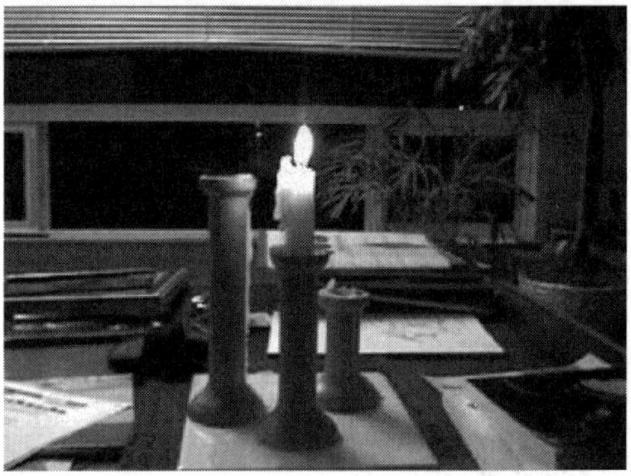

Figure 3.4 These two shots are similarly framed, but look at the plant in the background to see how the two approaches differ.

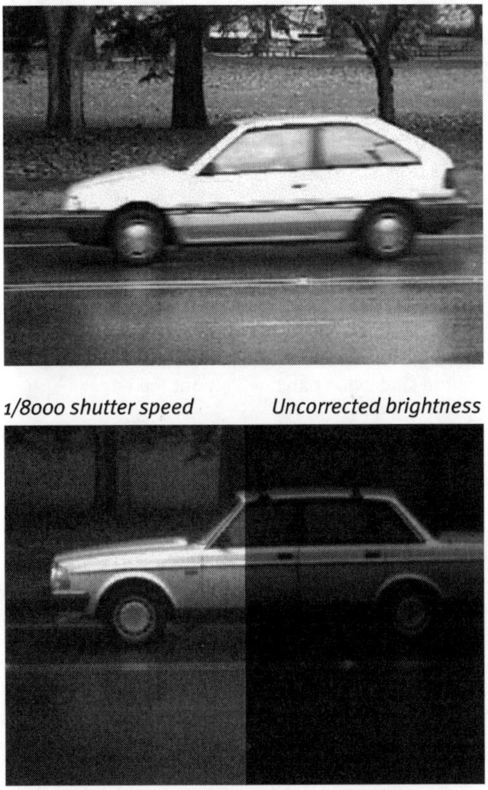

Figure 3.5 Higher shutter speeds can make fast-moving objects appear clearer. However, it also requires more light—I had to boost the brightness of the bottom image in an image editor to make it easier to see (the original is on the right).

Changing Shutter Speed

Your camcorder doesn't have a shutter in the traditional sense. There's no little door that opens and closes quickly to control the amount of light that gets through the lens. However, camcorders can simulate shutter speed by controlling how quickly the CCD sensors refresh the image being recorded, which is measured in times per second. A normal shutter speed is approximately 1/60th of a second, meaning the CCD samples an image 60 times per second.

Why change shutter speed? Using a higher setting is good for capturing fast-moving action like sporting events. The blur caused by moving objects is substantially reduced at speeds of 1/4000 or 1/8000, creating frames that contain very little blurring (**Figure 3.5**). You'll need to experiment with your camera's settings, though; a high shutter speed can also make the image appear to strobe, or flash artificially.

✔ Tips

- Faster shutter speeds require more light. If you think of a traditional shutter, not as much light enters the camera when the shutter is closing more times per second. So a dimly lit room can appear even darker at a high shutter speed.
- Your camcorder is probably changing shutter speeds without your knowledge. On Auto setting, it detects what kind of light is present, and if it detects fluorescent lighting—which flickers imperceptibly to our eyes, but can cause havoc on a digital recording—the shutter speed automatically changes to compensate.

Panning

Film has the great advantage of width: its wider aspect ratio captures landscape images in a way your video camcorder can only dream about. However, you can pivot the camera left or right to shoot that landscape and not disrupt the scene with too much motion. This side-to-side movement is called panning, and is a common tool in a director's box of shots. A similar shot, tilting, moves the camera up and down, though it's not used as frequently.

To pan a scene:

1. Set your camera up on a tripod for best results, or hold it as steady as you can.
2. Determine where the pan will begin and end.
3. Begin recording at the first point, and pivot the camera left or right at an even pace. If your camera is not mounted on a tripod, swivel your body steadily at the hips.
4. When you reach the end point of your pan, stop recording.

Pan ahead of subjects

A panning shot often follows a subject from one side of the screen to the other, but think of your composition as you do this. Don't just center the subject in the frame. Instead, provide space into which the person can walk by panning ahead of him (**Figure 3.6**).

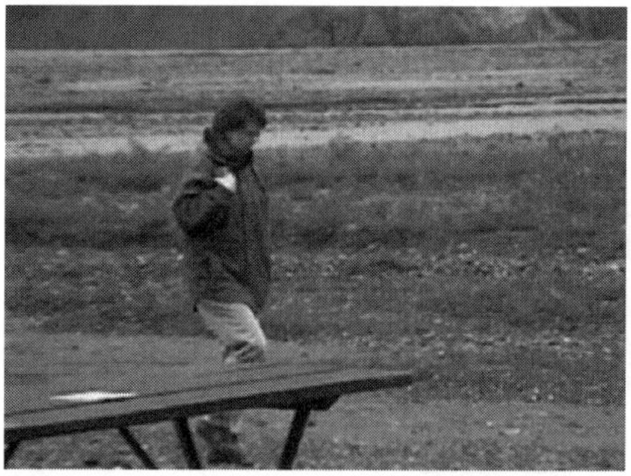

Figure 3.6 Frame your shots so that subjects walk into the shot when panning, not out the edges.

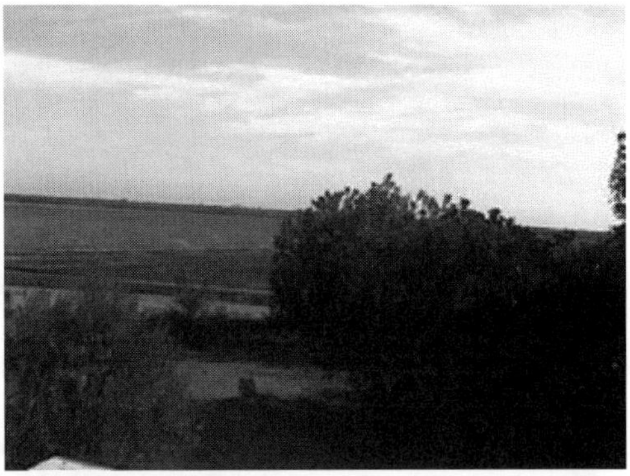

Figure 3.7 It's either you or the camera—the world just doesn't naturally tip like that.

✔ Tips

- To help stabilize the camera while you're holding it, pull your elbows in close to your body, hold the camera with both hands, and keep a wide stance.
- If you're using a tripod, be sure to get a fluid-head tripod. It's more expensive than your standard unit, but allows for much smoother motion.
- As it turns out, the biggest problem with panning isn't moving the camera smoothly. Your top concern should be: is the horizon level? If the camera isn't exactly even with the horizon, panning will give the effect of moving uphill or downhill (**Figure 3.7**).
- Panning doesn't have to involve rotating the camera around a central axis. Use a dolly setup (see "Dollying," earlier) to move the camera from side to side.

4

Lighting

Unless you plan to shoot with the lens cap on, you'll have to come to grips with lighting in your videos. Put simply, you want to have enough light to see what's being filmed, but not so much that it blows out the camcorder's sensors with pure white. You also don't want scenes that are so dark you can't see what's going on.

When a Hollywood film crew shoots a movie, the lighting you see is enhanced (or outright artificial—even the most natural-looking sunlight coming through a window is likely a big spotlight on the other side of the wall). You don't need to go to those extremes, of course. Most often your lighting rigs will entail the sun, some lamps, and maybe a spotlight or two.

What's important is that you know how basic lighting works, and how to take advantage of it to ensure that the objects you're shooting don't turn out to be dark talking blobs when you're editing.

Hard and Soft Light

There are infinite possible combinations of light, which can seem daunting when you're shooting video. Fortunately, for our purposes we can break light down into two broad categories: hard and soft.

- **Hard light.** The term hard light refers to the light produced by a direct source, which creates shadows with clearly defined edges (**Figure 4.1**). Hard light tends to be bright, like the sun at midday.
- **Soft light.** In contrast, soft light isn't as direct, and produces shadows that are blurred at the edges or fade away (**Figure 4.2**). Soft light is typically light that's filtered by artificial means (such as hoods and filters attached to the light) or by natural means (such as clouds, fog, or shade).

In general, soft light is better to film by, because it gives you more levels of brightness and accentuates natural textures. Hard light creates a lot of contrast, limiting the brightness levels because you see either high-intensity light or deep, dark shadows.

✔ Tip

- If lighting is particularly important to a scene, add a video monitor to your list of equipment to bring on a video shoot. Although your camcorder offers a viewfinder and an LCD, you won't know how the image will look on a TV screen until you see it projected on a monitor. The camera's LCD is great for viewing the content you're capturing, but LCDs can often display images brighter than they're being recorded; or, if you're outside, the LCD's pixels can get washed out by the sunlight.

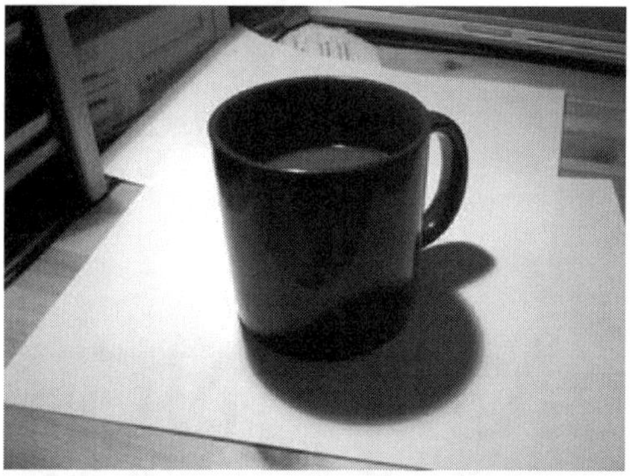

Figure 4.1 Hard light creates sharp, clearly defined shadows. A bright halogen lamp is providing the light.

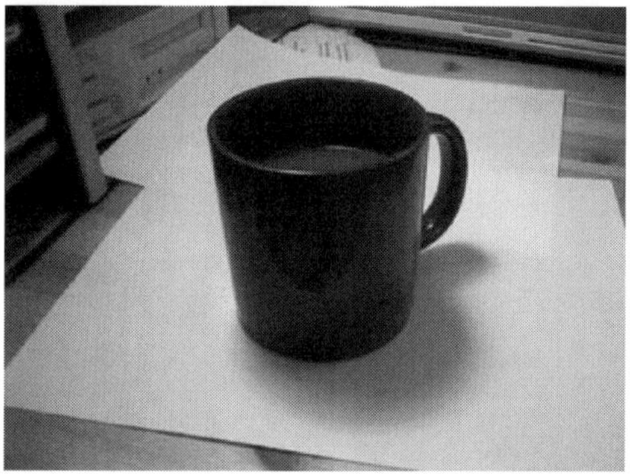

Figure 4.2 Soft light diffuses the shadows, making them blurry or even fade out gradually. In this case, a white t-shirt was put in front of the halogen bulb to dampen its intensity. (Hey, we're real high-tech at the Carlson world headquarters.)

White balance, indoors

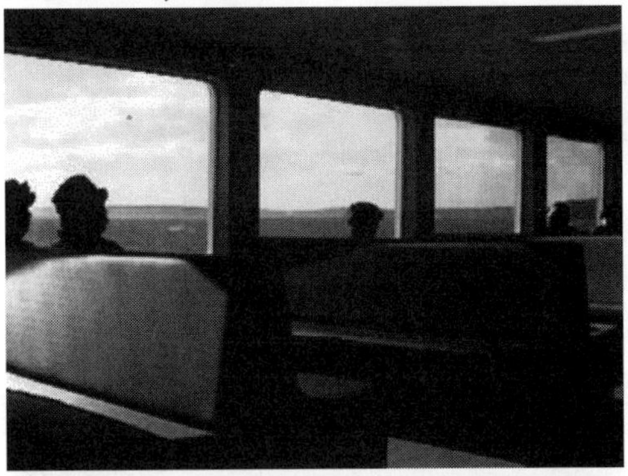

White balance, outdoors

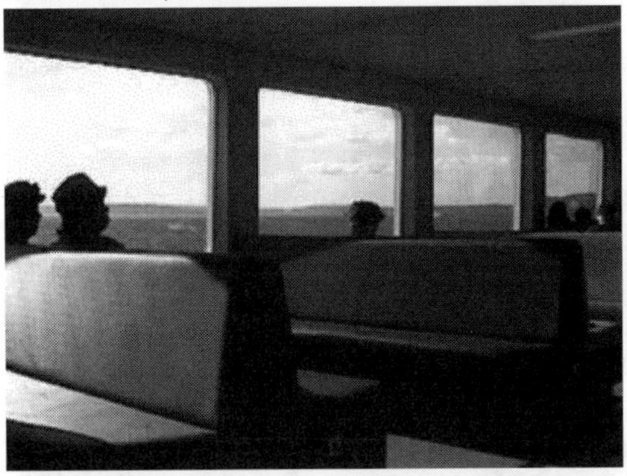

Figure 4.3 Many camcorders feature the capability to adjust the color temperature it displays. It's difficult to tell from these black-and-white images, but the top picture has a blue cast, while the bottom picture appears a warmer red. (You can see these frames in color at `www.necoffee.com/imovievqs/`.)

Color Temperature

White light is a combination of all the colors of the spectrum, as you've seen when playing with a prism or looking at a rainbow. As such, it's not going to always be white while you're filming—a myriad of factors can make images appear with a colored cast, leading to video footage that looks a little too green, or blue, or any number of shifts.

Your camcorder automatically adjusts to compensate for this *color temperature* of the light by setting the white balance. Essentially, this is the color that the camera sees as white, causing the camera to adjust the display of the rest of the colors based on this setting. You probably have a few basic controls for changing the setting, such as Auto, Indoor, or Outdoor presets (**Figure 4.3**).

You may also be able to manually specify the white point by selecting Manual and filming a sheet of white paper in the environment where you'll be shooting; the camera will use the values it captured as the basis for the other colors.

Three-Point Lighting

If you have more control over the way your scene is lit, try to use a basic three-point lighting setup. This allows for plenty of light to illuminate the scene, while also reducing deep shadows. A three-point setup consists of a key light, a fill light, and a back light (**Figure 4.4**).

The key light is the primary light source in your scene, and usually the brightest. The fill light is softer, filling in the shadows and adding texture, and is often dimmer than the key light to avoid washing out the image and flattening it. The back light is often small, focused, and used to help separate the scene's subject from the background.

As an easy example, let's say you're setting up to shoot an interview (**Figure 4.5**). Remember this is just a basic configuration—you can position the lights any way you choose.

To set up three-point lighting:

1. With the camera facing the interview subject, position the key light to the right and slightly forward of the camera. Raise the light so that it's at a 35- to 45-degree angle pointing down at the subject.
2. Position the fill light to the left of the camera and subject, approximately halfway between the two. The fill prevents deep shadows caused by the key.
3. Place the back light behind the subject, raised a bit higher than the key light, and aimed so that it illuminates the back of the subject's head and shoulders.

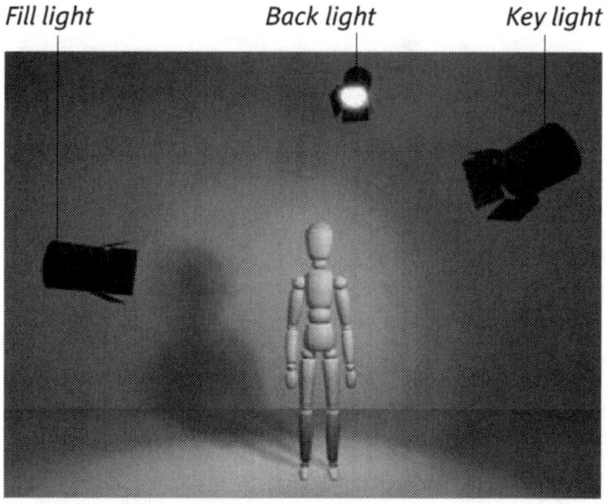

Figure 4.4 A basic lighting setup involves three lights, though of course you can use more (or less).

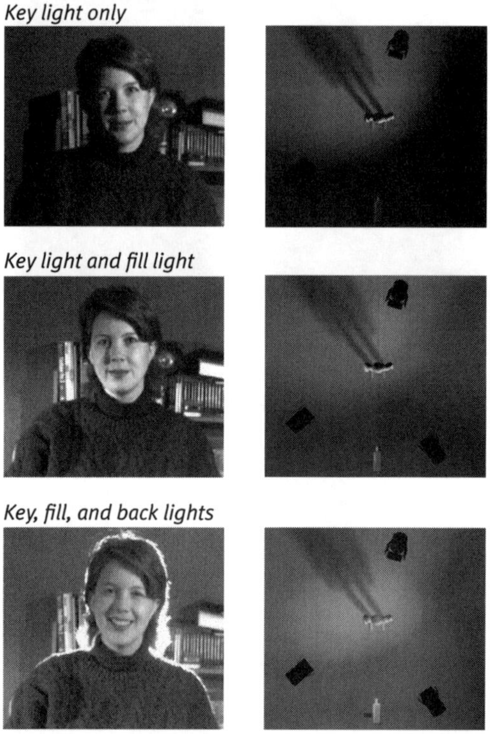

Figure 4.5 You could use just a key light, a fill and key, or any other combination of lights. Shown here is the progression of adding lights.

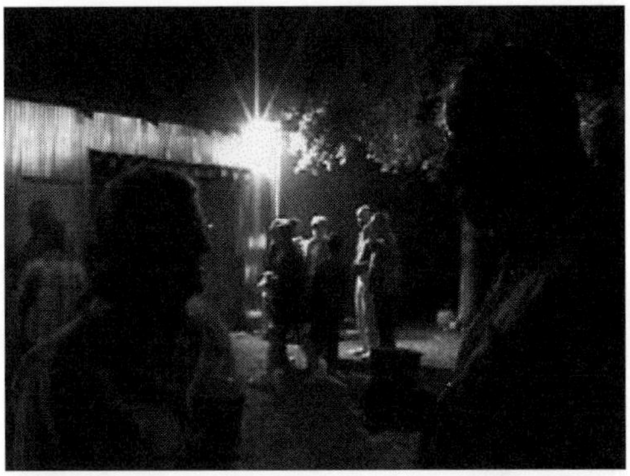

Figure 4.6 A strong light source behind your subjects can easily make them appear as silhouettes.

✔ Tips

- Your camcorder is programmed to automatically adjust the exposure (the amount of light coming in) by opening or closing its iris. You've probably seen this happen when you move from a bright area to a dark one, as details come into view after a second or two. To minimize this extreme change of contrast, break up your shots so that the camera can make the adjustment when you're not filming.
- You've seen the silhouettes. When the key light is behind your subject—whether it's the sun, an especially bright white wall, or a lamp in the background—the camera picks up on the light area in favor of the dark, and pretty soon the person in your video looks like a mob informant protecting his identity (**Figure 4.6**). Try to shoot with the light coming from behind you or from one side so the light is falling on the person or object you're filming.
- When a back light spills directly into the frame, you get the visual artifact known as lens flare. Repositioning your light usually fixes the problem.
- Keep in mind that you don't need to raid a professional camera store and stock up on lighting equipment. You probably have all the lights you need at home or in your office, if you're willing to move things around a bit. Just be careful to not shed too much light onto a scene, which will make it appear flat and less interesting.
- Three-point lighting is a good minimum starting point. On some productions, dozens of light sources may be used to properly light a scene.

Bounce Cards and Reflectors

You don't need a truckload of lights to illuminate your scene. A common and easy solution for shedding more light on your subject is to use a bounce card or reflector (**Figure 4.7**). These are either pieces of cardboard, cloth, or wood colored white, gray, or silver that are used to reflect light into shadowy areas. You can buy inexpensive flexible reflectors that twist into a compact circle for storage. You could also create your own reflectors—white poster board covered with aluminum foil on one side, for example.

Have someone hold the reflector, or mount it on something, and aim its reflection as you would with a fill light.

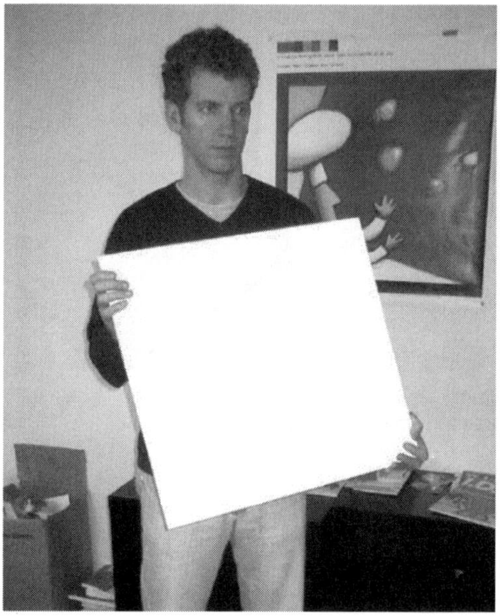

Figure 4.7 A bounce card can be anything that reflects and directs light. In this case, a piece of foam board is being put to good use.

✔ Tips

- Bounce light onto a person's face, but don't bounce it into their eyes. Yeah, it's a mean thing to do, but more importantly (for our purposes, anyway), it makes him squint, which hides the eyes, which are often the most compelling part of a person being interviewed.
- iMovie includes an effect for adjusting the brightness and contrast in a movie clip, but it won't fix a poorly lit scene. In fact, cranking up the brightness often washes out the image, because the setting is applied evenly throughout the frame. See Chapter 13 to learn how to apply effects in iMovie.

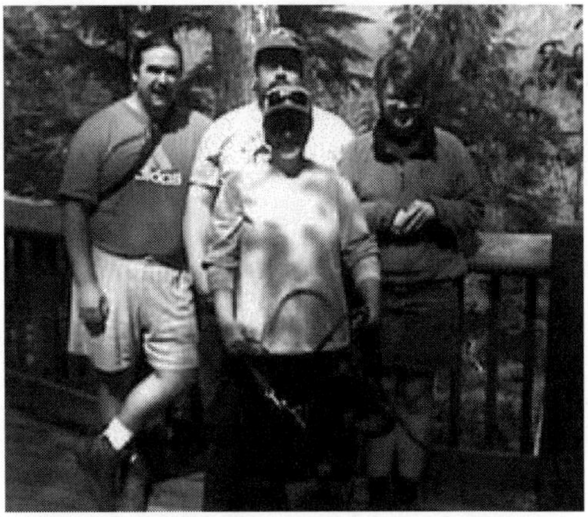

Figure 4.8 Shooting in the middle of the day can create sharp shadows.

Shooting Outside

It's one thing to configure lighting in a dark room where you have absolute control. But the rules become much more slippery when you're filming outside, where the sun and clouds can change the lighting from moment to moment. No matter where you're filming, you can make choices that take advantage of the weather.

- Avoid shooting in the middle of the day when the sun is directly overhead. A key light from above casts shadows down across the face, which obscures a person's eyes and generally gives the appearance of Frankenstein with a hangover (**Figure 4.8**, with apologies to my friends).
- Clouds are your friends. A good layer of cloud cover is an excellent diffuser of sunlight, providing a more even level of light in your scene. Coupled with a few well-placed bounce cards and a fill light, a typical cloudy day can provide warmer tones than you might expect.
- Shade is also your friend. Again, you want to minimize high-contrast key lighting and enhance the balance between shadows and fill light. Move to the shade of a tree (which can also provide its own unique shadow textures, depending on the tree) or to the side of a building.
- To maximize natural light, shoot early or late in the day, when the sun is near the horizon. The light isn't as harsh, you can get some very intriguing shadows, and the color of the scene is generally warmer and more inviting.

✔ Tip

- If you must shoot in the middle of a sunny day, put some light-colored fabric above your subject to act as a diffuser.

5

Capturing Audio

Video gets all the attention. When new camcorders are released, companies hype the image resolution, the color fidelity, the zoom ratios, optics...oh, and there's a microphone in there somewhere, too.

Well, you'll discover soon enough how important audio is. You can spend hours setting up your lighting and composition, but if your sound is poor, your scene is poor. The good news is, for most casual shooters, the built-in mic will capture what you're filming. Some cameras include controls for varying input levels, while most others offer automatic gain control (AGC) to manage the input without your involvement. However, even if you're going to be filming informally, consider purchasing a microphone.

As with lighting, you can spend your life learning the complexities of audio production. This chapter is intended as an overview of some options available for capturing audio.

Headphones

If sound is at all important to you, pack a pair of headphones when you go shooting (**Figure 5.1**). You can use almost any old pair (earbud-style headphones, for example, are extremely portable), but what's important is that you can hear what your camcorder is recording.

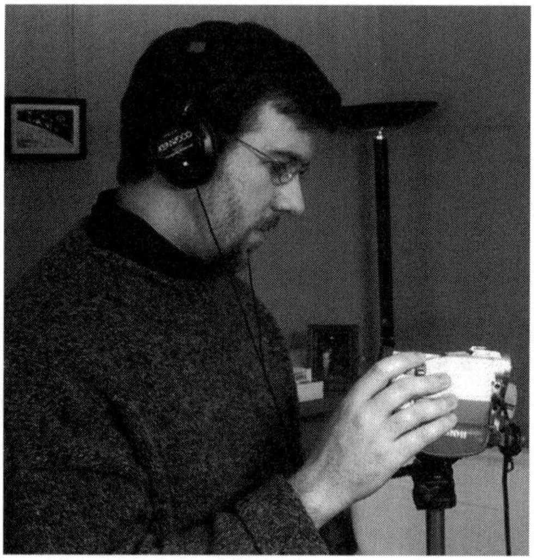

Figure 5.1 Wearing headphones while shooting is the only accurate way to know what your camera is recording.

When you're standing behind the camera, your ears are naturally picking out the audio in the scene and ignoring other ambient noises. Your camera's microphone isn't nearly as sophisticated, and does its best to maintain a level input based on all the noise in the immediate vicinity. Camcorder mics can also be sensitive to movement, picking up the sound of you shifting the camera or adjusting the focus.

A pair of headphones screens out the noise around you and gives you a direct bead on what the camera is hearing. And, it's the best audio troubleshooting device on the market: if you can't hear your subject, you'll know right away instead of later on when you're editing in iMovie.

Built-in microphone

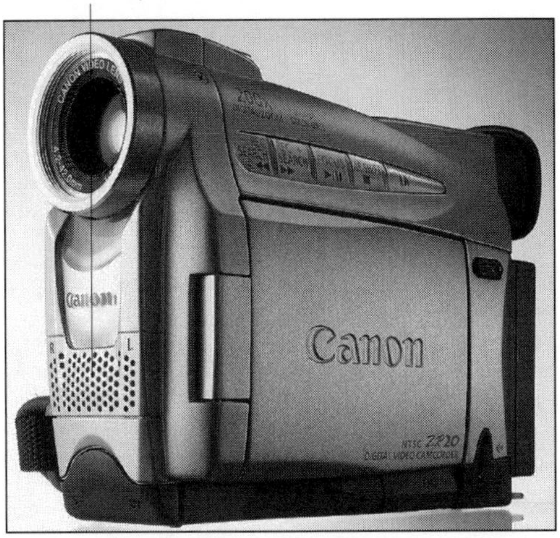

Figure 5.2 The camera's built-in microphone is good, but it's susceptible to picking up noise from the camera and doesn't record distant subjects too well.

Your Camcorder's Microphone

I don't want to give the impression that a camcorder's built-in microphone is a flimsy afterthought. On the contrary, it's a sophisticated device that does the best it can given the circumstances. Where it falls flat at times is with its placement: Because camcorders are so small, there isn't much room for a microphone (**Figure 5.2**), so you're bound to pick up sounds that the camera is making (such as the motor advancing the tape, or the zoom control adjusting the lens).

Another limitation is distance. The most important factor when recording audio is the distance between the microphone and subject—the closer the better. If you're filming a birthday party, for example, you're likely to be right in the action and will pick up audio pretty well. But what about when you're doing an interview? You want the person's comments to be picked up clearly, but you don't want the camcorder to be in her face. If you're shooting from a moderate distance away (see "Depth of Field" in Chapter 2), the microphone won't pick up the sound clearly.

12-bit versus 16-bit audio

Most likely, your camcorder includes the option to record in 12-bit or 16-bit audio. When you're recording in 12-bit, the microphone is grabbing sound in stereo and saving it to two separate channels (left and right), leaving two more channels to record more audio in the camera later.

If you choose to record in 16-bit audio, the quality is a bit better than what you'd hear from a CD—you're sampling more audio data than in 12-bit mode. (See this book's companion Web site at `www.necoffee.com/imovievqs/` for samples of each output.) However, that extra data occupies the available channels, so you can't add more audio to that footage (but see the tip on the next page). More data also means that your footage will take up more disk space in iMovie than 12-bit footage.

Wind Screen mode

Here's a good general tip: read your camcorder manual before you go on vacation. If I hadn't been in such a hurry to take a break, I would have discovered the Wind Screen feature of my camcorder, which does a decent job of cutting down the extra noise produced by wind blowing into the microphone. It's not a perfect solution (what is?), but it would have made some of my footage sound less like I was in the middle of a tornado.

✔ Tips

- Your camcorder can probably let you dub more audio into your footage (for example, if you want to add some narration to a scene), but don't bother. You can do it much better, with less hassle, in iMovie. See Chapter 10 for more on editing audio.
- Recording 12-bit audio sounds more flexible, offering two channels free for more sound. However, the advantage is moot because iMovie doesn't recognize separate channels the way other video editing software (like Final Cut Express) does. So the main benefit you're getting out of using 12-bit is the hard disk savings compared to recording in 16-bit.
- That said, you'd think recording in 16-bit would be the way to go all the time. After all, you want to make sure your audio is the highest quality, right? Well, it depends on how your video is going to turn out. If you're shooting primarily with QuickTime distribution in mind (see Chapter 15), much of the audio quality is likely to be compressed down to make sure your file sizes aren't insanely large.

Microphones

Remember earlier how I said you could spend years mastering the art of capturing audio? As with any specialized field, you could also spend a fortune on microphones and audio equipment. The good news is that you can also spend around $20 at Radio Shack and get what you need. Since it's unlikely that you'd spend tens of thousands of dollars on microphones to use with an $800 camcorder, I'm going to stick with a few realistic options.

Lavalier

A simple and portable solution is to purchase a lavalier microphone (**Figure 5.3**). It clips to your subject's shirt or tie, and often has a small battery-powered amplifier, making it a condenser mic, which is how your camcorder's documentation refers to it. (See `www.necoffee.com/imovievqs` for examples of audio captured with and without a lavalier microphone.)

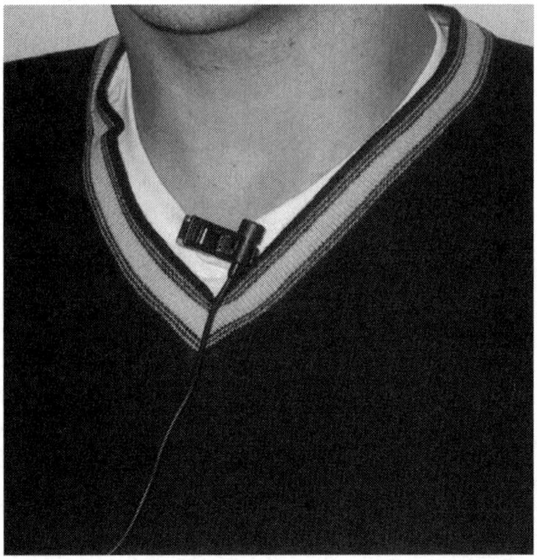

Figure 5.3 A simple clip-on lavalier microphone can greatly increase the quality of your recorded audio.

Directional

Directional microphones come in a number of shapes and sizes, and are built to pick up sound in some areas and not others. For example, cardioid microphones minimize sound coming from the sides and block sound from behind.

A shotgun mic, like the ones found on higher-end camcorders (**Figure 5.4**), picks up audio only in front of the camera (or whatever the mic is pointed at) while ignoring sound from behind the mic (therefore reducing the likelihood of recording camera noise).

Directional microphone

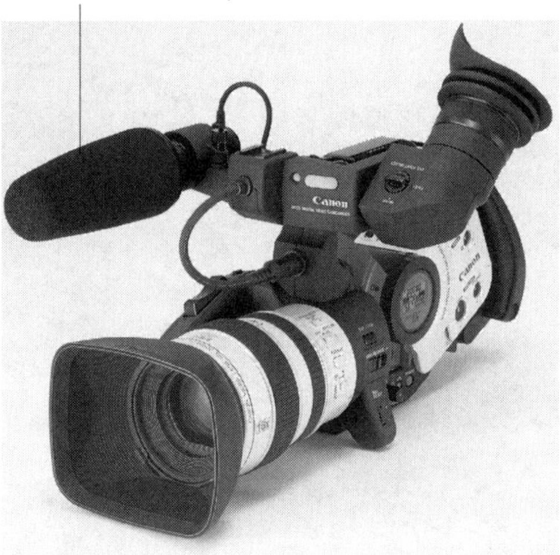

Figure 5.4 Higher-end digital camcorders are outfitted with directional microphones that aren't as likely to pick up camera (or camera operator) noise.

An omnidirectional microphone, on the other hand, picks up sound from all sides and is good to use when you're not focused on any one particular subject.

Wireless

Wireless microphones also come in a variety of shapes and sizes, but aren't tied to an audio cable that snakes back to the camcorder. They're portable, allowing you more freedom to shoot your video while moving, or from anywhere in the room. The biggest drawback to using a wireless mic is that it's more likely to pick up interference from other radio sources, so be sure to test the output before you start filming, and use headphones to monitor the recording while shooting.

✔ Tips

- Check your camcorder's specifications for attaching external microphones. Some require that the mic is amplified, calling for an external power source. Other cameras can use the camcorder's battery to provide power.
- If you don't entirely trust your camcorder's mic, or just want to be sure you have a backup source of audio, consider purchasing a MiniDisc recorder so you can make an additional recording of a scene's audio while you're filming. It stores audio digitally, which you can import into iMovie and add to your movie, or use in place of audio that didn't record clearly (due to the placement of the microphone, for example). If you're dubbing dialogue, you may have to break the audio into several clips in iMovie and synchronize the timing often, but that's a better solution than trying to re-create the original shoot. See Chapter 10 for more on editing audio.

Ambient Sound

Your biggest concern is likely to be capturing the audio of your main subject, but don't forget about ambient noise. The sounds that surround you can be just as important as the main audio to establish mood or place. It's also good for maintaining *consistent* noise. For example, I took some footage on the airplane en route to my aforementioned vacation, but when I brought it into iMovie, the engine noise differed depending on when the video was shot (when we started to descend) and even what side of the plane I was filming. However, I was able to use a sample of ambient noise in the background to provide an even level of noise (and also to adjust the audio so it wasn't as dominant). Record ambient noise whenever you can—you can spend a few minutes before or after your primary shooting and get plenty of material to work with later in iMovie.

This applies to "quiet" rooms as well. Even an empty room has its own audio signature—it's never completely silent. Grab a minute or two of quiet noise, too.

Part 2
Editing

6

iMovie Overview

Being a fan of the moviemaking process, I enjoy reading "behind the scenes" articles about how films are produced. In nearly all cases, the reporter interviews cast and crew at the movie set during shooting (and invariably makes it sound more exciting than it usually is). But filming is only one part of the production.

Rarely reported on is the editing stage, when the editor and director spend long hours in a dark editing room—sometimes for many months—shaping hours of raw footage into what we eventually see in a theater. They grab the best takes from each day's shooting, assemble them according to the storyline, and then add transitions, audio, special effects, and whatever else is required for that particular flick.

The process of making your digital video is the same (minus the reporters). By this point you've shot your footage, but that doesn't mean you have a movie. Here's where iMovie and digital non-linear editing can take your mass of video and audio and turn it into a movie. This chapter introduces iMovie, making sure you have the tools you need to get started, and giving you an overview tour of the program's unexpectedly powerful yet simple interface.

Getting iMovie

If you've purchased a new Macintosh within the last couple of years, you should have a free copy of iMovie on your hard disk or on an accompanying CD-ROM.

In January 2003, Apple introduced iMovie 3 as a free download or as part of iLife, its $50 suite of digital hub applications (`www.apple.com/ilife/`). You don't need to purchase iLife to get iMovie—the price mostly covers iDVD 3, which is too large to offer as a free download (see Chapter 16 for more on iDVD).

Working with Projects

The first thing to do is launch iMovie. This step may seem absurdly obvious, but stick with me for a minute. Go to your Applications folder in the Finder and launch iMovie by double-clicking its icon. After the program's interface appears, a dialog box offers the following options (**Figure 6.1**):

- **Open Existing Project** loads a project in progress. In the dialog box that appears, locate the project file on your hard disk.
- **Quit** exits the program. (When this dialog box is displayed, the Quit command under the iMovie menu is disabled.)
- **Create Project** starts an iMovie project from scratch. After clicking the button, give your project a name and decide where it will live on your hard disk.

✔ Tips

- iMovie 3 includes a PDF-based tutorial if you want a short step-by-step walkthrough of the program. Choose iMovie Help from the Help menu, then click the Tutorial option (**Figure 6.2**).
- To reclaim about 55 MB of your hard disk, delete the help files of languages you don't use in the Library > Documentation > iMovie folder.

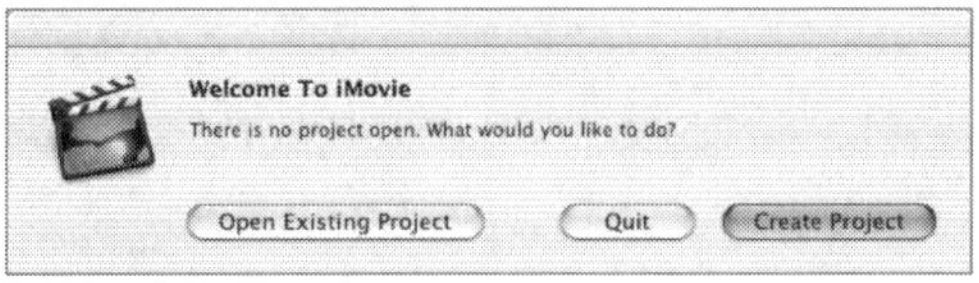

Figure 6.1 Launching iMovie for the first time gives you three simple options.

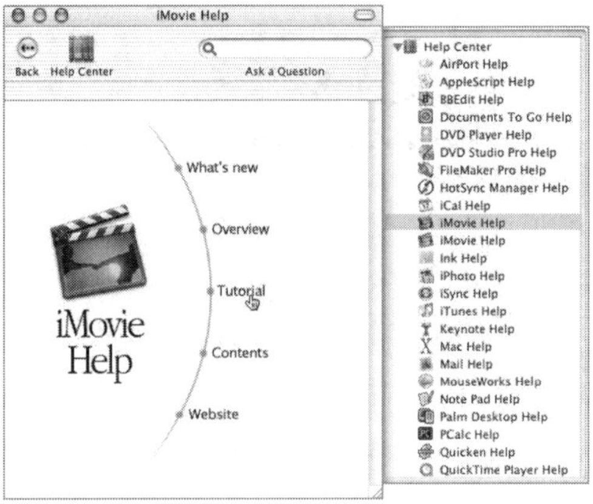

Figure 6.2 iMovie comes with no manual—instead, follow along with the online PDF-based tutorial.

iMovie 3 is for Mac OS X Only

iMovie 3 is the first version to run only under Mac OS X, and even then only under version 10.2 ("Jaguar") or higher.

If you're still running Mac OS 9, you can still use iMovie 2, which most likely came with your computer; unfortunately, it's not available as a download.

Although most features are similar in iMovie 3, if you need to stick with iMovie 2 I suggest you buy a copy of this book's predecessor, *iMovie 2 for Macintosh: Visual QuickStart Guide.*

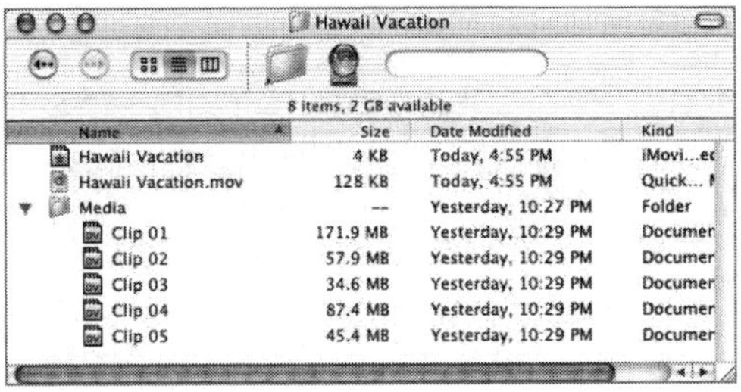

Figure 6.3 An iMovie project is comprised of a small project file, a QuickTime movie, and a Media folder.

Upgrading from iMovie 2

Upgrading to iMovie 3 is easy, but I recommend keeping a copy of iMovie 2 available, too. Before you run the iMovie installer, locate the iMovie program in your Applications folder and copy it to another hard disk, or duplicate it (press Command-D in the Finder) and rename it "iMovie 2".

Why make a copy? Unfortunately, the early release of iMovie 3 had some bugs and performance issues (though some users reported no problems at all), but there's no easy way to switch back to iMovie 2 if the iMovie 3 installer has already replaced it.

I didn't say it was impossible, however. Your Mac should have come with a set of Software Restore discs that let you install a fresh Mac OS X system—the entire thing. Instead, download the shareware utility Pacifist (`www.charlessoft.com`), and use it to locate the iMovie installation package on one of the Software Restore discs.

Naturally, there are exceptions. If your Mac came with a separate iMovie 2 install disc, as my original PowerBook G4 did, then you can just install from that. If your Mac is brand new, your only option is iMovie 3.

Opening and closing projects

Most programs, such as Microsoft Word or Adobe Photoshop, work with individual files you can create, open, and save. iMovie works just a tad differently.

An iMovie project comprises a project file and its associated media files. The project file is miniscule in comparison to the others: in the example in **Figure 6.3**, the "Hawaii Vacation" project file is 4K, while the contents of the Media folder total 397.5 MB. The project file is small because it only records how you've arranged and edited the media files (I'll go into more detail about this in Chapter 8).

When you begin working within iMovie, you'll soon notice something different from other programs: there is no Close command. Once you've created or opened a project file, the only way to close it is by creating or opening a different project, or by quitting the program.

On the other hand, iMovie remembers which project you're working on between sessions, so your current project automatically loads the next time you launch the program, thereby skipping the initial dialog box.

✔ Tip

- Another file appears in the project folder: a QuickTime movie sharing your project's name. This is a DV-format rendition of the movie you're assembling. You can view it using QuickTime Player, import it into another iMovie project, or use it in another application (such as iDVD 2). It's almost the same file you'd get if you export your movie at the highest QuickTime movie settings, except that this is a reference movie that points to the source files in the Media folder, not a self-contained movie (see Chapters 15 and 16 for more information).

iMovie's Interface

In iMovie, everything happens in one big window (**Figure 6.4**). The nice thing about iMovie 3 is that the window doesn't monopolize the entire screen as in previous versions. Use the resize control in the lower-right corner to change the window's size, or click the green Zoom button in the upper-left corner to maximize the window.

The interface comprises three main areas: the Monitor, where you view video clips; the Shelf, where clips are stored; and the Liquid Timeline, which combines the Clip Viewer and Timeline Viewer, where you assemble your movie.

✔ Tips

- To help improve performance, try reducing iMovie's window to its minimum size. If the Monitor is smaller, iMovie doesn't need to expend as much processing power drawing video on the screen.
- If you're fortunate enough to have a large display, such as Apple's giant Cinema HD Display, the Monitor enlarges when you increase the size of iMovie's window. However, the Shelf doesn't display more columns, which would be a nice added treat.

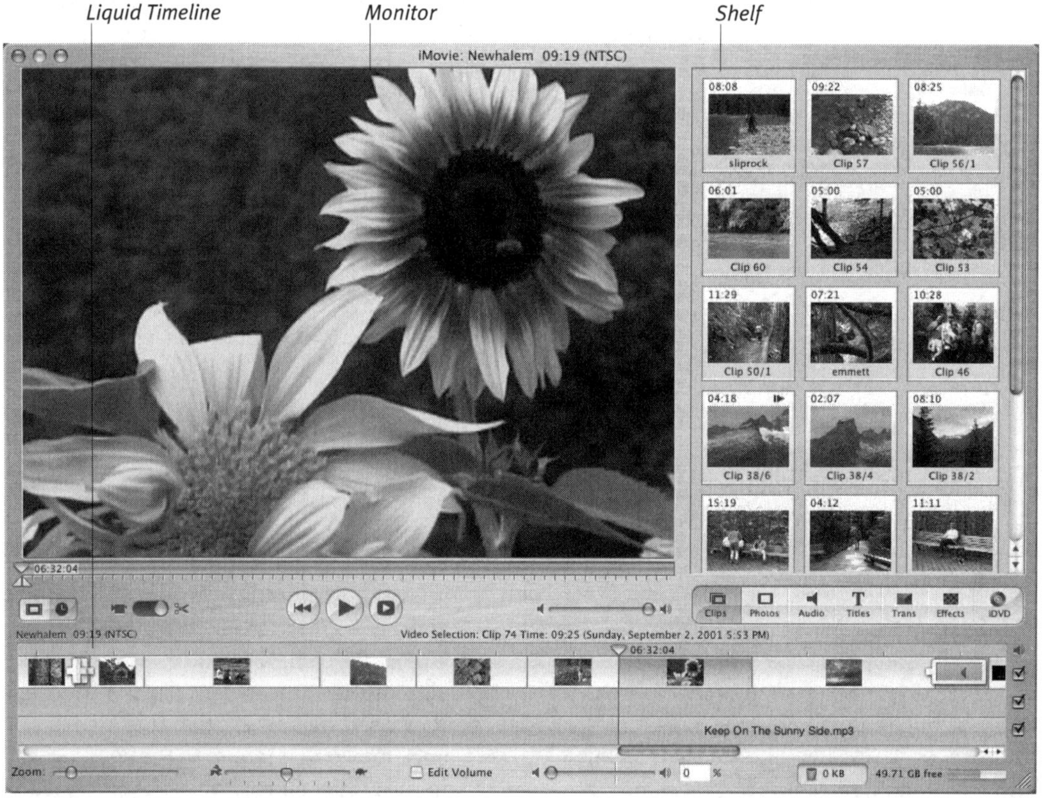

Figure 6.4 iMovie is broken down into three main sections: the Monitor, the Shelf, and the Liquid Timeline, which can switch between the Clip Viewer and the Timeline Viewer (shown here).

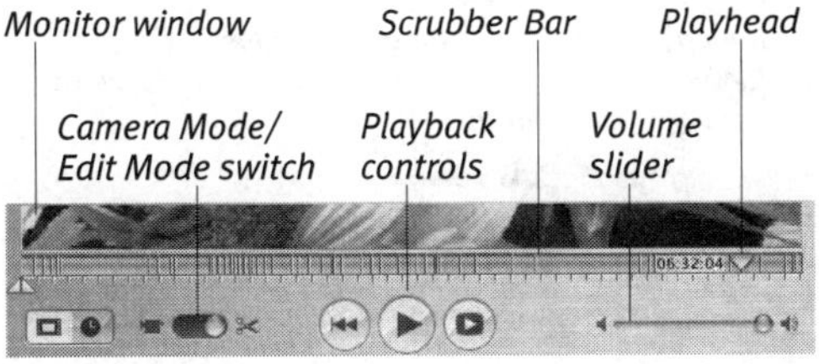

Figure 6.5 iMovie groups its Monitor controls into a relatively small space.

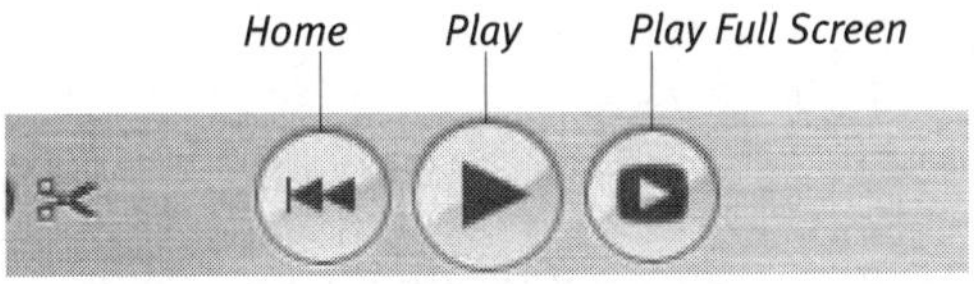

Figure 6.6 Use these Monitor controls when you're in iMovie's Edit Mode. To rewind or fast-forward through a clip or movie, use the Scrubber Bar.

Review and Fast-Forward

Unlike iMovie 2, there are no buttons for reviewing (rewinding) and fast-forwarding your movie during playback. However, the functionality is still there: press Command-[(left bracket) to review, and press Command-] (right bracket) to fast-forward. To stop playback, hit the keys again or press the spacebar.

These features are always good for a laugh, too, when you've been editing for hours without a break: the audio plays at the same sped-up rate.

The Monitor

The Monitor is where you view and edit clips. A few controls, such as the Scrubber Bar, affect how you edit your clips (**Figure 6.5**). The playback controls are context-sensitive, and can play clips (**Figure 6.6**) or control a camcorder (**Figure 6.7**, next page).

Monitor controls

- **Monitor window.** View clips and incoming video from a camcorder.
- **Camera Mode/Edit Mode switch.** Toggle between these modes to either import or edit video footage.
- **Volume slider.** Set the playback volume by dragging the knob or clicking a spot on the slider.
- **Playhead.** Drag the Playhead to any point within your movie or clip; the numbers beside it indicate the time location within the movie.
- **Scrubber Bar.** When viewing an entire movie, the Scrubber Bar includes lines marking clips and transitions. This is also where you can select portions of clips and cut, copy, or crop them (see Chapter 8).

Playback controls (Edit Mode)

- **Home.** Click here to move to the start of the movie. (If you select a single clip, even in the Shelf, clicking this button takes you to the beginning of your movie and deselects the clip.)
- **Play.** Click this button to play the video in real time. Click it again to stop playback (or hit the spacebar).
- **Play Full Screen.** This button expands the video to fill the entire screen.

Playback controls (Camera Mode)

- **Import.** With a camera attached, click this button to begin saving the video to your hard disk. Click it again to stop capturing.
- **Rewind/Review.** Click this button to rewind the camcorder's tape. If the tape is playing, click to review (play backwards) the footage quickly. You can also click and hold to review, then release the button to resume normal playback.
- **Stop.** This button stops the camcorder's tape and ceases playback.
- **Play.** Click this button to play the video in real time.
- **Pause.** Click this button to pause, but still view, the camera's playback. Click it again to resume.
- **Fast Forward.** Click to advance the tape without playing it. As with the Rewind/Review control, if the tape is playing, click to view the playback quickly; or, click and hold to play back, then release the button to resume normal playback.

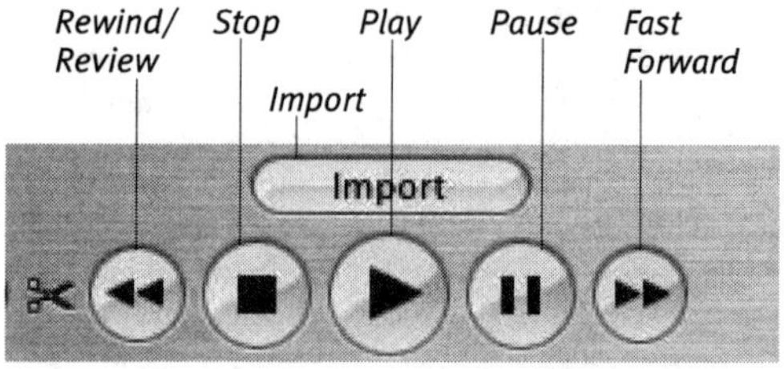

Figure 6.7 With Camera Mode enabled, the buttons control the camera's playback functions.

✔ Tips

- When switching between Camera Mode and Edit Mode, simply click the icons—you don't have to "move" the switch.
- In Edit Mode, the spacebar activates and deactivates the Play button. In Camera Mode, the spacebar activates the Import button.
- Use the left and right arrow keys to move the video in one-frame increments when you're in Edit Mode. Hold Shift and use the arrow keys to move 10 frames at a time.

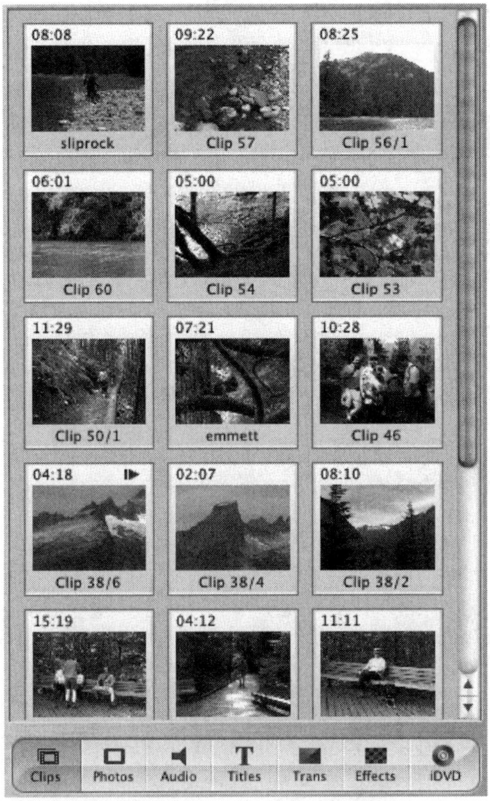

Figure 6.8 The Shelf, in addition to storing clips, serves as the pane for controlling other features such as transitions, effects, and titles.

The Shelf

Think of the Shelf as a big rack filled with lots of videocassettes, photos, and audio reels (but much better organized); this is where you store your raw footage in preparation for editing (**Figure 6.8**). It's also where you find controls for working with photos, transitions, titles, effects, audio, and DVD chapter markers.

Shelf components

- **Clips panel.** The purpose of the Shelf is to store your clips, which are arranged in a grid on the Clips pane. Use the scroll bar at right to view more clips.
- **Panel buttons.** The Shelf doubles as the control center for the Photos, Audio, Titles, Transitions, Effects, and iDVD panes. Click one of the buttons to activate its pane. (Each of these panes is discussed at length throughout the book.)

The Liquid Timeline

The Shelf may hold all of your raw video clips, but you don't have a movie until you start moving them to the Clip Viewer or Timeline Viewer, which in iMovie 3 reside in the sexy-sounding "Liquid Timeline." Consider them to be two different methods of looking at the structure of your movie.

The Clip Viewer displays clips in the order that they play, with large thumbnail previews to help identify them (**Figure 6.9**). The Timeline Viewer arranges the clips in order and also depicts their lengths (**Figures 6.11** and **6.12**). The Timeline also includes audio tracks and controls for changing aspects of a clip, which I'll discuss in the next few chapters.

Clip Viewer components

- **Clip Viewer button.** Click the filmstrip icon to display the Clip Viewer.
- **Project title and movie length.** Located at the top-left corner of the Clip Viewer, these labels tell you which project is open, and the total length of the movie. The type of movie, either NTSC or PAL, is shown in parentheses.
- **Transitions.** When you add a transition to your movie, an icon indicates which clip it's attached to (see Chapter 10).

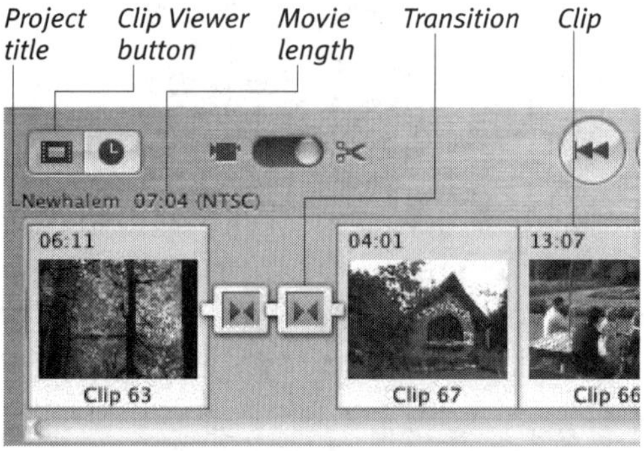

Figure 6.9 Using the Clip Viewer is often easier than the Timeline Viewer when adding clips.

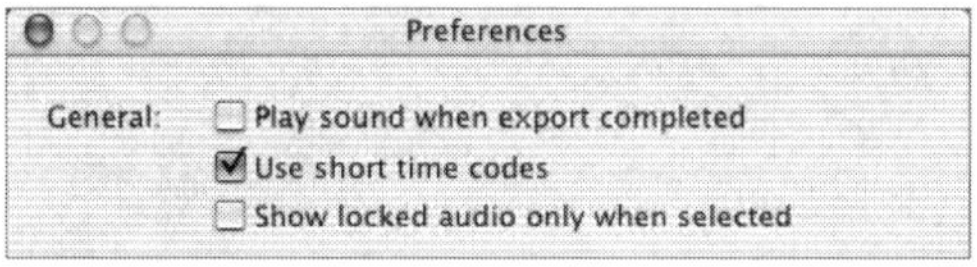

Figure 6.10 A few of iMovie's preferences affect how clips appear in the Clip Viewer and Timeline Viewer.

Changing View Preferences

You can tweak some of the ways clips are displayed by setting options in iMovie's preferences (**Figure 6.10**).

- **Use short time codes.** This option truncates time codes; a 10-second clip appears as "10:00" instead of "00:10:00".
- **Show locked audio only when selected.** You can lock audio clips individually, which are then shown with a pin icon (see Chapter 10). This option shows the icon only when the clip is selected.

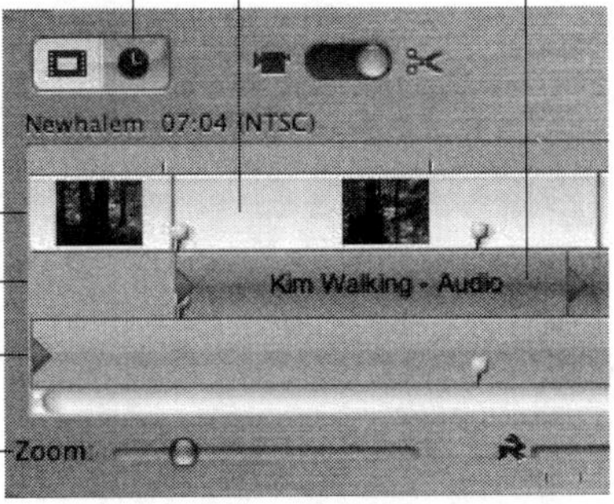

Figure 6.11 The Timeline offers a better sense of how much time a clip occupies.

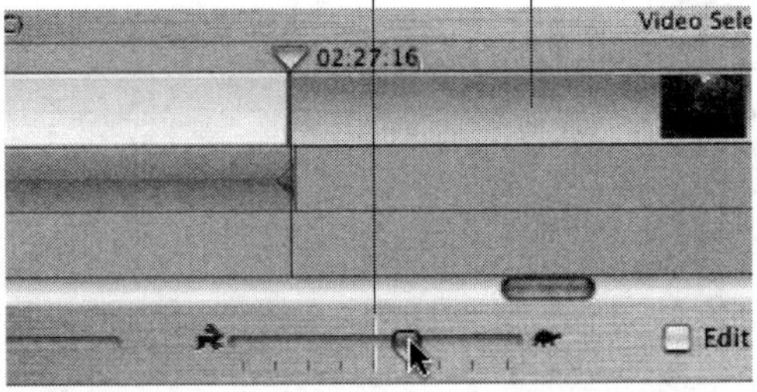

Figure 6.12 Speed up or apply slow-motion to a clip using the Clip Speed slider.

Timeline Viewer components

- **Timeline Viewer button.** Click the clock icon to bring this viewer to the front.
- **Video track.** The top horizontal bar represents the video track, where clips are displayed according to their lengths. Transitions also appear here, with an icon similar to those found in the Clip Viewer.
- **Audio tracks.** iMovie gives you two separate audio tracks to work with, just below the video track. Audio can be extracted from video clips or imported and edited on these tracks.
- **Zoom slider.** This control determines how much of the Timeline is shown in the viewer: with the slider at the left, the entire movie appears in the Timeline; with the slider button at full right, you may see only a few seconds, depending on your movie's length. Zooming in is helpful when you're editing small clips or transitions.
- **Clip Speed slider.** When a clip is selected, use this slider to control how fast or slow the clip plays. The Video Selection information at the top of the Timeline displays the length of the selected clip.

continued on next page

- **Clip-specific sound controls.** The Edit Volume checkbox and slider only apply to a selected clip (**Figure 6.13**). See Chapter 10 for more on editing audio.
- **Mute switches.** Uncheck a box to turn off the volume in its associated video or audio track (**Figure 6.14**). This doesn't affect any volume adjustments you've made to particular clips.

Project Trash and free space indicator

- **Project Trash.** When you delete clips, they're sent to the Project Trash. However, this trash doesn't operate the same as the Trash in the Finder: you can't open it and pull things back out. The reason for this is a bit convoluted and explained in Chapter 7. For now, just be aware that the size of the Project Trash is indicated to the right of the icon. Clicking the Trash gives you the option to empty the trash (but really, go read Chapter 7 first!).
- **Free space indicator.** The bar fills from left to right according to the amount of available space on the hard disk where your project is stored. A green bar indicates plenty of free space; yellow warns you that you're getting low; and red means you're critically low on space.

✔ Tip

- To see just how "liquid" the Timeline can be, use the Zoom slider: the clip previews and names slide around like crazy. What's going on? It's actually simple and sensible: operating the Zoom slider centers the Playhead in the Timeline, then zooms the clips from that middle point. To make sure a clip is visible when you zoom, place the Playhead within that clip before you start slip-sliding away.

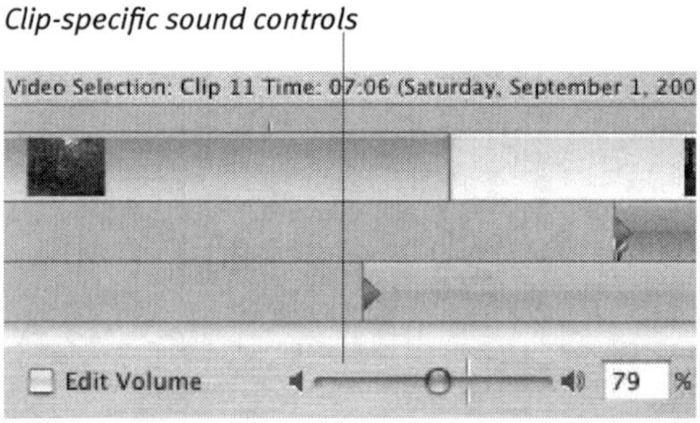

Figure 6.13 The sound controls at the bottom only apply to selected clips.

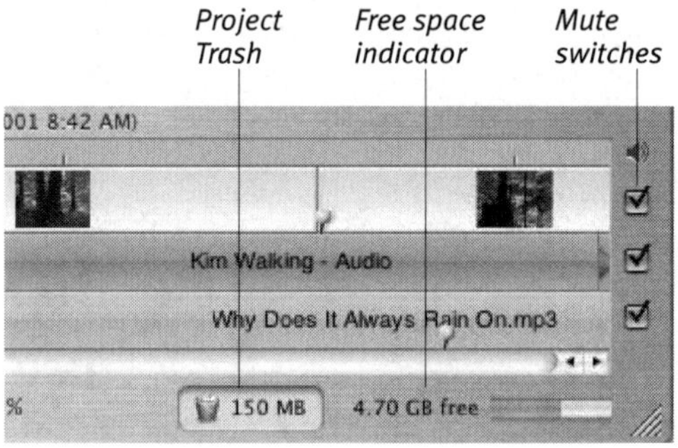

Figure 6.14 Mute switches turn audio on and off for an entire track. The Project Trash and free space indicator appear in the Clip Viewer as well.

Monitoring Your Movies

iMovie's Monitor window is invaluable, and the Play Full Screen feature is helpful when you need to get a better feel for how the movie will display. However, consider hooking up an external television or AV monitor so you can see how your movie will really look to your audience (**Figure 6.15**). (If your movies are destined only for display on the Web or via email, you may not want to go to this trouble.)

You'll need your computer, a television or AV monitor with RCA-style input jacks, and your digital camcorder. You'll also need the FireWire cable to hook up your camcorder to your Mac, and the AV cable that came with your camcorder, which allows you to view movies on a TV (it normally has three connectors on one end—yellow, red, and white—and a single connector that plugs into the camera).

To hook up an external monitor:

1. Connect the camera to your computer via the FireWire cable.
2. Connect the television to your camera using the AV cable.
3. Switch the television's mode from TV to Video, if necessary.
4. In iMovie, choose Preferences from the iMovie menu.
5. Click the Video Play Through to Camera checkbox.
6. Close the Preferences window. Your movie should now appear on the TV.

✔ Tips

- Plug in the camera's AC adapter while you're working, so you don't drain the battery.

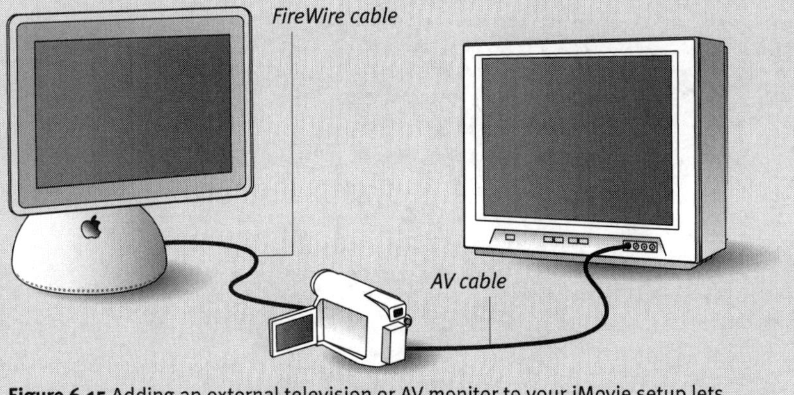

Figure 6.15 Adding an external television or AV monitor to your iMovie setup lets you see how the video appears on a real video screen.

7

Importing Footage

When I first began looking into buying a camcorder, cost was definitely a main consideration. I found several analog cameras in the $200 to $300 range, which was acceptable. However, all signs point to a digital future—but the cameras cost around $700 or (in some cases much) higher. Sure, digital is definitely the future, but did I really need to edge into that higher price range? I wanted the camera primarily for vacations and special events, so the quality and features of a digital camcorder probably weren't worth the extra money...right?

Wrong.

If you're planning on doing any type of video editing (and I'm assuming you are, since you're reading this book), spend the extra bucks and go digital. I can't stress this point enough. The convenience of hooking your camera directly to your Mac and just letting the video flow is worth the money you put out up-front. You also get the benefit of clearer video and audio, since the footage is entirely digital and therefore doesn't need to undergo any analog-to-digital conversion.

However, don't let my digital zeal frighten you. If you already own an analog camcorder, you can still use iMovie to edit your video, as I'll discuss later in this chapter.

Importing Clips

Getting footage into iMovie is a snap: connect your digital camcorder to your Mac via FireWire, and start importing. You don't even need to shut down your Mac to plug in the FireWire cable (as we needed to do in the days of SCSI devices). Your only practical limitation is space on your hard drive—make sure you have plenty (see the sidebar on the next page).

To connect via FireWire:

1. Quit iMovie if it's running. Apple recommends quitting iMovie before you plug or unplug FireWire cables. This step isn't essential—I've had no problems with iMovie 3 recognizing my camcorder—but it's not a bad idea anyway.
2. Plug the FireWire cable into the Mac and the camcorder.
3. Switch the camcorder to VCR or Play mode.
4. Launch iMovie. If you don't have a project file yet, create a new one and name it. The Monitor switches to Camera mode and displays "Camera Connected" (**Figure 7.1**).

To import footage from the camcorder:

1. Use the Monitor's Playback controls to rewind or forward the camcorder's tape to the spot where you want to begin.
2. Click the Import button. The imported footage is stored as clips in the Shelf (**Figure 7.2**).
3. Click the Import button again to stop.

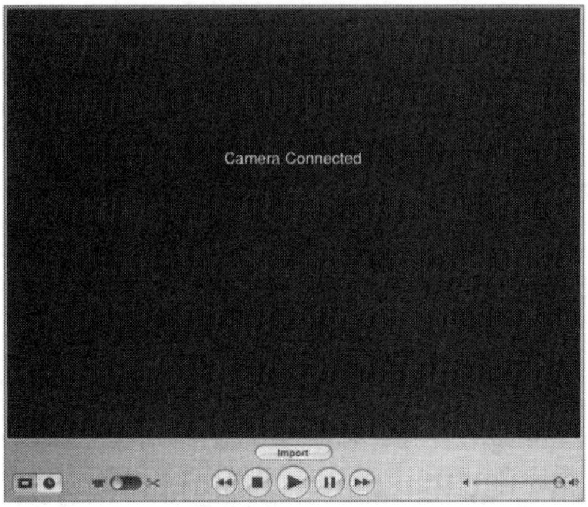

Figure 7.1 Connecting the camera to your Mac via FireWire automatically switches iMovie's Monitor to Camera mode.

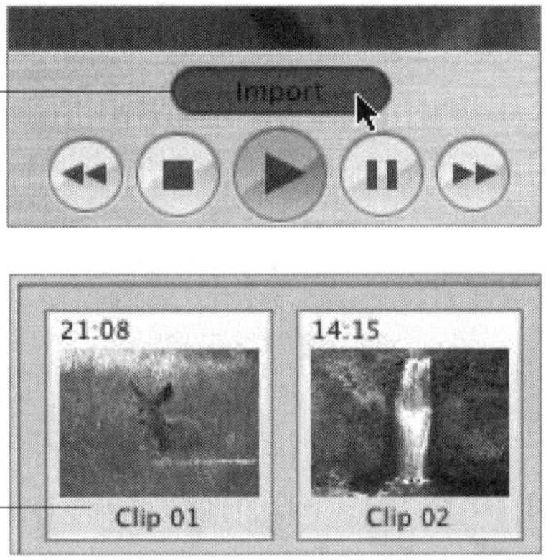

Figure 7.2 iMovie can automatically detect when scenes begin and end, and split them into clips.

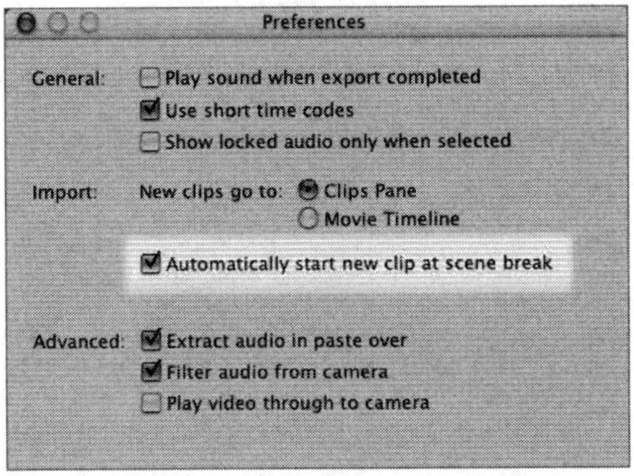

Figure 7.3 Turning off the Automatically start new clip at scene break option reduces the number of clips created from your footage when you import.

The Biggest Hard Drive Isn't Large Enough

When you begin working with digital video, your concept of hard disk space changes forever. For example, one second of footage equals 3.6 MB on disk.

Fortunately, hard drives are getting cheaper: a quick search for an 80 GB drive turns up prices between $150 and $200 as of this writing (try `www.dealmac.com`). Here's one way to estimate how much storage you need, courtesy of Jay Nelson's *Design Tools Monthly* newsletter (`www.design-tools.com`):

To determine a disk's DV capacity:

1. Divide the disk capacity by 3.6 MB, which is the amount of space required to save one second of digital video.
2. Divide that result by 60 to convert from seconds to minutes.

For example, a 60 GB hard disk can hold 277.77 minutes of digital video (60,000 MB / 3.6 MB = 16,666.67 seconds / 60 = 277.77 minutes).

By default, iMovie creates a new clip for each scene, which is calculated based on the time stamps stored on the tape. If you prefer, the video can be stored in fewer clips, giving you the option to *manually* control where clips are split. (iMovie limits the clip size to 2 GB, which is about 9 minutes of video, so you can't just import all your footage as one gigantic clip.) However, I've found that leaving iMovie's automatic scene detection on saves time later when I'm editing.

To turn off automatic scene detection:

1. Choose Preferences from the iMovie menu to open iMovie's preferences.
2. Deselect the option labeled Automatically start new clip at scene break (**Figure 7.3**). Click OK.

✔ Tips

- Are are you you hearing hearing double double? There's a slight lag between the camera and the Mac when importing. Turn the volume all the way down on either the camcorder or in iMovie.
- If you want to import your video to an external FireWire hard drive, make sure the drive has a speed of at least 7,200 RPM. Although some users report that 5,400 RPM drives work fine, a faster drive is less likely to drop frames or audio when iMovie is importing.

In addition to importing video from the camcorder's tape, you can grab live footage directly from the camera.

To import live footage from the camcorder:

1. With the camera connected to your Mac, launch iMovie.
2. Switch the camcorder to Camera or Record mode.
3. In iMovie's preferences, click the Play video through to camera option, then close the window (**Figure 7.4**).
4. Switch iMovie to Camera mode and click the Import button. You don't need to use the camera's Record button.
5. Click the Import button again to stop.

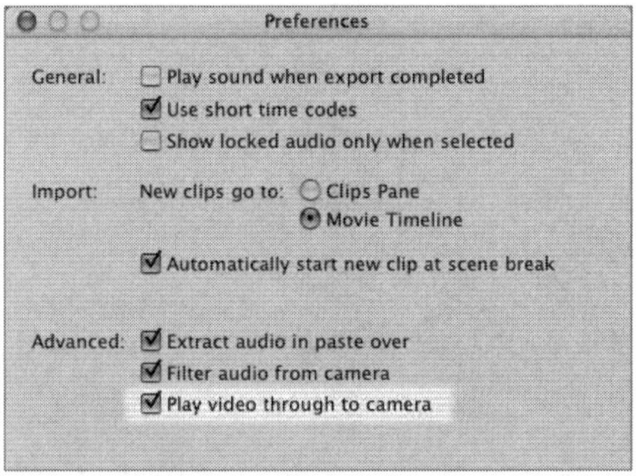

Figure 7.4 The Play video through to camera option enables you to import video as you record it. In fact, you don't even need to record footage to tape on your camcorder in this mode.

As clips are imported, they're stored in order on the Shelf with the expectation that you're going to crop and rearrange them when they're put into the movie. But suppose you're importing footage that's already been edited, or is otherwise in the correct order? You can save a few steps by importing the clips directly to the Timeline.

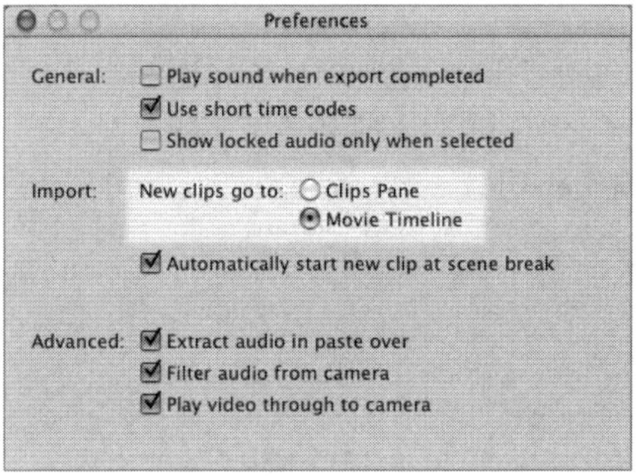

Figure 7.5 Set the New clips go to preference to Movie Timeline to import footage directly to the Timeline.

To import to the Timeline instead of the Shelf:

1. Open iMovie's preferences.
2. In the Import area, click the Movie Timeline radio button (**Figure 7.5**). Close the window.
3. Click the Import button to begin capturing the footage, then click Import again to stop.

✔ Tip

- You can have either the Clip Viewer or Timeline Viewer active when importing directly to the Timeline.

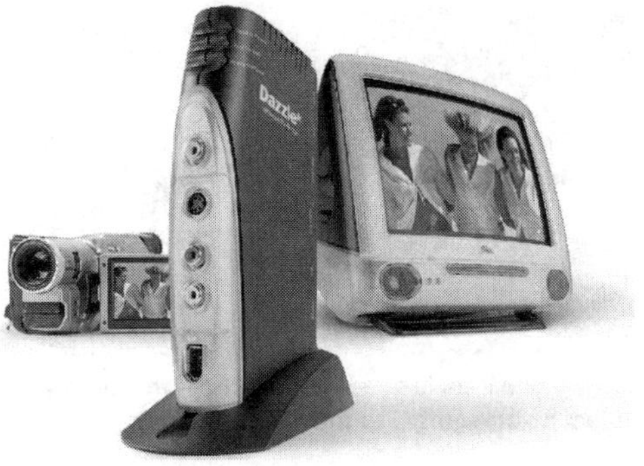

Figure 7.6 Analog-to-video converters enable you to use a non-digital camcorder with iMovie.

Importing Footage from an Analog Camcorder

The process of importing footage from an analog camcorder in iMovie is much the same as when importing from a digital camcorder. However, you need a go-between device that converts the camcorder's analog signal to digital information on the Mac. Products such as Dazzle's $250 Hollywood DV-Bridge (`www.dazzle.com`) feature a FireWire port for connecting to your computer and RCA-style inputs for connecting to your camcorder; some devices may also include an S-Video port (**Figure 7.6**).

Since you're importing converted analog data, iMovie doesn't automatically split clips according to scenes. You'll have to use iMovie's editing tools to trim and organize the clips, or manually start and stop importing according to scenes.

To import from a non-DV camcorder:

1. Connect the conversion device to the Mac via FireWire, and to the camera using RCA or S-Video cabling.
2. Switch the camcorder to VCR or Play mode.
3. Push the camcorder's Play button.
4. Click the Import button in iMovie.
5. When finished, click Import again to stop capturing video, and press the Stop button on the camcorder.

Importing Old VHS Tapes Using a DV Camcorder

If you have a digital camcorder, but still have some older VHS (or other format) tapes, you can bring that footage into iMovie to edit or even just store digitally. Connect your VCR to your camcorder and record the contents of the VHS tape to the DV tape. Then you can import your footage into iMovie normally.

Another option is to use a recent Sony DV camcorder, which performs the analog-to-digital conversion.

Analog tape doesn't last forever—save your wedding/graduation/school play on disk (and maybe even edit out a few of those more embarrassing moments).

Importing QuickTime Movies

iMovie is built on QuickTime, Apple's technology for playing and creating all sorts of digital audio and video. iMovie 3 gains the capability to drag and drop QuickTime movies onto the Shelf or Timeline.

To import a QuickTime movie into iMovie:

◆ Drag a QuickTime movie file from the Finder to iMovie's window (**Figure 7.7**).

or

1. In iMovie, choose Import from the File menu, or press Command-Shift-I.
2. Locate the file in the Import dialog box, then click the Open button (**Figure 7.8**). The clip appears on the Shelf.

✔ Tips

- Most QuickTime movies are small in size and compressed, which is great for viewing on the Web but not so good-looking compared to a DV clip taken from a video camcorder (**Figure 7.9**). So don't be surprised if the clip looks highly pixelated or blocky.
- You can import media files from other iMovie projects, which are in the DV format and feature full resolution.

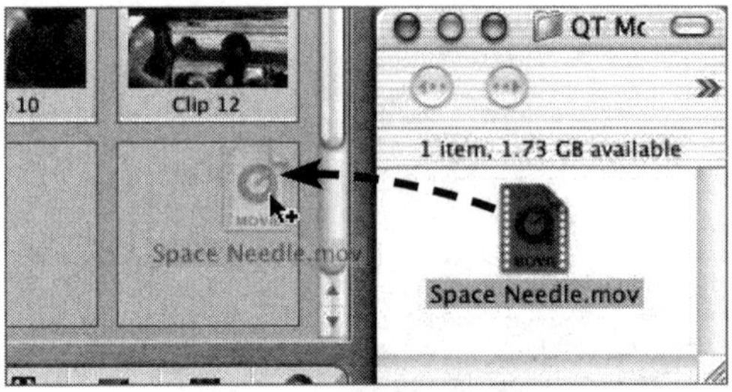

Figure 7.7 In iMovie 3, add a QuickTime movie to your project by dragging it to the iMovie window.

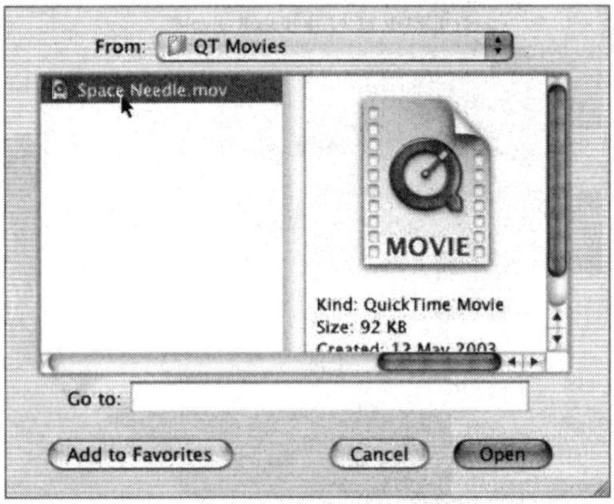

Figure 7.8 Instead of dragging a file into iMovie, use the Import command to locate a QuickTime movie.

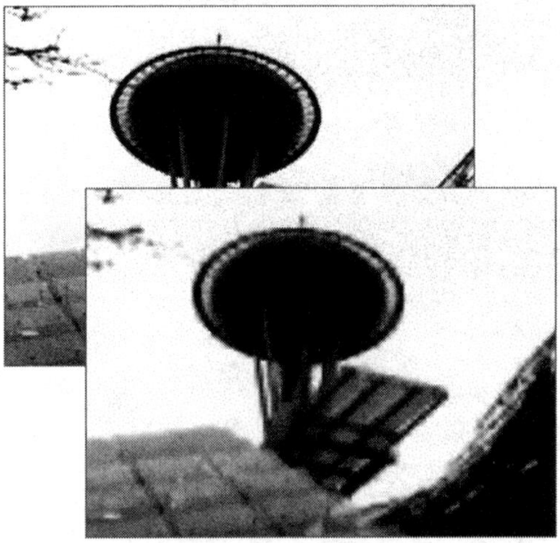

Figure 7.9 To compare image resolution, I exported some DV footage (top) as a QuickTime file, then imported the file back into iMovie (bottom).

Importing QuickTime Movies

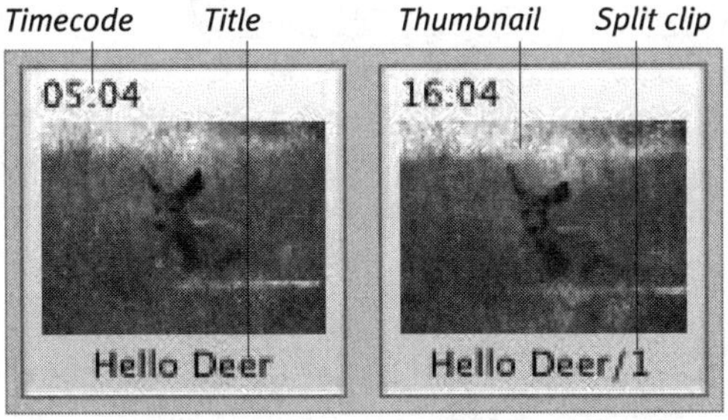

Figure 7.10 Each clip contains a thumbnail image of the first frame in the video. If a clip has been split, iMovie adds a number to indicate it's a section from the original.

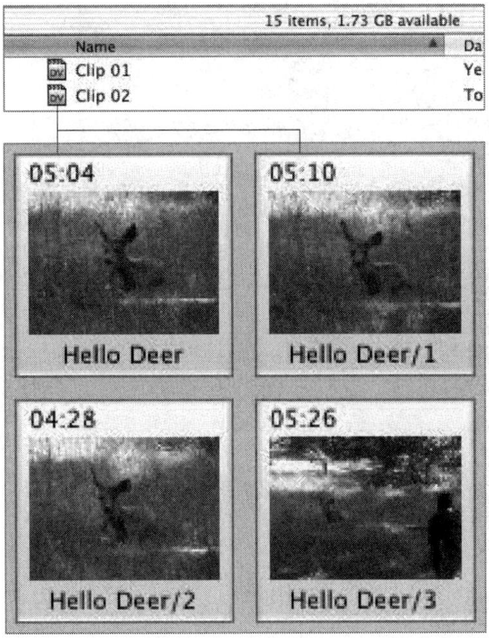

Figure 7.11 The original clip, "Clip 02," was renamed "Hello Deer" and split into four separate clips, but the Clip 02 source file is not renamed or split on the hard disk.

How iMovie Manages Clips

If you're casually flipping through this chapter, I'll understand it if you skip everything else—*except this section.* It's important to understand how iMovie handles clips as you're working with them, especially when you begin deleting unused clips.

Clips can be made up of either video footage or imported still pictures. Each clip includes a thumbnail image of the clip's first frame, a timecode noting the clip's duration, and a title that you can edit (**Figure 7.10**).

When you import footage, iMovie creates a new clip for each scene, which then adds a new clip file to your hard disk. However, even if you rename, split, reverse, or otherwise edit a clip in iMovie, *the media file stays the same* (**Figure 7.11**). iMovie actually records only the *changes* made to the clip, and doesn't alter the clip's original media file.

This clip management style comes in handy in several ways as you use iMovie.

Advantages of iMovie's method of managing clips

- **Undo.** iMovie offers 10 levels of Undo, enabling you to recombine split clips, move clips back to their original locations, and other actions.
- **Deleting clips.** iMovie's Trash is something of a digital Roach Motel: clips go in, but they don't come out! This doesn't mean the clips are gone for good, though (see "Moving Clips to the Trash," later in this chapter).
- **Restoring clips.** If you're not happy with your edits, or something has gone horribly wrong, you can always restore the clip to its original state, because the original data is always on file. See the next chapter to learn how to restore clips.

Managing Clips

Clips are named sequentially during import (such as "Clip 01"), but you can rename them with more meaningful titles. If you split a clip (explained in the next chapter), iMovie adds a slash and a number to indicate it's part of the original, such as "Mountain/1".

To rename a clip:

1. Click the clip's title, which selects the text. Or, either double-click the clip or press Command-Shift-I to display the Clip Info dialog box (**Figure 7.12**).
2. Type a new name and click OK.

The Shelf features slots for storing clips, but it doesn't matter in what order they appear. You'll find yourself moving them frequently as you assemble your movie.

To reorder clips in the Shelf:

1. Click the clip(s) you wish to move. To grab a range of clips, Shift-click multiple clips or click and drag a box around them with the pointer (**Figure 7.13**).
2. Click and drag the clip(s) to a new location in the Shelf.

✔ Tips

- Renaming a clip only changes its name in iMovie. The original media file is still named "Clip 04" (or similar). Do not rename the media file on disk or iMovie will lose track of it.
- Since you can drag clips anywhere in the Shelf, use this capability to visually group scenes or related materials before you add them to your movie.

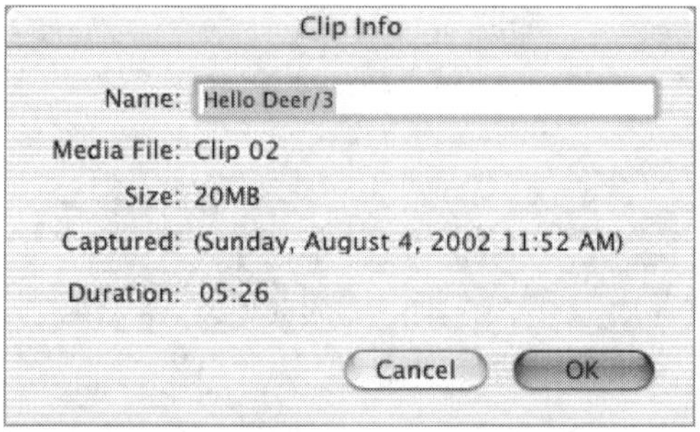

Figure 7.12 Double-clicking a clip displays the Clip Info dialog box, which reveals the media file's name.

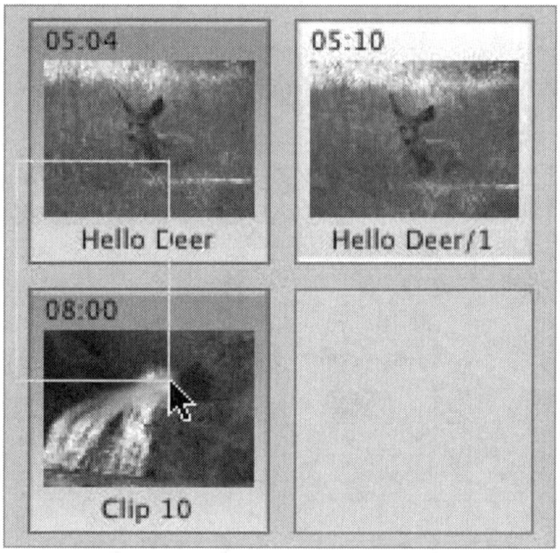

Figure 7.13 Click and drag your pointer in the Shelf's background area to select multiple clips.

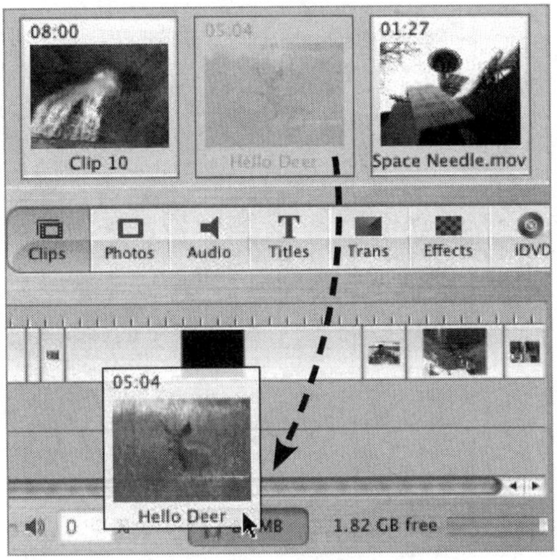

Figure 7.14 To delete a clip, drag it to the Trash; or, simply select the clip and press the Delete key.

Figure 7.15 As clips are added, the Trash indicates how much footage is marked for deletion.

Figure 7.16 I usually think reminder dialog boxes are annoying, but this is one I always pay attention to.

Moving Clips to the Trash

One of the few elements of iMovie that vexes me is the Trash, which seems at first straightforward, but doesn't act the way you would expect. You can easily delete clips, which are sent to the Trash, but there's no way to open the Trash and pull a deleted clip out (a behavior that every Mac user is accustomed to in the Finder).

To delete a clip:

1. Select a clip.
2. Press the Delete key, or click and drag the clip to the Trash icon (**Figure 7.14**).

So far, so simple. Remember that iMovie isn't actually deleting any file from your hard disk, only keeping track of which portions of clips have been sent to the Trash (**Figure 7.15**).

Emptying the Trash

If you know you're not going to need any of the deleted clips later, you can empty the Trash. This action permanently deletes the media files (or portions of the files, depending on what was cut), and frees up the amount of disk space indicated next to the Trash icon.

However, emptying the Trash also permanently affects most of your clips—you can't use the Undo command, or restore clips to their original state. So unless you desperately need to reclaim some hard disk space, *don't empty the Trash until your movie is finished.*

To empty the Trash:

1. Choose Empty Trash from the File menu, or click the Trash can icon.
2. iMovie displays a warning (**Figure 7.16**). Click OK to empty the Trash, or click Cancel to leave its contents untouched.

continues on next page

✔ Tips

- Levels of Undo don't transfer between your editing sessions. When you quit iMovie then launch it again later, your last 10 actions are forgotten.
- One way to restore clips you've trashed is to quit iMovie without saving changes to your project (**Figure 7.17**). When you launch it again, the clips you threw away will be intact again (though you lose all other edits you made since the last save). Another way is to use the Restore Clip command, which is detailed in Chapter 8.
- Don't forget that even if you empty the Trash, you still have a backup of your clips: the original footage stored on your camcorder's tape.
- Sometimes it can take a while to empty the Trash, due to the way iMovie stores the clip media files. Deleting a short section at the beginning of a clip, for example, makes emptying the Trash take longer because iMovie must first copy the clip's remaining data, calculate the time between the new beginning and the ending, then delete the original file. Trashing a section from the end of a clip is quicker, because iMovie already knows the clip's beginning point.

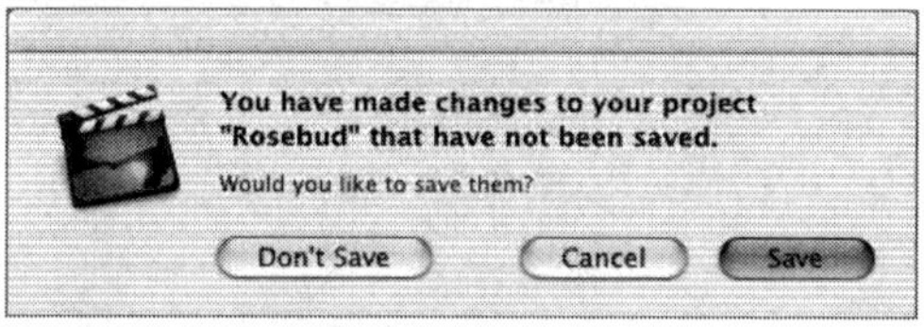

Figure 7.17 Resurrect your trashed footage by quitting iMovie without saving any changes.

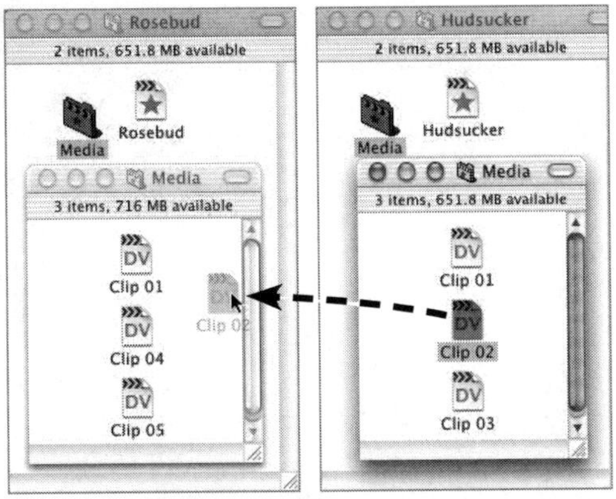

Figure 7.18 Perform a little quick-change act to move clips between projects—iMovie figures it out.

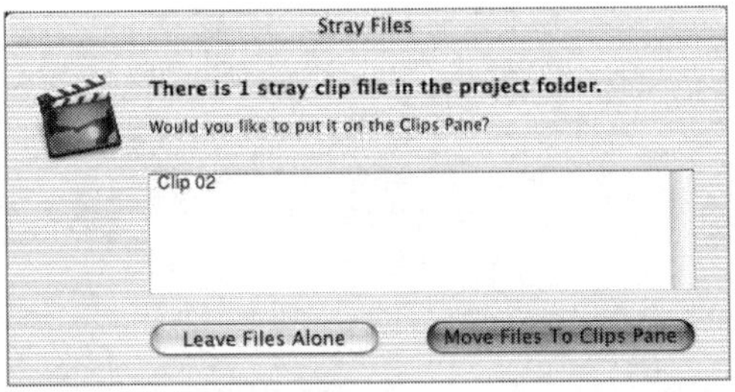

Figure 7.19 iMovie notices the new media file and builds a thumbnail for the clip.

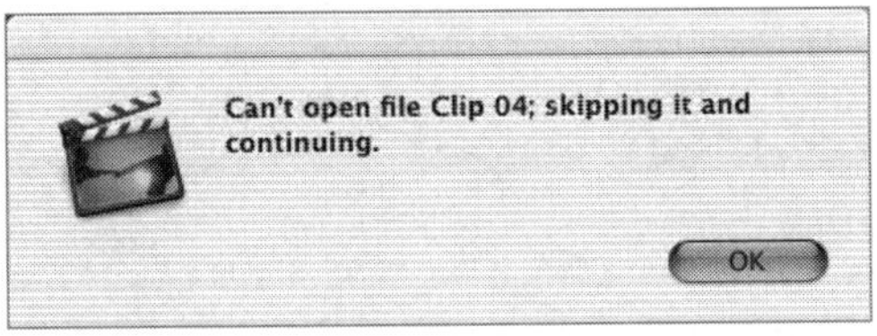

Figure 7.20 When you open a project, iMovie scans the Media folder to see if there have been any changes. If a file goes missing, you get this message.

Transferring Clips to Other Projects

As you'll learn in the next chapter, non-linear editing means you don't have to stick to the chronology of the camcorder's tape. What if you want to insert your great bear sighting that you took days earlier? Moving clips is easy, though a little rough around the edges.

To transfer a clip to another project:

1. Open the project that contains the clip you want.
2. Identify the clip's media file by double-clicking the clip and noting its name.
3. Switch from iMovie to the Finder and locate that media file in your project's Media folder.
4. Drag and drop the file to your destination project's Media folder (**Figure 7.18**).
5. Open the destination project. A dialog box tells you that iMovie has found clips that weren't originally there (**Figure 7.19**). Click Move Files To Clips Pane.
6. Save your project, then open the other project where the clip originated. iMovie displays a dialog box telling you that the clip's media file could not be found and was skipped (**Figure 7.20**). Click OK.
7. Open the destination project again, where the clip now appears on the Shelf.

✔ Tips

- Unfortunately, if you've moved several clips, you must confirm a dialog box in the original project for each missing media file.
- Use this technique to split larger project folders into smaller ones when copying to smaller-capacity hard disks.

8

EDITING VIDEO

The first movies were pure documentaries. Armed with new technology, camera operators shot what they saw: trains leaving the station, people at work, the movement of animals. Motion pictures didn't need to tell a story because the story was in the reproduction. The first movie created by brothers Louis and Auguste Lumière was the action spectacular *Workers Leaving the Lumière Factory*, depicting exactly that.

However, filmmakers soon realized that their "flickers" didn't need to be just linear slices of life. They could shoot movies in any order and assemble them to tell a story, or even combine totally unrelated scenes for dramatic effect. Lev Kuleshov, an early Russian filmmaker, filmed a closeup of an actor wearing a neutral expression. He then intercut a scene of an empty bowl, prompting audiences to praise the actor's subtle portrayal of hunger. Kuleshov took the same neutral footage and intercut scenes of a dead woman in a coffin, then a girl playing with a doll, and in each case audiences were amazed to see the actor's grief or joy. Editing became a vehicle for expressing emotions or ideas that weren't necessarily present during filming.

Today, iMovie and non-linear editing give you the capability to use the visual language of film to tell stories, whether fiction or simply a day at the park. The fun begins here!

Timecode

In Chapter 2, I explained how timecode works as it applies to a camcorder. Although it operates the same in iMovie, you're going to run into slightly different versions of it in various places while editing.

Timecode in iMovie

- **At the Playhead.** The Playhead's timecode always shows the time relative to the entire movie. So, for example, positioning the Playhead two seconds into a clip that appears in the middle of your movie displays something like "08:04" instead of "02:00" (**Figure 8.1**). The only exception is when you select a clip on the Shelf, which isn't yet part of your movie.
- **In the Clip Viewer.** In addition to showing timecode of individual clips, the Clip Viewer and Timeline Viewer display the movie's total length. The Thumbnail Playhead, a red inverted T, indicates where the Playhead appears (**Figure 8.2**).
- **In the Timeline Viewer.** Although the Playhead in the scrubber bar shows a timecode, you often need to refer to the Timeline Viewer (and its Playhead) when editing. Individual clips include a timecode indicating their length, as space permits (**Figure 8.3**).

✔ Tips

- By default, iMovie displays short timecode, displaying only seconds:frames (such as "02:07") instead of minutes: seconds:frames ("00:02:07"). To switch between short and long timecode display, go to iMovie's preferences and toggle the checkbox marked Use Short Time Codes.
- See Chapter 2's sidebar "iMovie Timecode versus Real-World Timecode" for a timecode refresher.

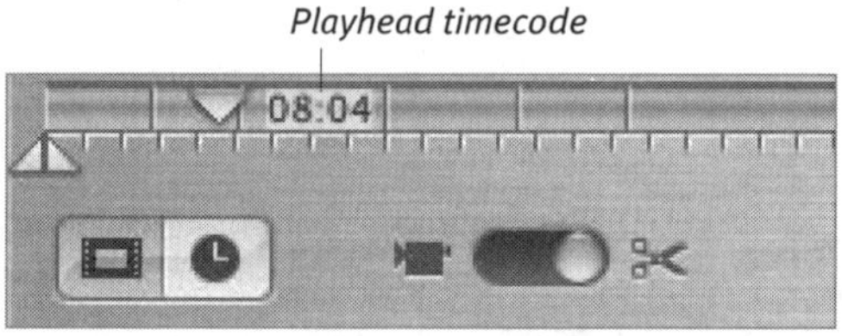

Figure 8.1 The Playhead timecode refers to time location within the context of the movie, even if only a single clip is selected.

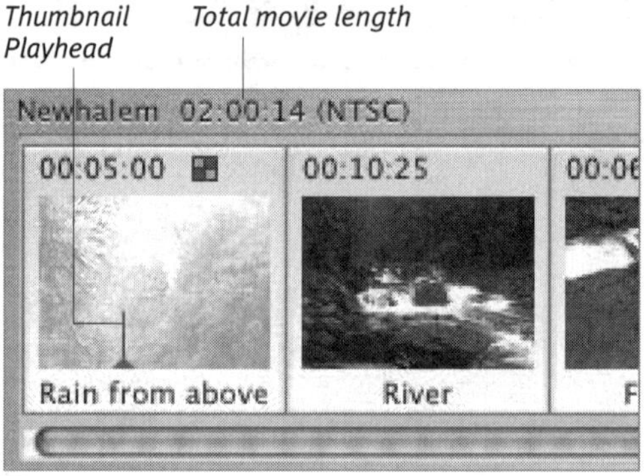

Figure 8.2 A Thumbnail Playhead appears in the Clip Viewer, but without a timecode indicator. (Note that I've turned off short timecode display in this example, so you can see the full timecode; see the tip at left.)

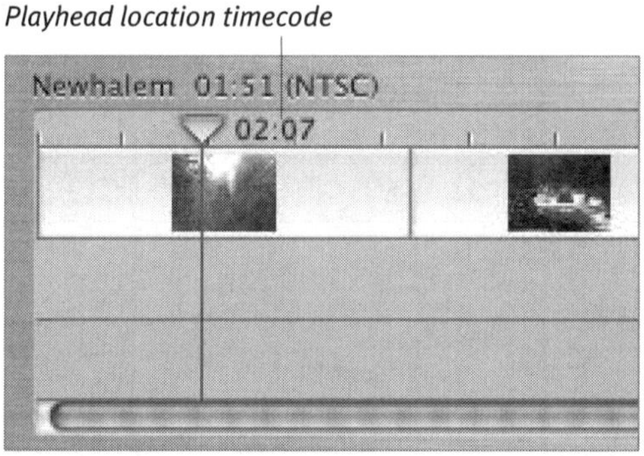

Figure 8.3 The Playhead in the Timeline Viewer includes its own timecode indicator, which is based on the movie's total time.

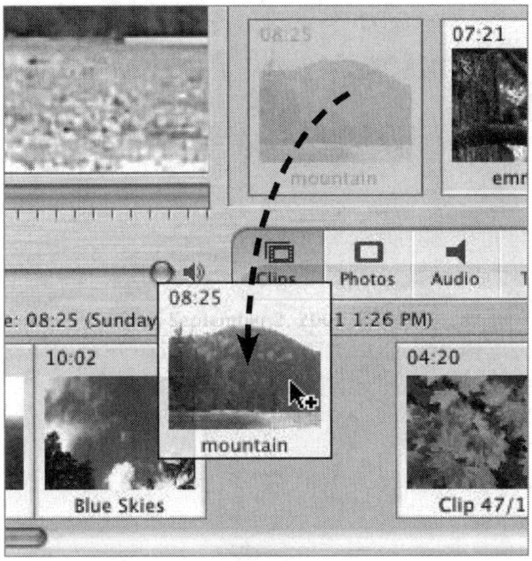

Figure 8.4 Drag clips from the Shelf to the Clip Viewer (shown) or Timeline Viewer to add them to the movie.

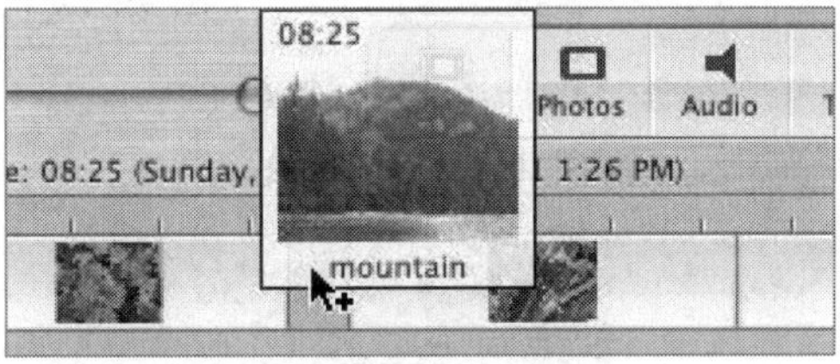

Figure 8.5 When adding clips to the Timeline Viewer, the clips in the movie scoot aside to indicate where you're about to drop the new clip.

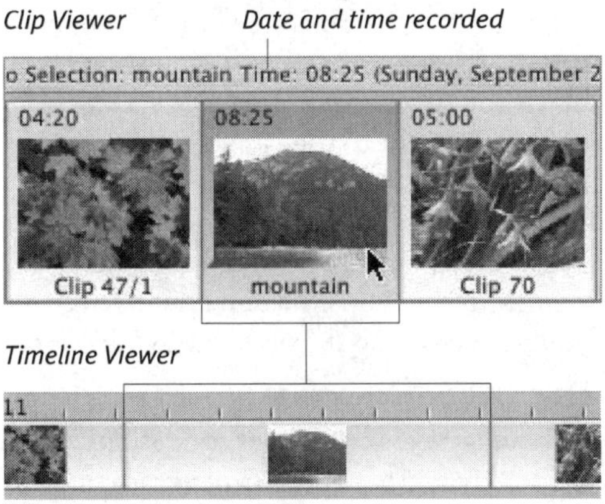

Figure 8.6 The two views shown here are of the same clip. The Timeline Viewer displays an approximation of the clip's length.

Adding Clips to the Movie

Even with a bunch of clips on the Shelf, your movie doesn't exist until you begin building it in the Clip Viewer or the Timeline Viewer.

To add clips to the movie:

1. Select one or more clips in the Shelf.
2. Drag the clip(s) to the Timeline Viewer or the Clip Viewer (**Figure 8.4**).

Ordering Clips

The movie's order progresses from left to right in the Viewers, so use the Clip Viewer to drag and drop clips in the order you wish them to appear; iMovie politely moves existing clips aside to indicate where you can drop your clip (**Figure 8.5**).

✔ Tips

- It's easier to assemble your movie by dragging clips to the Clip Viewer where each clip icon is the same size. The Timeline Viewer displays clips in different sizes based on their lengths (**Figure 8.6**).
- As editor, you have power over time. Clips can appear in any order, no matter when the events happened chronologically. (Most studio movies are rarely—if ever—shot in chronological order.)
- You can rearrange a movie's clips only in the Clip Viewer. The Timeline Viewer creates black frames if you try (see later in this chapter for more on black frames).
- If you need to determine when a clip was originally filmed, select it and look to the top of the Clip Viewer or Timeline Viewer. iMovie notes the date and time the clip was recorded (**Figure 8.6**).

Editing Clips

Remember in Chapter 2 when I advised you to shoot plenty of footage? Take a moment to look back on those lingering, leisurely days, because in this chapter you're going to chop your film into the smallest pieces you can, and still keep it comprehensible. Part of your job as editor is to arrange the many pieces into a unified whole, but you also want to keep your audience awake.

iMovie offers four methods for editing clips: splitting, which divides a clip where the Playhead is located; trimming, which deletes a selection of frames; cropping, which deletes the frames that aren't selected; and copying and pasting, which creates a new clip based on selected frames. These actions can be performed on clips that are on the Shelf or in the Viewers.

Remember that you can use Undo to easily cancel up to the last 10 edits you've made. Also, you can always resurrect clips that have been cut up (see "Restoring Clips" at the end of this chapter).

To split a clip:

1. Position the Playhead at the point where you want to split the clip.
2. Choose Split Video Clip at Playhead from the Edit menu, or press Command-T.
   A new clip is created and placed next to the original (**Figure 8.7**). iMovie appends a slash and number to the name to indicate it's a partial clip (such as "Trees/1").

✔ Tips

- This command works wherever the Playhead is located—you don't need to select a clip in order to split it.
- After splitting, the two clips are still selected. To deselect the clips, click the top of the Viewer, or select another clip.

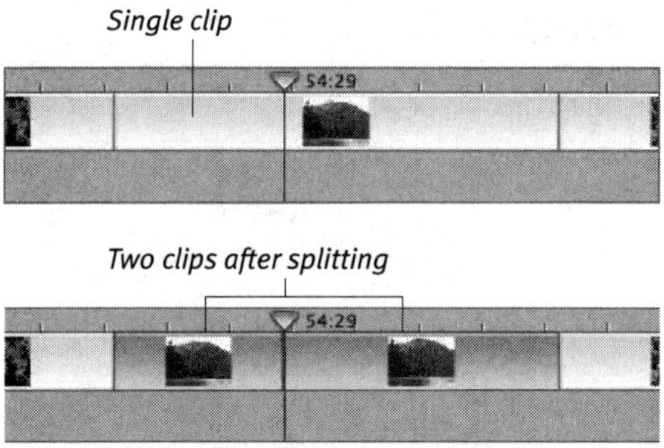

Figure 8.7 Use the Split Video Clip at Playhead command to slice a clip into two separate clips.

Get In, Get Out

There are times when long, lingering shots can define a scene or even an entire movie—but not many. When you're editing, concentrate on making your movies *tight*, showing only the essential shots within your scenes. For example, it's a good idea to have an establishing shot of a room, and perhaps a person opening the door. But you don't need to show him closing the door, walking to the center of the room, and beginning a conversation. Jump right to the conversation, since that's probably the core action of the scene. This advice applies to all types of movies: for your trip to the zoo, jump straight to the lions; we don't need to see you bounce along the pathway looking for directions.

Of course, there are always exceptions (watching *2001: A Space Odyssey* immediately comes to mind), but a tighter film is almost always a better film.

Crop markers

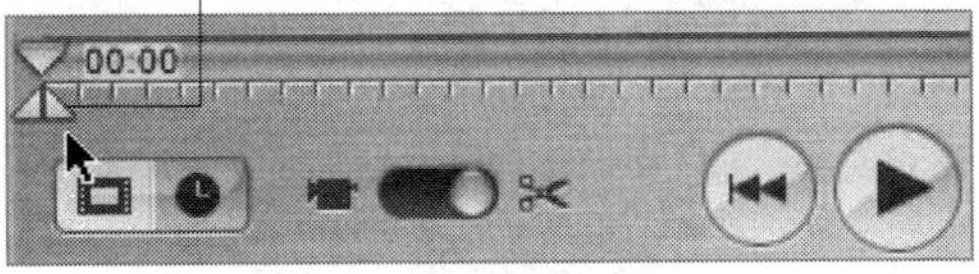

Figure 8.8 Unlike iMovie 2, the crop markers are always visible in iMovie 3.

Drag to make a selection

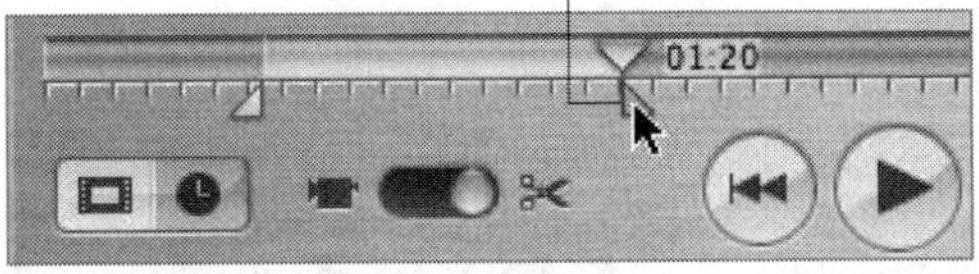

Figure 8.9 Click and drag to create a selection, which appears in yellow.

Right crop marker dragged past left one

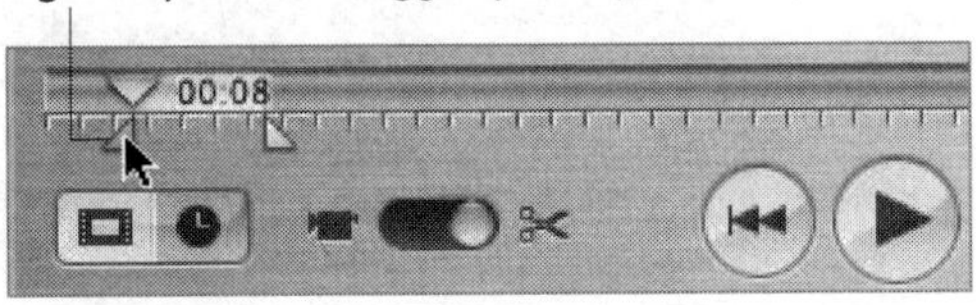

Figure 8.10 Dragging one crop marker past the other swaps their positions (right becomes left, or left becomes right). This allows you to make a different selection in only one mouse move instead of several.

To select portions of a clip:

1. Locate the crop markers at the left side of the scrubber bar (**Figure 8.8**).
2. Click and drag to make a selection, which is highlighted in yellow (**Figure 8.9**). The Monitor playback follows your pointer so you can see the frames being selected.

   or

   Shift-click in the scrubber bar to make a selection.
3. Move the crop markers to fine-tune your selection.

✔ Tips

- Click on another clip or at the top of the Timeline Viewer to deselect the frames. You can also choose Select None from the Edit menu (Command-Shift-A).
- If you move the right crop mark past the left crop mark, it becomes the left mark (**Figure 8.10**). However, if you use the Shift-click method, the selection is extended in the direction based on which crop mark is closest.
- With a selection made on the scrubber bar, choose Select All from the Edit menu (or press Command-A) to highlight all the frames in the clip; conversely, choose Select None from the Edit menu (or press Command-Shift-A) to cancel your selection. This only works when you have a single clip selected; otherwise it selects or deselects all clips in your movie.
- The crop markers can be finicky at times. If you're positioning your pointer beneath the scrubber bar and not seeing the ghosted markers, try clicking and dragging anyway to force their appearance.

To trim a clip:

1. Select a portion of a clip.
2. Choose Clear or Cut from the Edit menu, or press the Delete key. The selection is removed (**Figure 8.11**).

   If you chose to cut the selection, it will be stored in your Mac's Clipboard.

To crop a clip:

1. Select a portion of a clip.
2. Choose Crop from the Edit menu, or press Command-K. The selection is retained, and the rest of the clip's frames are deleted (**Figure 8.12**).

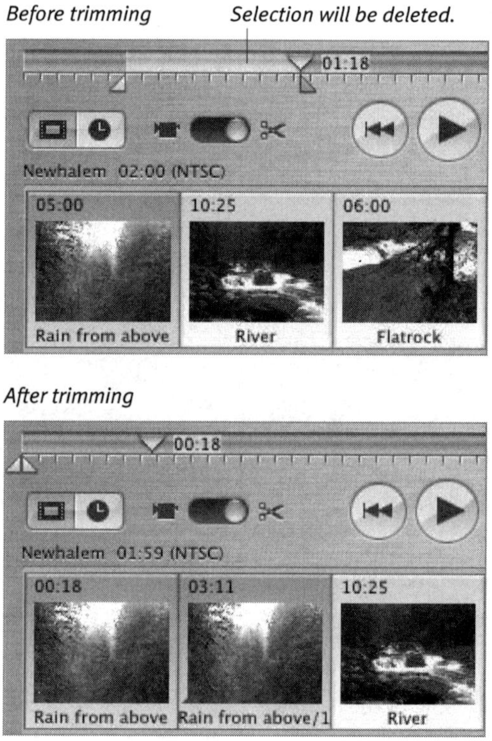

Figure 8.11 Trimming deletes selected frames. The remaining segments become two separate clips. (If you trim from the beginning or end of a clip, you end up with just one smaller clip.)

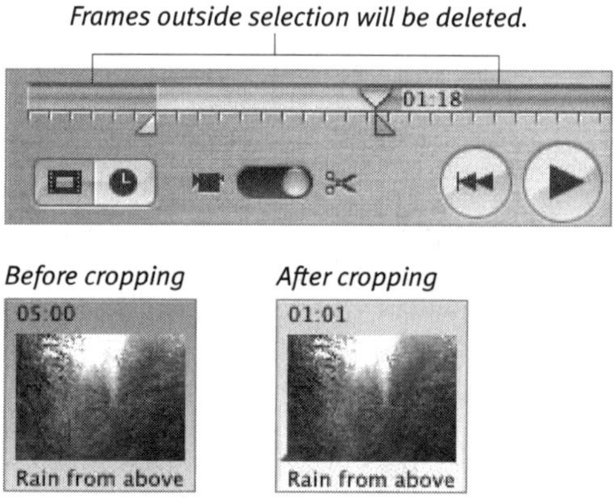

Figure 8.12 Cropping works opposite to trimming. The frames outside the selection are deleted.

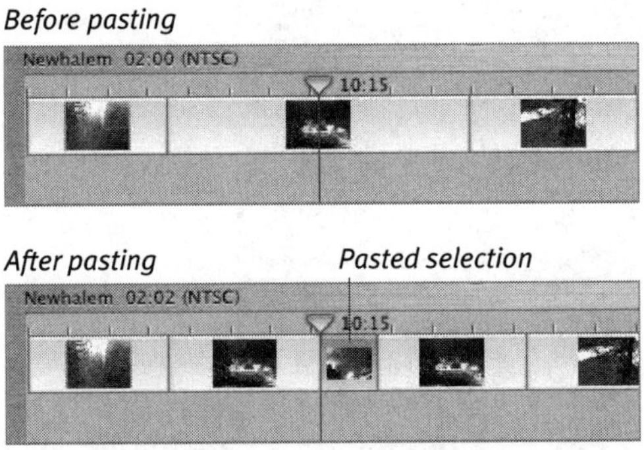

Figure 8.13 When pasting a copied selection into your movie, the new clip splits any existing clip at the Playhead and pushes its parts out of the way.

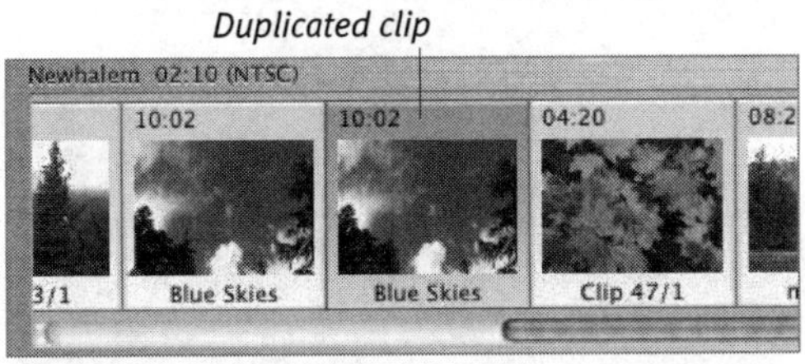

Figure 8.14 Duplicating a clip creates an exact clone of the original, which is why it's a good idea to rename the new clip.

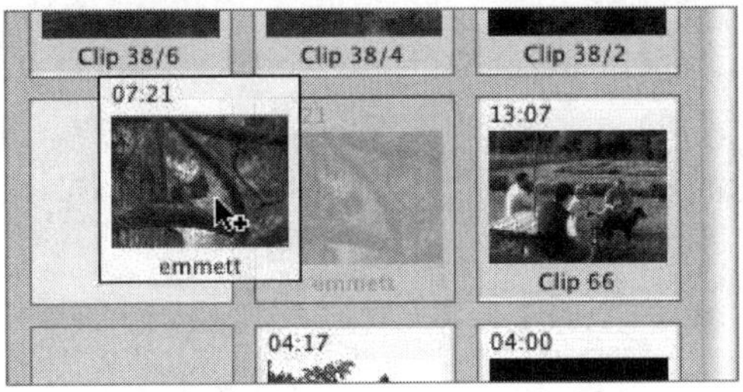

Figure 8.15 In the Shelf, hold down Option and drag a clip to an empty slot to duplicate it.

To copy and paste a selection to a new clip:

1. Select a portion of a clip.
2. Choose Copy from the Edit menu, or press Command-C. The selection is stored in your Mac's Clipboard.
3. Select any clip on the Shelf, then choose Paste from the Edit menu (Command-V). iMovie creates a new clip.

   or

   Position the Playhead in your movie to the location where you want the clip to appear, then paste it. iMovie inserts the new clip at that point, splitting any clip that was present and pushing its remaining footage to the right (**Figure 8.13**).

To duplicate a clip:

1. Select the clip in the Timeline or Shelf.
2. Choose Copy from the Edit menu.
3. Choose Paste from the Edit menu. A new, identical clip appears beside the original (**Figure 8.14**).

To duplicate a clip by Option-dragging:

1. Select the clip in the Shelf.
2. Option-drag the clip to an empty space on the Shelf (**Figure 8.15**).

✔ Tips

- Consider renaming your new dragged or pasted clip, since it will share the original's name.
- You can edit clips by trimming, cropping, or cutting and pasting in the Shelf. However, what's nice about doing it in the Clip Viewer or Timeline Viewer is that the new clips are already positioned within your movie.

Pasting Clips over Clips

In addition to pasting a whole clip into your movie, which inserts it and pushes aside other footage, you can also replace a section of an existing clip (or clips). This is an easy way to show different visuals while retaining a clip's original audio, such as when someone is narrating a flashback (**Figure 8.16**). You can choose to make the sound of both clips editable or not.

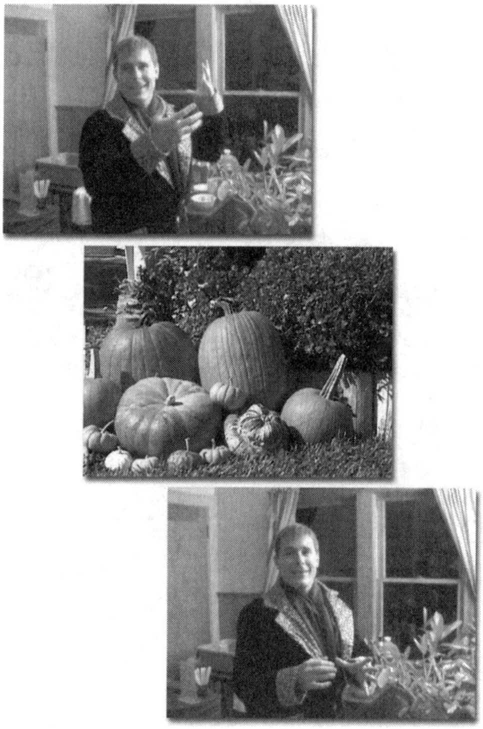

Figure 8.16 Using the Paste Over feature, you can add a flashback (middle) without interrupting the audio of your subject speaking.

To set the audio preference:

1. Open iMovie's Preferences.
2. To be able to edit the audio of the original video clip, enable the Extract audio in paste over option, if it's not already active (**Figure 8.17**). If you want to substitute in the audio of the pasted clip, disable Extract audio in paste over. Close the Preferences window.

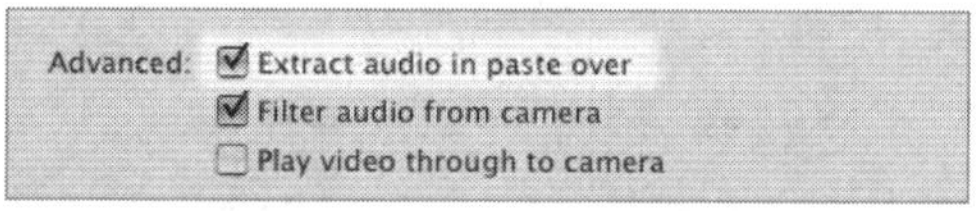

Figure 8.17 To make sure the original clip's audio plays, enable the Extract audio in paste over option in iMovie's preferences.

To paste a clip over another clip:

1. Select and cut or copy some footage or a clip.
2. Position the Playhead where you want the pasted footage to begin, or select a range of frames to be replaced.
3. Choose Paste Over at Playhead from the Advanced menu, or press Command-Shift-V.

   The pasted clip appears directly on top of the clip that was there before, with its sound clip—colored purple—added to the first audio track (**Figure 8.18**). The audio clip actually belongs to the original clip, and is what you hear when you play the sequence. The clip you inserted still has its soundtrack embedded, and you can hear the volume from each. However, you can now edit the audio levels and control which clip's sound is louder or softer (see Chapter 10).

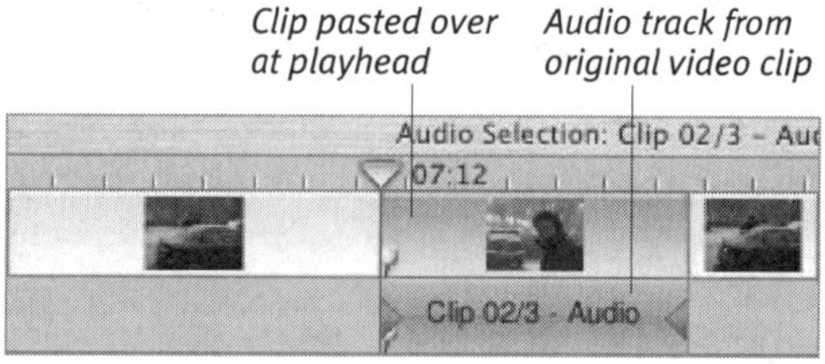

Figure 8.18 The original clip's audio is extracted so you can edit it independently of the pasted-over clip.

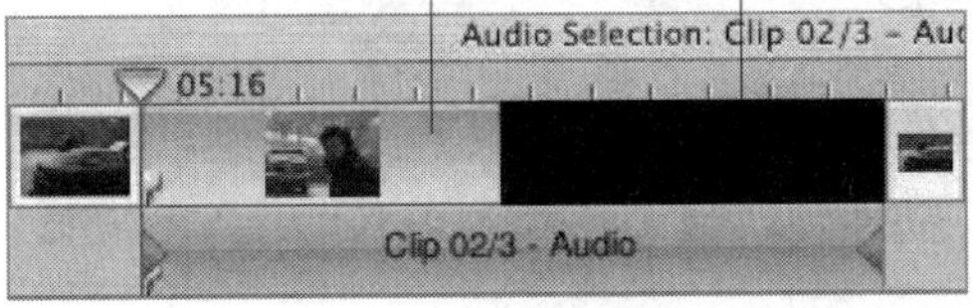

Figure 8.19 iMovie automatically adds black frames if the Clipboard contents are shorter than the selection in your movie.

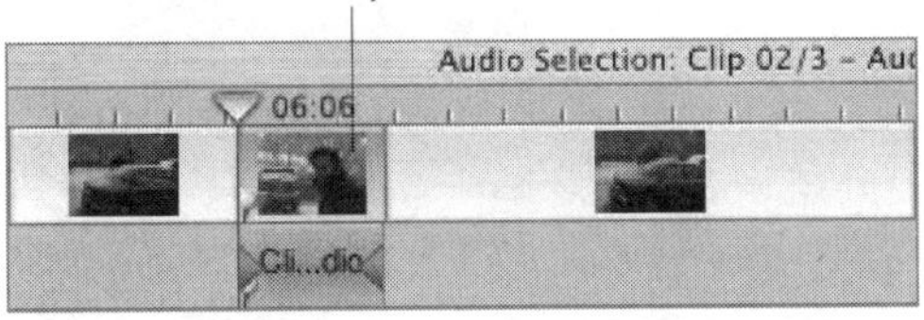

Figure 8.20 If you've made a selection in your movie that's shorter than the contents of the Clipboard, iMovie only pastes over as much as will fit.

✔ Tips

- Selecting a range of frames in the existing clip and then using the Paste Over at Playhead command can create a number of interesting results.
  - ▲ If the number of frames in both clips matches exactly, the footage is added with no worries, mate.
  - ▲ If the selection is longer than the footage on the Clipboard, black frames are added to make up the difference (**Figure 8.19**).
  - ▲ If the selection is shorter than the footage on the Clipboard, iMovie pastes only as much footage as will fit into the selection (**Figure 8.20**).
- When you use the paste-over technique, you're actually overwriting the existing footage (versus overlaying something such as a title; see Chapter 12). This means that if you delete the pasted-over clip, you don't get the existing footage back. The only way to get the lost footage back is to use Undo, or completely restore the clip media (explained at the end of this chapter).
- If you're looking for a Robert Altman-esque audio effect where the audio from both clips is playing simultaneously, use the Paste Over at Playhead command. Click the pasted clip (which retains its embedded audio track if the Extract audio in paste over option is enabled), then edit its volume (see Chapter 10).

Reversing Clip Direction

Playing a clip backwards can be good for more than just comic value or special effects. This feature comes in handy more often than I ever thought: a clip played in reverse can sometimes blend better into the next scene (for example, zooming out of a landscape). Then again, I find it hard to resist tweaking reality by making a spilled glass of milk clean itself, or coaxing waterfalls to rush upwards.

To reverse clip direction:

1. Select a clip.
2. Choose Reverse Clip Direction from the Advanced menu, or press Command-R. A triangle icon appears on the clip to indicate that it's reversed (**Figure 8.20**).

   To restore the clip's direction later, simply choose Reverse Clip Direction again.

✔ Tip

- Reversed clips feature backwards audio as well as visuals. You'll probably want to make the clip silent and play some other audio track in its place.

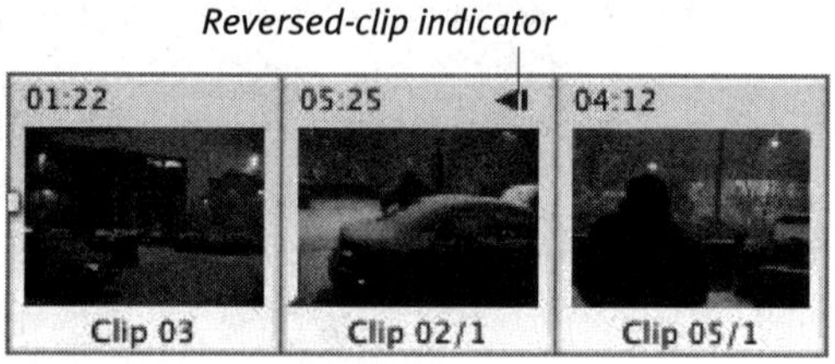

Figure 8.21 Look for this triangle icon to see which clips have been reversed.

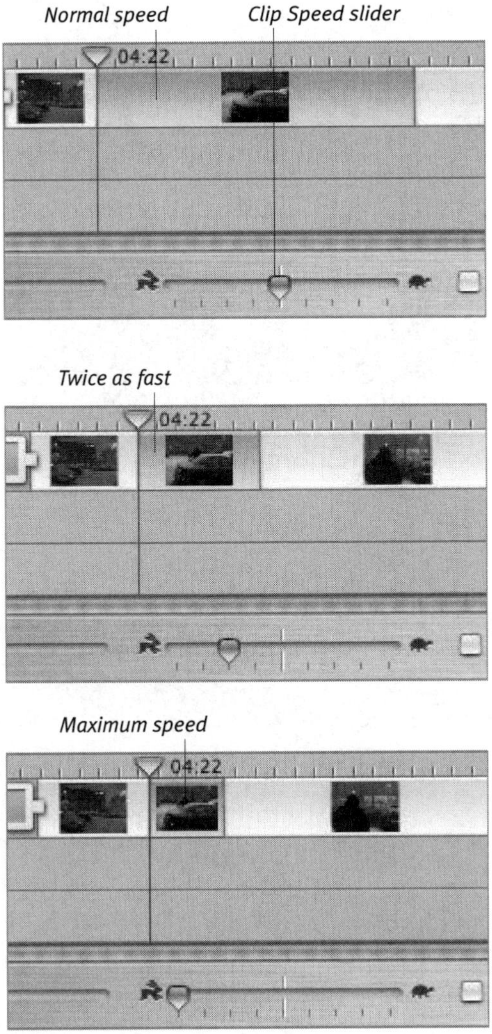

Figure 8.22 As you increase the Clip Speed slider, the clip shrinks to indicate how much time it occupies.

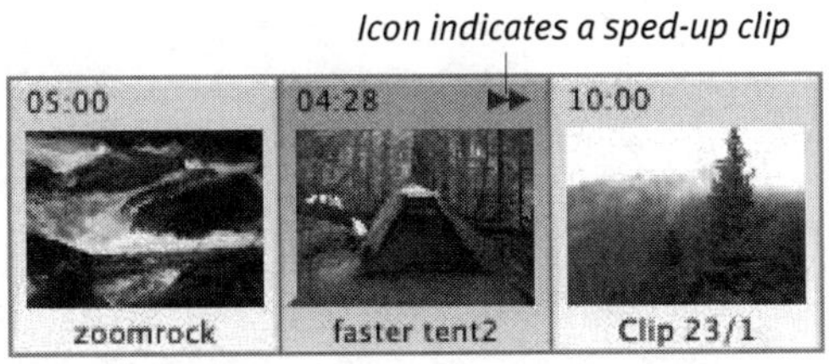

Figure 8.23 This clip has been sped up, exported to tape, re-imported into iMovie, and sped up again. You've never seen me set up a tent so fast!

Changing Playback Speed

Creating sped-up or slow-motion imagery used to involve changing a camera's shutter speed (the faster the film moved, the more individual pictures could be shot, creating slow motion, for example). In iMovie, all you have to do is move a slider.

To speed up or slow down video:

1. Select the clip you wish to alter in the Timeline Viewer.
2. Move the Clip Speed slider toward the rabbit icon (to speed up) or the turtle icon (to slow down). The clip contracts or expands in the Timeline to indicate its new duration as you move the slider (**Figure 8.22**).

iMovie's Clip Speed slider can make a clip five times faster or five times slower than the original speed. If you need a clip that's faster or slower than that, follow these steps.

To make clips super fast or super slow:

1. Speed up or slow down the footage in your movie as described above.
2. Export the footage to your camera's tape or to a QuickTime file (see Chapter 15).
3. Re-import that footage into iMovie. Since it's regular footage now, iMovie considers its speed to be normal.
4. Use the Clip Speed slider to change the speed of the new clip (**Figure 8.23**).

✔ Tips

- You can also simply click a portion of the slider's scale to adjust the speed, instead of moving the slider knob.
- Changing clip speed is especially helpful on clips of scenery or backgrounds. Draw out scenes you shot too quickly, or speed up long pans to improve pacing.

Inserting Black Frames

When you add clips to your movie, they're inserted end to end without any gaps. But sometimes you want to start a clip at one specific point. While you're experimenting with the timing of your movie, you can insert placeholder clips consisting of black frames to pad sections of the movie.

To insert black frames:

1. In the Timeline Viewer, select the clip that immediately follows the section where you want to add black frames.
2. Click and drag the clip to the right. A black clip appears (**Figure 8.24**).
3. Continue dragging until the black clip is the duration you want.

   or

   After the black clip has been created, double-click it to bring up its Clip Info dialog box, then change the time in the Duration field. That said, this *should* work based on iMovie 2's behavior, but it's broken in iMovie 3.0.3 (the latest version available at this writing).

✔ Tips

- If a transition precedes the clip you need to move, you'll need to delete the transition first.
- Black-framed clips don't need to be just placeholders. If you need some black footage longer than what's available using a transition such as Fade In or Fade Out, for example, insert a black clip. You can even paste the clip over footage to keep the audio playing while the screen is dark (see "Pasting Clips over Clips" earlier in this chapter). Another benefit of this is that, unlike using black footage you shot with the camera, black clips don't occupy hard disk space.

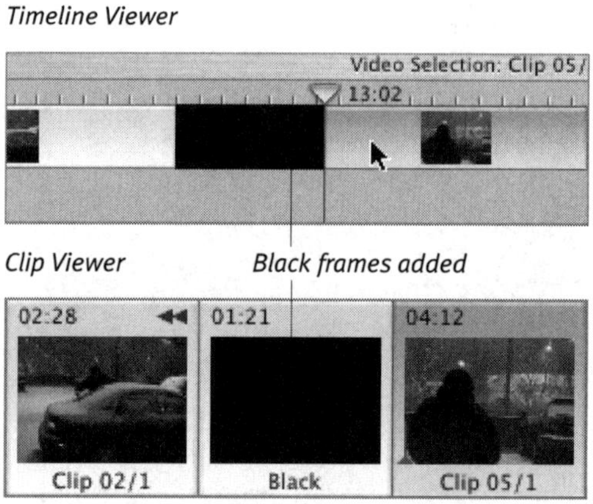

Figure 8.24 Dragging a clip to the right adds a clip composed of black frames before it.

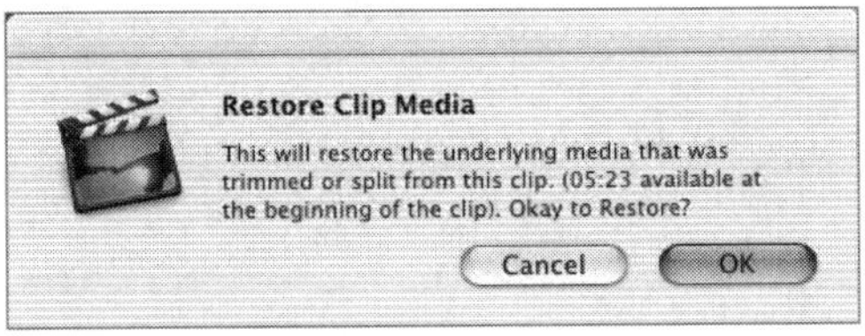

Figure 8.25 No matter how many times you chop up a clip in iMovie, the Restore Clip command is ready to pick up the pieces.

Restoring Clips

It's not uncommon for me to chop up a single long clip into so many little pieces that I've lost track of where they are. Some thrown away (in a Trash I can't open), some trimmed and reversed, some on the Shelf, and even a few in the movie itself. So imagine my frustration when I realize that I really need about two seconds of footage from the beginning that is now scattered throughout my project. Is all that work gone?

No way. iMovie has a last-ditch method of getting it all back, thanks to the way it stores files. As I mentioned in Chapter 6, clips you create don't actually exist as new files on your hard disk. Instead, iMovie simply notes what changes have been applied to clips, and grabs the necessary information from the clip's original data file. Using the Restore Clip Media command, iMovie can recover the clip as it was when you first imported it.

To restore a clip:

1. Select a clip in your movie or on the Shelf that you want to restore.
2. Choose Restore Clip from the Advanced menu. A dialog box explains the amount of footage that will be restored if you proceed (**Figure 8.25**).
3. Click OK to restore, or Cancel to dismiss the dialog box.

✔ Tips

- I like to make a copy of an altered clip before I restore it, just in case I need that edited snippet again.
- Say you take a clip and split it in half, then make edits to the second half. If you decide you want the entire clip back, restore the first half—the edits you made to the second half are retained.

Trash Warning!

If you've emptied the Trash, you can't restore your clips. As part of emptying the Trash, iMovie deletes the actual portions of the data files that have been deleted. So be certain you want to empty the Trash before you do it.

9

EDITING STILL PICTURES

After purchasing a camcorder, I didn't immediately throw away my trusty digital still camera. In fact, on a day-to-day basis, I find myself taking more photos than shooting video footage, purely because my still camera (a tiny Canon PowerShot 200) is easier to carry around.

iMovie makes it easy to incorporate those stills into your movie projects, whether you're creating a slideshow, adding a series of pictures to accentuate video footage, or creating graphics or Photoshop-enhanced title screens. With iMovie 3, it's a snap to add any image from your iPhoto library.

This chapter also includes information about the new—and highly touted—Ken Burns Effect, a pan-and-zoom operation that adds motion to otherwise static images.

Importing Pictures from iPhoto

iMovie can easily import photos you've scanned or taken with a digital still camera. iMovie 3 makes this process easier by giving you access to your iPhoto library of pictures.

To import pictures from iPhoto:

1. Click the Photos button to switch to the Photos pane (**Figure 9.1**).
2. Your entire photo library is shown in the preview area. If you want to access a specific photo album, choose its name from the popup menu.
3. Click on a photo to select it for importing.
4. Set the clip's length by using the Duration slider or type a value in the Duration field (in timecode's seconds:frames format).
5. Drag the picture from the Photos pane to the Timeline, where it appears as a regular clip (**Figure 9.2**).

✔ Tips

- Check to see if the Ken Burns Effect is activated before you import still photos (see "Adding Motion with the Ken Burns Effect," later in this chapter). If you want the photo to appear without any motion applied, uncheck the Ken Burns Effect checkbox if it is active. Or, you can type Command-period to cancel the effect after the image imports (the render status bar on the clip disappears).
- You can add multiple photos at once: Command-click to select the ones you want, then drag them to the Timeline.
- The number to the right of the popup menu indicates the number of pictures in the selected photo album.

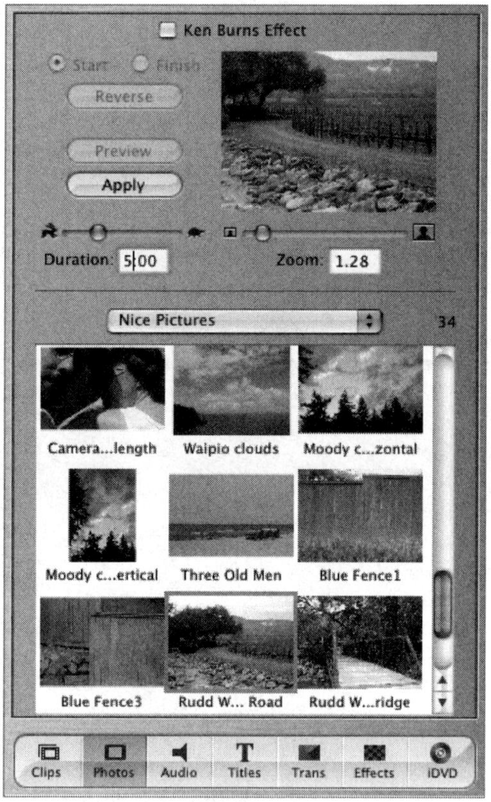

Figure 9.1 All the pictures in your iPhoto library are accessible from within the Photos pane.

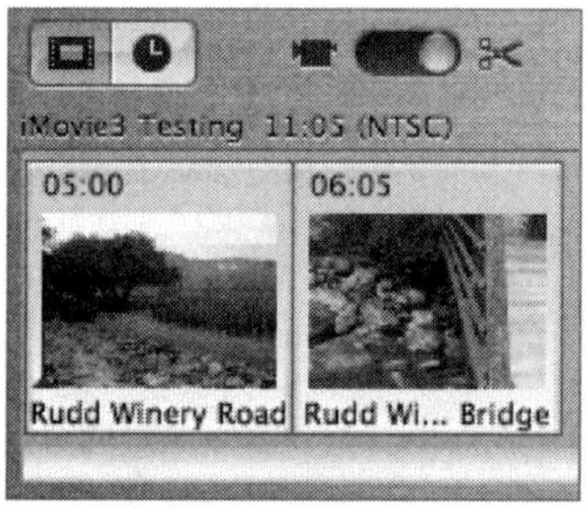

Figure 9.2 Imported photos appear in the Timeline as video clips.

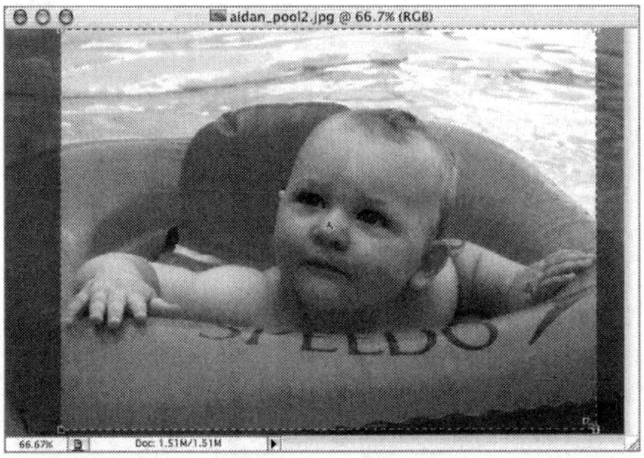

Figure 9.3 To fit correctly into a movie, still images must measure 640 by 480 pixels.

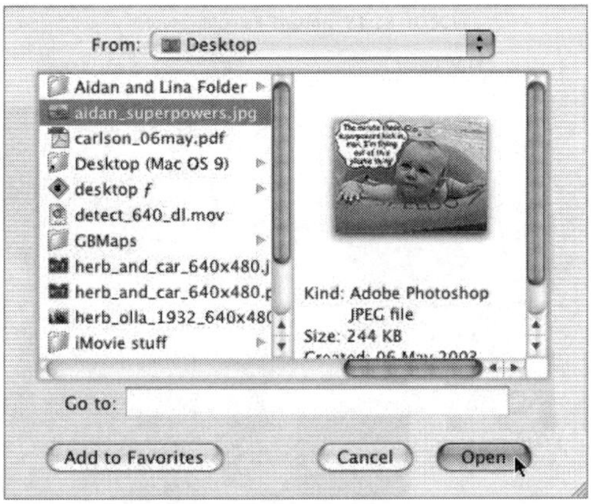

Figure 9.4 Using the File menu's Import command shows you a preview of your image.

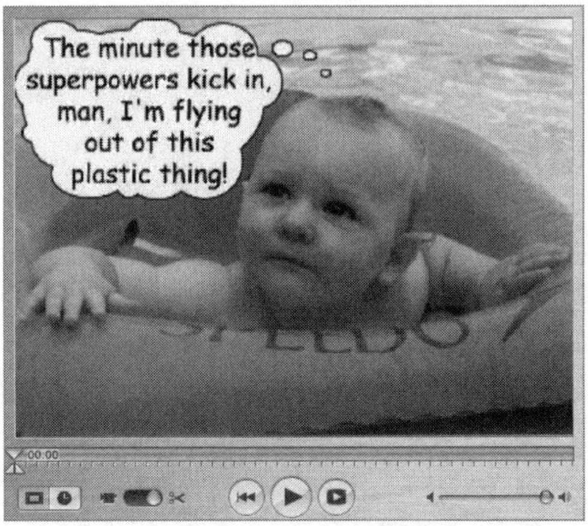

Figure 9.5 Come on, did you honestly think I could write an iMovie book and not include a baby picture?

Importing Pictures from Other Sources

iMovie can easily import photos you've scanned or taken with a digital still camera—or better, images that you've modified in an image-editing program such as Adobe Photoshop (`www.adobe.com/products/photoshop/`) or GraphicConverter (`www.lemkesoft.com`). But first, make sure it's ready to be imported.

To prepare a still picture for import:

1. Open the image in your favorite image-editing application.
2. Size the image so that its dimensions are 640 by 480 pixels (**Figure 9.3**). Make any other changes you see fit.
3. Save the image as a JPEG file.

To import a still picture:

◆ Drag an image file from the Desktop to iMovie's Shelf or Timeline.

or

1. In iMovie, choose Import File from the File menu (or press Command-I).
2. In the Import File dialog box, select the still image you want (**Figure 9.4**) and click the Open button.

   The image appears as a clip on the Shelf, which can be added to your movie like any other clip (**Figure 9.5**).

✔ Tips

- Imported images that don't measure 640 by 480 pixels appear with black bands on the sides or top and bottom.
- iMovie 3 doesn't display PICT image files correctly—best to avoid them entirely.
- The duration of imported images is set by the Duration value in the Photos pane.

Creating a Still Clip from a Video Clip

Thousands of still images flicker by as we're watching video—sometimes too quickly. Perhaps you'd like to linger on a sunset or highlight the one short moment when everyone in your family was looking at the camera. You can create a still clip from a single frame of video.

To create a still clip:

1. Position the Playhead at the frame you wish to use.
2. Choose Create Still Frame from the Edit menu, or press Command-Shift-S. A new 5-second clip appears on the Shelf, named "Still 03" or similar—iMovie sets the number in the title (**Figure 9.6**).

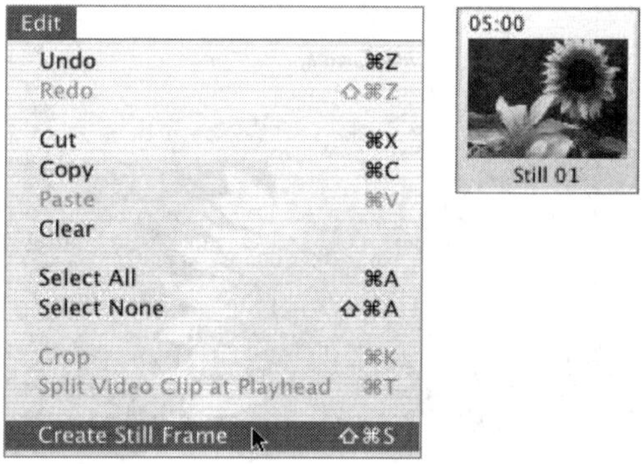

Figure 9.6 A new 5-second clip appears on the Shelf when you choose Create Still Frame.

How to Set a Default Still Clip Duration in iMovie 3

iMovie 3 removed the capability to specify a default duration for still clips that you create using Create Still Frame—but is it really gone? Time to hack iMovie's preference file!

First, quit iMovie. Then, using a text editor such as Apple's TextEdit or Bare Bones Software's BBEdit, open the file named *com.apple.iMovie3.plist* in your [User]/Library/Preferences folder. (It's a good idea to make a copy of this file before editing it.) Scroll down until you see this:

```
<key>DefaultStillDuration: %4.2f
</key>
<real>5.000000e+00</real>
```

The last decimal number represents the default duration of 5 seconds. To make all new still clips 3 seconds, for example, change it to `<real>3.000000e+00</real>`. If you prefer 03:15 (three seconds and 15 frames, or three and a half seconds), use `<real>3.500000e+00</real>`.

Save the file, launch iMovie, and use Create Still Frame to view your handiwork.

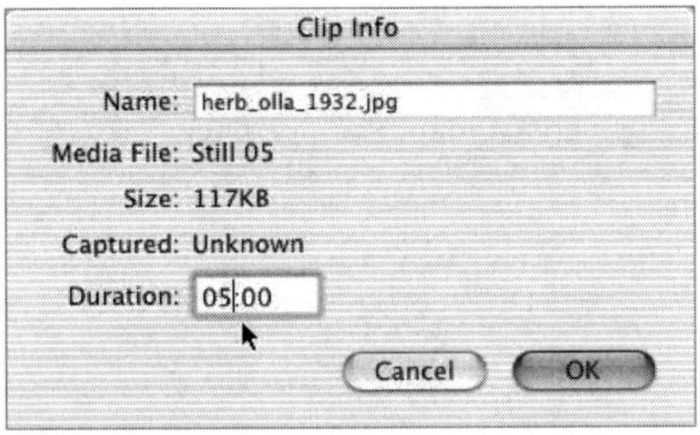

Figure 9.7 Double-click a still clip to access the Clip Info screen, where you can change the duration value. Other video clips do not have an editable Duration field.

Changing the Duration of a Still Clip

Now that your picture has been added to iMovie, it can be edited like any other clip (see Chapter 8). However, if you haven't applied the Ken Burns Effect (see the next page), the change you're most likely to make is to the clip's duration. Instead of trimming the clip, simply tell iMovie how long the clip should be.

To change a picture's duration:

1. Double-click the still clip, or choose Show Info from the File menu (or, press Command-I).
2. In the Clip Info dialog box, enter a new value into the Duration field (**Figure 9.7**). The field uses timecode format (seconds: frames, though you could go ahead and enter a full hours:minutes:seconds:frames value such as 01:34:25:19 if you wanted).

Adding Motion with the Ken Burns Effect

Who says still photos must remain still? A common effect used by documentary filmmakers is *pan and zoom*, where the camera moves across a still image, zooms in on (or out of) a portion of the image, or performs a combination of the two.

To apply the Ken Burns Effect:

1. Select an image in the iPhoto preview area.
2. Click the Ken Burns Effect checkbox at the top of the Photos pane.
3. Set a duration for the effect using the Duration slider or field.
4. Click the Start button to set the appearance at the first frame of the sequence.
5. Specify a zoom setting using the Zoom slider or field (**Figure 9.8**). A setting of 1.0 displays the entire image on screen.
6. Click the image in the preview window and drag it to define the portion of the picture that initially appears. (If you're not zoomed-in at all, you probably don't need to do this.)
7. Click the Finish radio button, then perform steps 5 and 6 to set the appearance of the last frame in the sequence (**Figure 9.9**).
8. Click the Preview button to watch the effect in the preview window.
9. When the effect is set up to your liking, do one of the following to add it to your movie:
   - ▲ Click the Apply button; iMovie adds the clip to the end of your movie.
   - ▲ Drag the photo from the iPhoto preview area to a location in the Timeline.

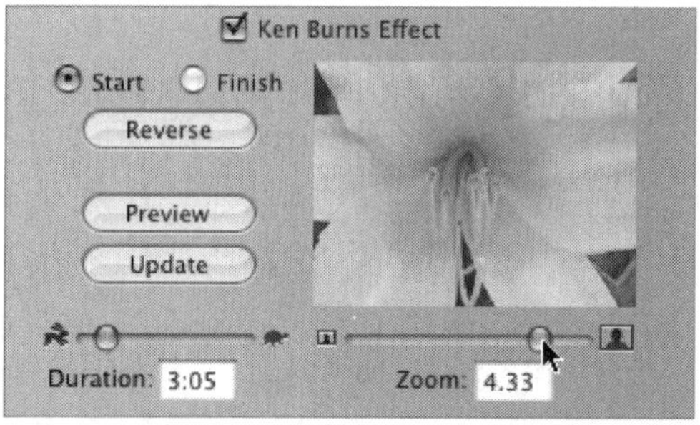

Figure 9.8 Click the Start button and set up the opening frame of the effect. Here, we're starting off with a zoomed-in close-up shot of a flower.

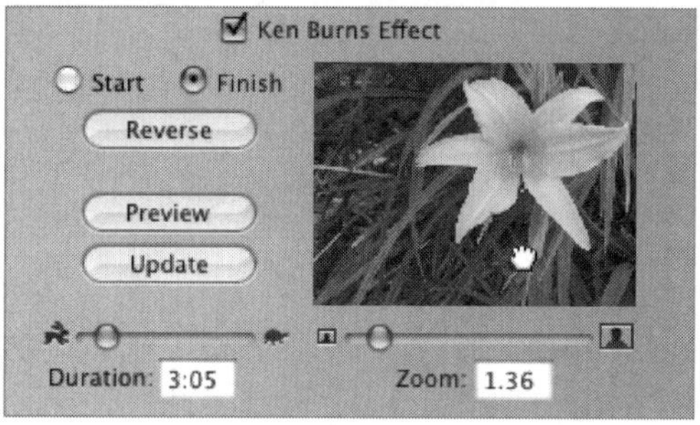

Figure 9.9 Now we're setting up the last frame of the effect—zoomed out and shifted to the right by dragging in the preview window.

Ken Who?

Ever one to capitalize on name recognition, Apple named this feature after Ken Burns, a documentary filmmaker who frequently employs the effect in his popular documentaries. Examples include *The Civil War, JAZZ,* and *Baseball.* For more information, see `www.pbs.org/kenburns/`.

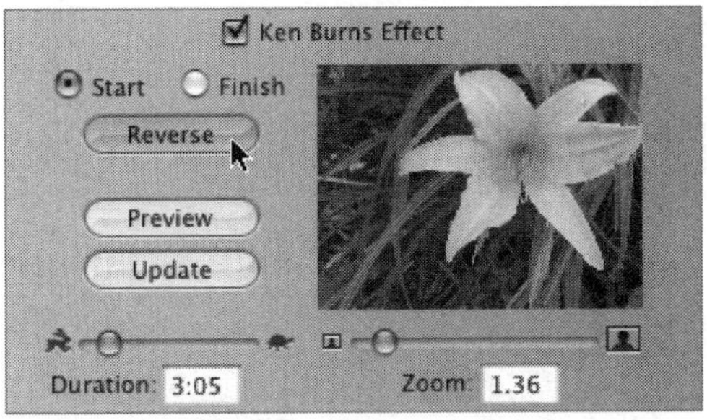

Figure 9.10 Click the Reverse button to quickly swap the Start and Finish settings.

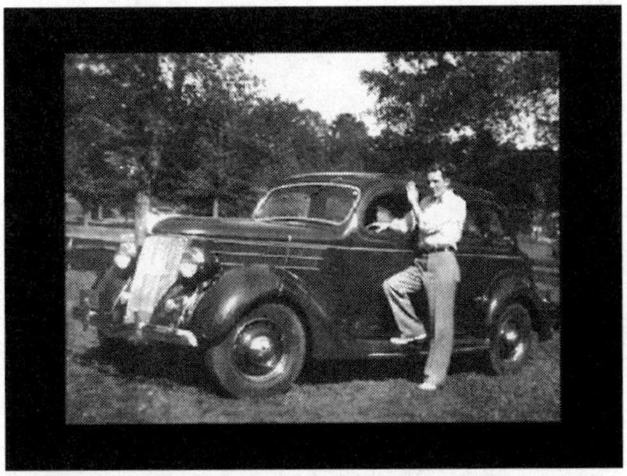

Figure 9.11 If a still photo has low resolution, iMovie compensates by keeping the image small and using a black frame to fill in for leftover space.

✔ Tips

- iMovie automatically plays the effect in the preview window; if the Finish button is highlighted, it means the preview has ended. Clicking the Start or the Finish buttons interrupts the preview.
- The Ken Burns Effect can only be applied to clips that are on the Timeline. Clicking the Apply button with a photo selected in the Photos preview area adds the picture to the Timeline.
- If you decide you want your effect to run backwards from the way you set it, click the Reverse button to swap the Start and Finish settings (**Figure 9.10**).
- You can use the Ken Burns Effect to crop photos. At the Start stage, specify a zoom amount. Then Option-click the Finish button to set the same zoom value. When you click the Apply button, the photo is added to the Timeline as a regular still photo, not a Ken Burns clip. You can also Option-click the Start button to apply the values of the Finish state.
- Higher-resolution photos generally display better than lower-resolution ones. Although iMovie does a good job of interpolating the image, zooming way in can cause blurry images.
- If your image doesn't start with much resolution, it appears in iMovie centered within a black border (**Figure 9.11**).
- For a different effect, drag the image out of the preview window entirely at the starting point, then drag it out of the opposite side of the frame for the finish point—the image glides across the screen as if it were in motion.

To apply the Ken Burns Effect to a non-iPhoto still picture clip:

1. Move the clip to the Timeline, if it's not already there, and make sure it's selected.
2. Switch to the Photos pane; the picture appears in the preview window.
3. Set the Start and Finish values (detailed on the previous pages) to define the pan and zoom effect.
4. Click the Preview button to see a rough version of the effect in the preview window.
5. Click the Apply button to render the settings and turn the picture clip into a video clip.

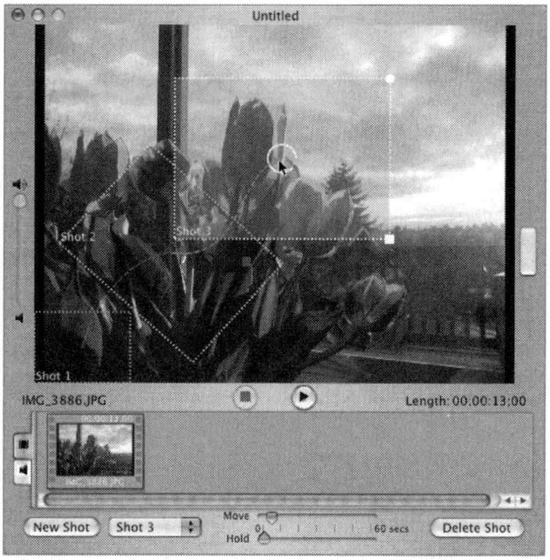

Figure 9.12 Granted Software's Still Life offers more control over pan and zoom effects.

✔ Tips

- iMovie 3.0.3, which appeared the day before this book was printed, broke the functionality described above. Hopefully, it will be fixed by the time you read this.
- If you want to change how the effect appears, make your changes and click the Apply button again.
- Unfortunately, you can't create a still frame from a video clip and apply the Ken Burns Effect to it. As a workaround, export the frame as a still image using the File menu's Save Frame As command, then re-import that file back into iMovie.
- For far more control over pan-and-zoom effects, look to third-party iMovie plug-in vendors. In particular, I like Still Life (`www.grantedsw.com/still-life`), which gives you the capability to rotate the camera, and add other photos and audio (**Figure 9.12**). You can then export the clip as a QuickTime or DV-formatted file to be imported into iMovie; or, you can even create a new iMovie project. See Appendix B for other companies, as well.

10

Editing Audio

How important is audio in a movie? If you ever get the chance to attend an advance test screening of a Hollywood movie, the answer may be painfully clear. I've been to screenings where the audio in some scenes consisted of just what was recorded on set—no background music, no sound mixing to balance actors' voices and dampen background noise, no re-recorded dialogue to enhance enunciation. Although quite a bit of work goes into editing audio, people tend not to notice it unless something is wrong.

I covered some methods for capturing quality audio in Chapter 5, which is the first step. But audio can be much more than just video's underappreciated sibling. In this chapter, you'll see how editing audio tracks can give depth to your movie by working independently of the video, and by adding music, narration, and sound effects.

Changing a Clip's Volume

When you import footage, the video and audio are combined in the Timeline Viewer's video track (**Figure 10.1**). So, as you're editing video clips, you're also editing the audio—splitting, trimming, and cropping it with the visuals. You can control how loud an individual clip plays, or change the volume level within the clip.

To set a clip's volume evenly:

1. In the Timeline Viewer, select the clip you want to edit.
2. Click the Edit Volume button, located below the video and audio tracks.
3. Use the volume control slider, or enter a percent value in the field, to set the clip's volume (**Figure 10.2**).

To change volume within a clip:

1. In the Timeline Viewer, select the clip you want to edit.
2. Click the Edit Volume button; a purple volume level bar appears within the clip.
3. In the Timeline Viewer, click on the volume level bar to set a marker where you want the volume change to occur (**Figure 10.3**). iMovie creates the marker (a yellow circle) and a beginning point for the marker (a small square).
4. Drag the marker up or down to increase or decrease the volume. All audio following the marker in that clip is affected.
5. Drag the marker's beginning point to the right or left to determine how quickly the volume change occurs.

To remove a volume marker:

1. Click a marker to select it.
2. Press the Delete key.

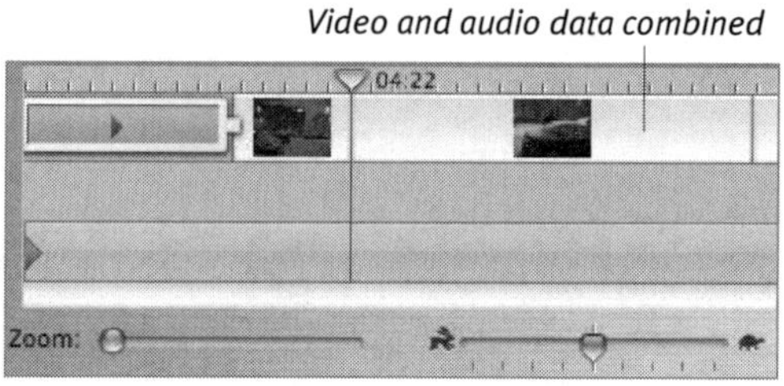

Figure 10.1 Although the top track is usually referred to as the video track, it also contains the clip's audio.

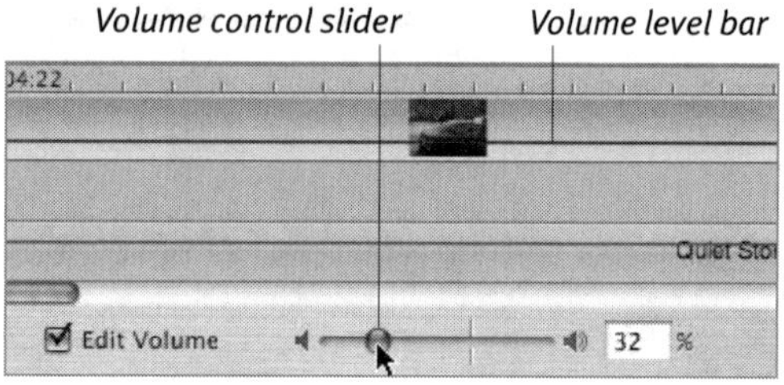

Figure 10.2 With a clip selected, click the Edit Volume button and drag the volume control slider to adjust the clip's volume uniformly.

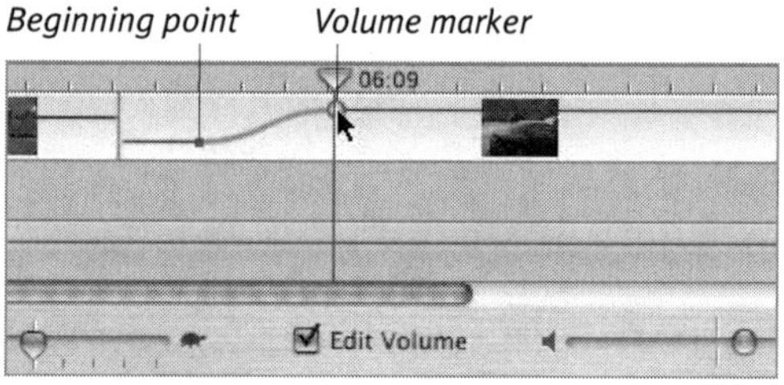

Figure 10.3 iMovie 3 introduced the capability to edit volume levels within a clip. The audio between the beginning point and the volume marker is automatically incremented smoothly to a louder or softer level.

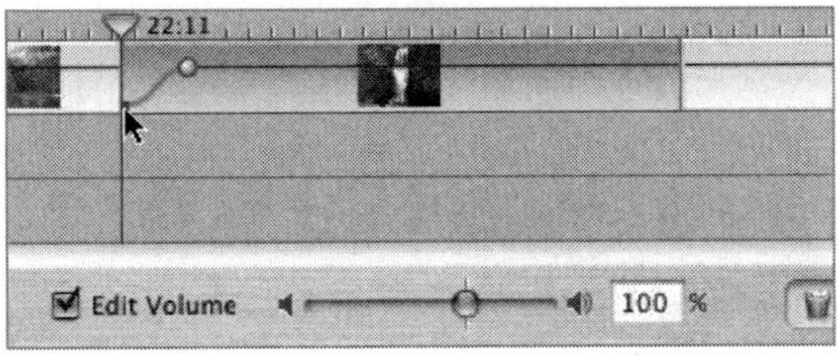

Figure 10.4 To fade in, move the beginning point to the bottom-left corner of the clip.

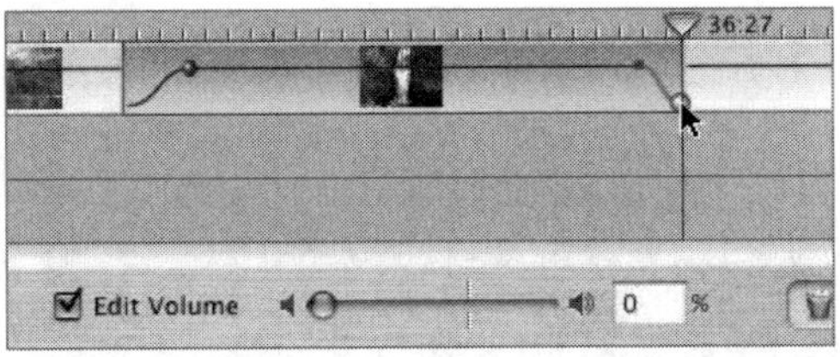

Figure 10.5 To fade out, move the volume marker to the bottom-right corner of the clip.

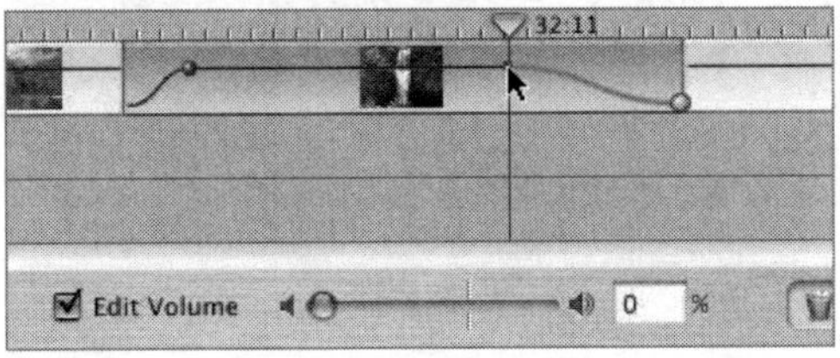

Figure 10.6 Move the beginning point left or right to determine the duration of the fade.

Fading Audio In or Out

iMovie 2 featured controls for creating audio fades—increasing the volume from silent to full strength (fade in) or dropping the volume from full to silent (fade out). With iMovie 3's improved volume controls, you don't need the old Fade In and Fade Out checkboxes, but sometimes you still want the effect. Here's how to do it.

To fade audio completely in or out:

1. Select a clip in the Timeline Viewer.
2. Click the volume level bar to create a new marker at the beginning or end of the clip, depending on which fade you want.
3. If you want a fade in, drag the beginning point (the square box) to the bottom-left corner of the clip (**Figure 10.4**).

   If you're looking to fade out, drag the volume marker to the lower-right corner of the clip (**Figure 10.5**).

To change the fade duration:

- Drag the the beginning point left or right to dictate the fade's length (**Figure 10.6**). You may have to first move the volume marker—which drags the beginning point behind it—then adjust the beginning point to extend the fade duration.

✔ Tips

- If you drag a marker so that it lines up with an existing volume level, a dotted line appears and the marker is automatically deleted.
- When you apply a Fade In or Fade Out transition (see the next chapter), the audio automatically fades to accompany the visual effect. But you can edit the volume levels in the transition, too (if you want the video to fade to black, but bring the volume down only halfway, for example).

Extracting Audio

So far, I haven't mentioned the two obvious audio tracks that appear in the Timeline Viewer. These are typically where you would work with sound effects or imported audio files, but they're also the sandboxes for playing with audio that comes with your video footage. Before we can play, however, we need to extract the audio from the video clip.

To extract audio:

1. Select the clip in the video track.
2. Choose Extract Audio from the Advanced menu, or press Command-J. An audio clip, represented as a purple bar, appears in the audio track beneath the video clip (**Figure 10.7**).

✔ Tips

- If you later delete an extracted audio clip, it's not gone forever. The original sound is still embedded in the video track, but its volume is turned down to zero so it does not interfere with the audio tracks. If you can't undo the deletion, select the clip and increase its volume to restore the sound. You can then extract the audio again, which places a new copy in the audio track.
- Extracting audio clips makes it possible to start playing audio before the visuals begin (or after they're done). For example, when editing the video of a recent camping trip, I wanted to portray how it felt to wake up one morning to rain (**Figure 10.8**). I opened on a few seconds of black frames with the sound of the rain pattering on a tarp, then faded in on the image of the wet tarp. The audio and visuals weren't synchronized, but that didn't matter because the clip was an establishing shot with background sounds.

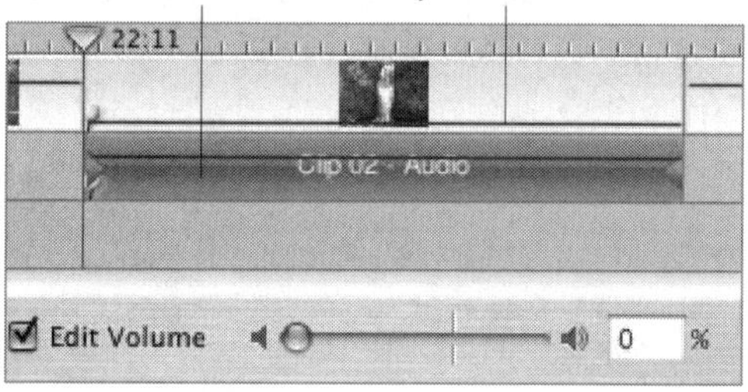

Figure 10.7 Extracted audio clips appear on the first audio track. The video clip becomes silent.

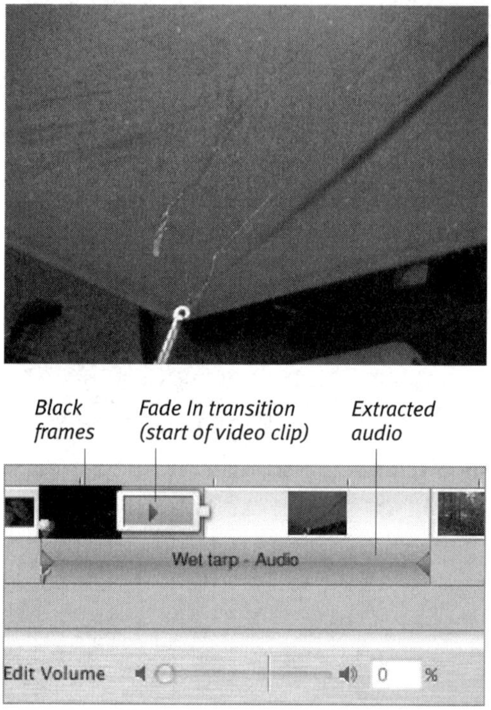

Figure 10.8 Extracting the audio from the "Wet tarp" clip allowed me to begin playing the sound of the rain during a few seconds of black frames, then fade in on the visual of the tarp itself (top). You can view this clip at www.necoffee.com/imovievqs/.

Locking and Unlocking Audio Clips

After you extract an audio clip, it appears with a pushpin icon at its far left. This icon indicates that the video and audio tracks are synchronized, or locked, at that point. But you can unlock the clip, then drag it elsewhere on the Timeline.

To unlock an audio clip:

1. Select the audio clip (not the video clip) in the Timeline Viewer. If you've just extracted the audio clip, it should be already selected.
2. Choose Unlock Audio Clip from the Advanced menu, or press Command-L.)If you don't see this command, it means the audio clip isn't selected.) The pushpin icon disappears (**Figure 10.9**).

Similarly, you can lock an extracted audio clip to any video clip in your movie. Locking it ensures that the sound remains synchronized, even if you add video clips later (**Figure 10.10**).

To lock an audio clip:

1. Position the audio clip where you want it to appear on the Timeline.
2. Move the Playhead to a spot where the audio and video clips overlap (it doesn't have to be at the beginning).
3. Choose Lock Audio Clip at Playhead from the Advanced menu, or hit Command-L. A new pushpin icon appears at the Playhead location (**Figure 10.11**).

✔ Tip

- Locking audio at the Playhead, instead of at the start of a clip, allows you to edit the video and audio clips without disrupting the synchronization.

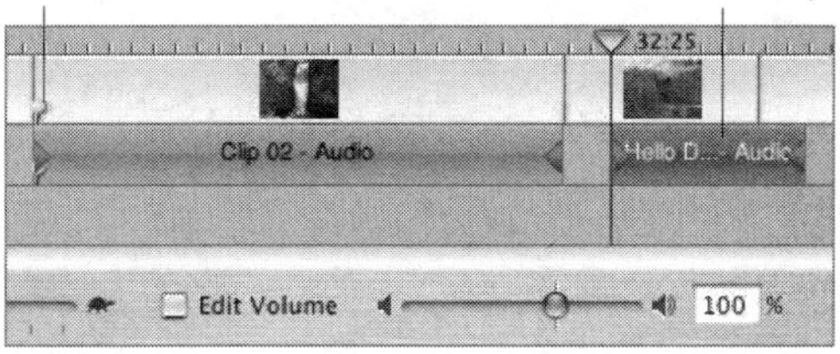

Figure 10.9 Once unlocked, you can position an audio clip anywhere in the movie. Here, the clip on the right is shifted out of sync with its video.

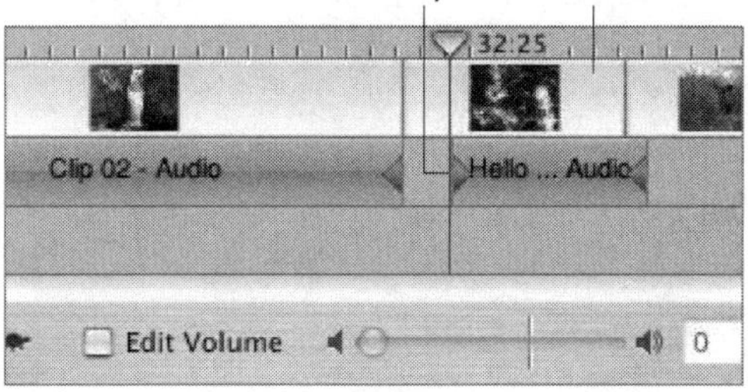

Figure 10.10 The unlocked audio clip gets pushed further out of sync when a new video clip is added.

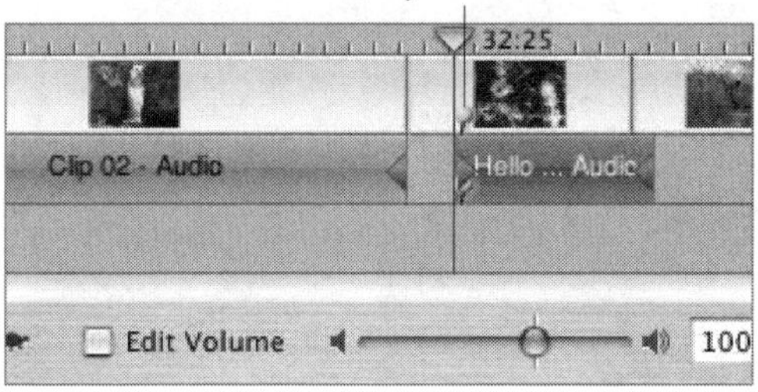

Figure 10.11 Choosing Lock Audio Clip at Playhead anchors the audio clip at a specific location.

Locking and Unlocking Audio Clips

Editing Audio Clips

When you extract audio, it becomes its own clip that you can edit independently of its original video clip.

To split an audio clip:

1. Select the audio clip. Unlike video clips, which are split at the Playhead even if they're not selected, audio clips must be selected with the Playhead in place.
2. Choose Split Selected Audio Clip at Playhead from the Edit menu, or press Command-T (**Figure 10.12**).

To rename an audio clip:

1. Double-click the audio clip to display the Clip Info dialog box.
2. Type in a new name in the Name field, then click OK.

   Note that as of iMovie 3.0.3, the Clip Info box doesn't work properly for audio clips: the name isn't shown in the Timeline, and the duration field doesn't work.

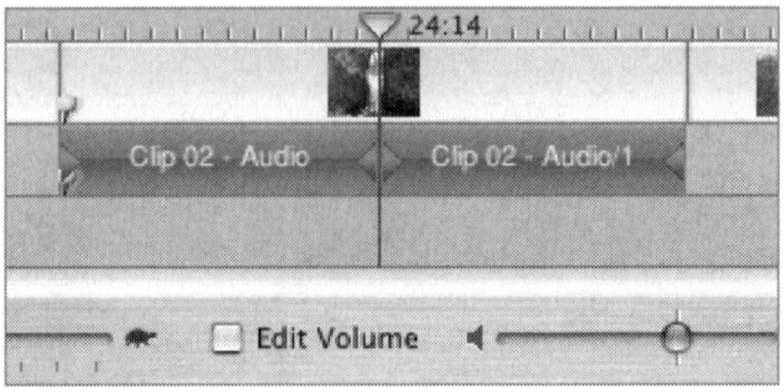

Figure 10.12 You can split an extracted audio clip without splitting the video clip to which it's attached.

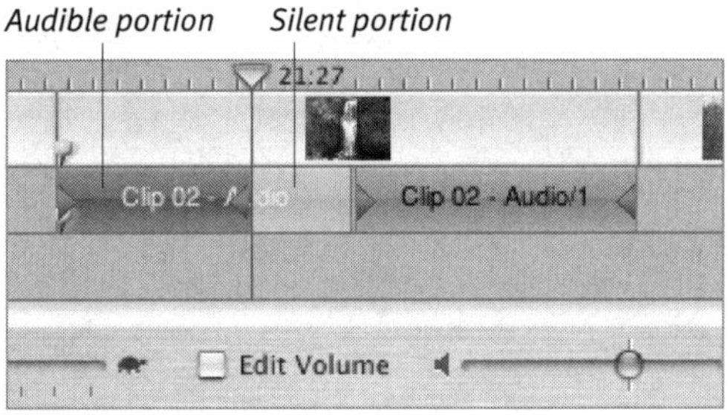

Figure 10.13 Drag an audio clip's crop markers to set which portion will be audible during playback.

Changing a clip's duration

Video clips use crop markers on the scrubber bar to select a range of frames. Audio clips, by contrast, feature crop markers at each end of the clip that determine at what point a clip becomes audible and when it goes silent. Simply drag the triangular crop markers to change the clip's duration (**Figure 10.13**). The highlighted section between the markers is what will be heard during playback.

If you prefer, you can leave the rest of the clip dangling in case you need to adjust the clip's duration in the future. However, this can lead to overlapping clips that are difficult to select. If you're satisfied with the clip's length, you can crop out the unused sections.

Audio clip cropped

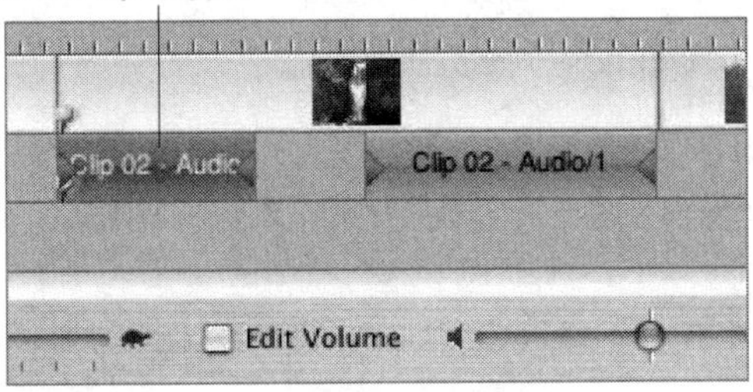

Figure 10.14 When you crop an audio clip, the unused portions are removed, not just kept silent.

Last video clip

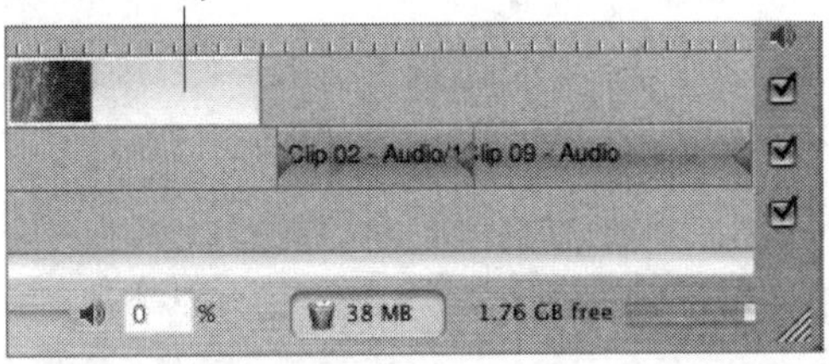

Figure 10.15 The end of your movie is a convenient location to temporarily store unused audio clips.

To crop an audio clip:

1. Set a clip's crop markers to your liking.
2. Choose Crop from the Edit menu, or press Command-K. The unused portions are removed (**Figure 10.14**).

✔ Tips

- Clips can go into either audio track in the Timeline Viewer, though iMovie tends to use the second track for imported audio.
- Although audio clips act like video clips in most respects, you can only edit them in the Timeline Viewer; there's no audio equivalent to the Shelf. However, you can temporarily store audio clips you aren't yet using: simply drag them beyond the end of the last video track (**Figure 10.15**).
- You don't have to select an audio clip before you adjust its crop markers. Grabbing a marker selects the clip for you.
- Audio is notoriously difficult to trim to the right length. Fine-tune your editing by using the left and right arrow keys: selecting a clip anywhere in the middle moves the entire clip when the keys are pressed, while clicking once on either crop marker makes it respond to your key presses.
- Unlike video clips, audio clips can overlap (though this can create audible gibberish, but that may be what you're going for).
- Editing audio is one area where the Timeline Viewer's Zoom control is especially useful. Zoom in to make precise changes.
- Experiment with overlapping clips that contain fades. This is an easy way to blend dialogue, for example (one quickie method for playing voices in a character's head), or even tighten scenes by reducing the amount of lag between speakers.

Adding Music from iTunes

When the first version of iMovie appeared, the idea of storing one's music as MP3 files on a hard disk hadn't yet caught on. Now, however, iTunes can rip and store thousands of songs, all of which are ready to be added to your iMovie project.

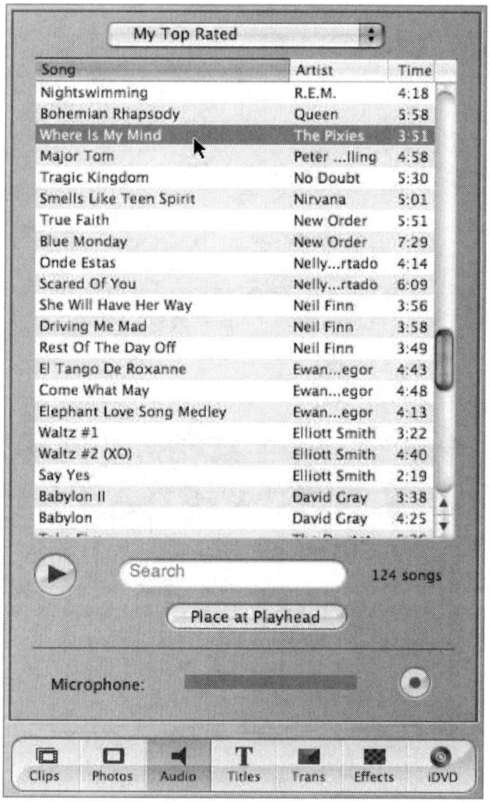

Figure 10.16 You don't have to leave iMovie to import your digital music—everything in iTunes is available.

To locate songs in your iTunes library:

1. Switch to the Audio pane. Your iTunes library is listed in the main window (**Figure 10.16**).
2. Scroll through the list to find the song you want to use, or click the popup menu to choose from your iTunes playlists (**Figure 10.17**).

   Or, type a word in the Search field if you're looking for a particular song or artist name. The list updates as you type (**Figure 10.18**). Click the Cancel button (with the white X on it) to clear the field and return to the full list.

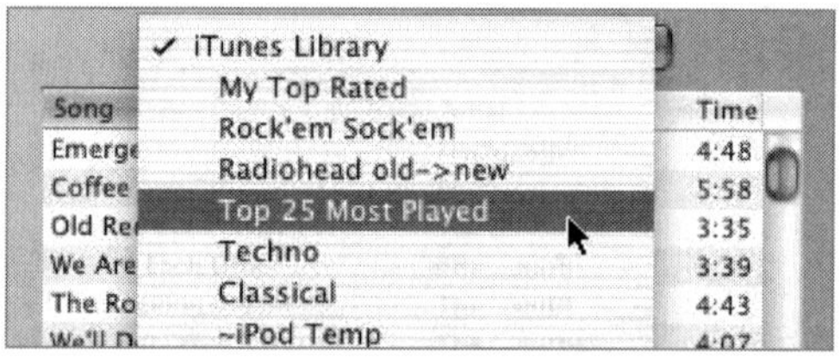

Figure 10.17 The popup menu lists your iTunes playlists to help narrow your search.

To listen to an iTunes song:

1. Select a song in the iTunes library.
2. Click the round Play Audio button to play the track from the beginning.

   Click the button again to stop playing.

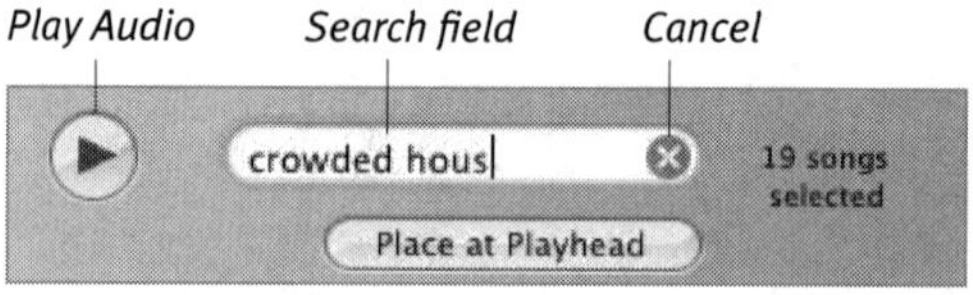

Figure 10.18 Type the name of a song or artist into the Search field to display only the matches in the list.

✔ Tips

- Set up a custom iMovie playlist in iTunes that contains the music you want to use for a particular project to help you find songs faster.
- The Search field only looks for song titles and artist names.

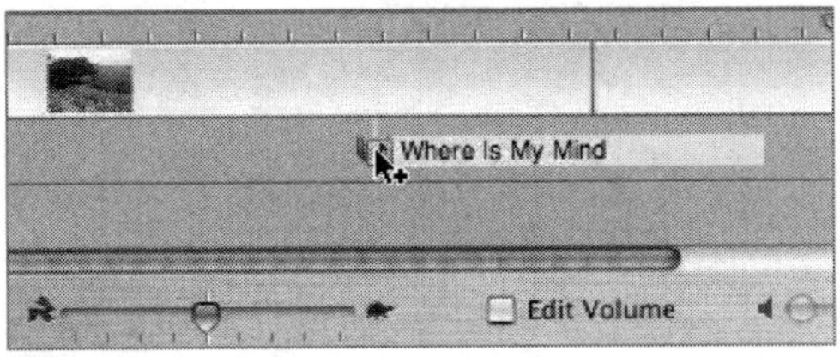

Figure 10.19 Drag songs directly from the Audio pane to the Timeline Viewer to add them to a movie.

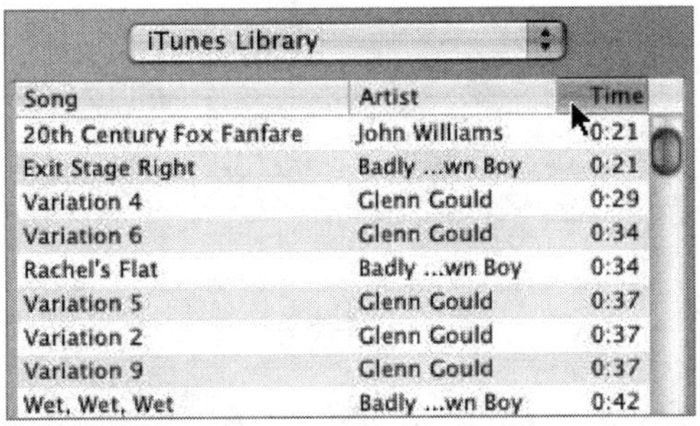

Figure 10.20 Sorting the iTunes library by time makes it easy to find music that matches the length of your video clips or sequences.

To add music from iTunes:

1. Position the Playhead in the Timeline Viewer where you want the song to begin.
2. Click the Place at Playhead button; the audio clip is imported and appears on the Timeline's lower audio track.

   or

   Drag one or more songs from the iTunes list to either audio track in the Timeline Viewer (**Figure 10.19**).

✔ Tips

- Click the column headings to sort the list. For example, I often click the Time column to find songs that fit within a given section of a movie (**Figure 10.20**).
- iMovie can import any file format that iTunes can play, so you're not limited to just MP3 files.
- Music encoded in MP3 or AAC formats in iTunes are compressed, meaning that some audio data have been removed to make the file size smaller. Most people probably won't notice the difference, but some audiophiles can tell. If you need to use the highest-quality music in your movie, import the songs in AIFF format within iTunes.
- It's worth pointing out that nearly anything you import from iTunes is probably copyrighted material. For most people this is no problem, since only friends and family are likely to see their edited movies. But if you're planning to distribute the movie or play it for a lot of people, you need to get permission to use the music.

Grabbing Music from an Audio CD

Nearly every kind of filmed creation—studio pictures, homemade shorts, even television commercials—uses background music at some point. In addition to importing music from iTunes, iMovie includes the capability to extract songs from any music CD you put into your Mac and turn them into editable audio clips.

To extract a song from an audio CD:

1. Insert the audio CD into your Mac's CD or DVD drive.
2. Click the Audio button in iMovie to bring up the Audio pane. If a CD is present, its tracks appear in the pane.
3. Drag a song title from the Audio pane to the position in the Timeline where you want it to begin playing (**Figure 10.21**). iMovie normally uses track 2, but you can drag the song to either track.

   The extracted track appears as an orange audio clip, and can be edited like other audio clips (**Figure 10.22**).

✔ Tip

- iMovie saves songs extracted from CDs as AIFF formatted files, which feature better quality but also occupy much more disk space. If you don't need that level of quality (for example, if you're creating a movie that will appear on the Web), you can save some disk space by importing the CD's tracks in iTunes and using an MP3 or AAC formatted song file.

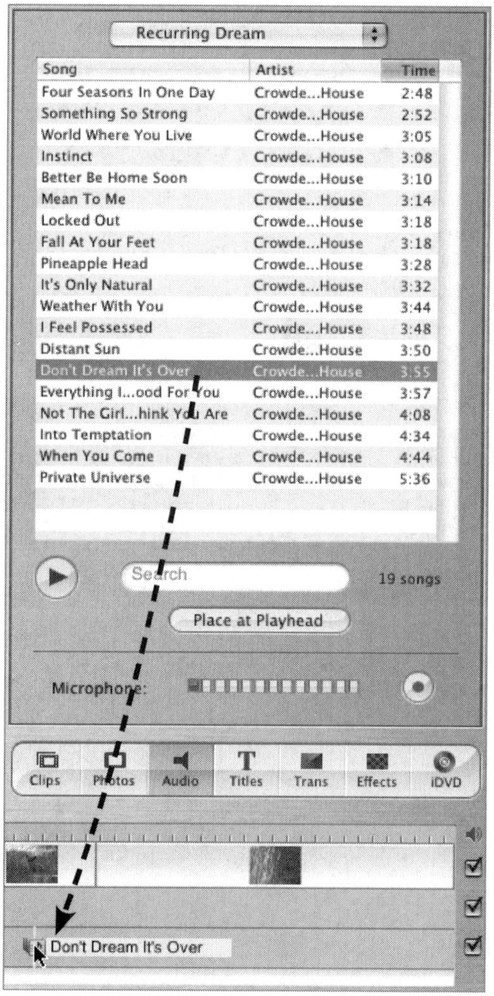

Figure 10.21 When you insert an audio CD into your Mac's media drive, the track list appears in iMovie. Simply drag a track name to the Timeline to copy it from the CD.

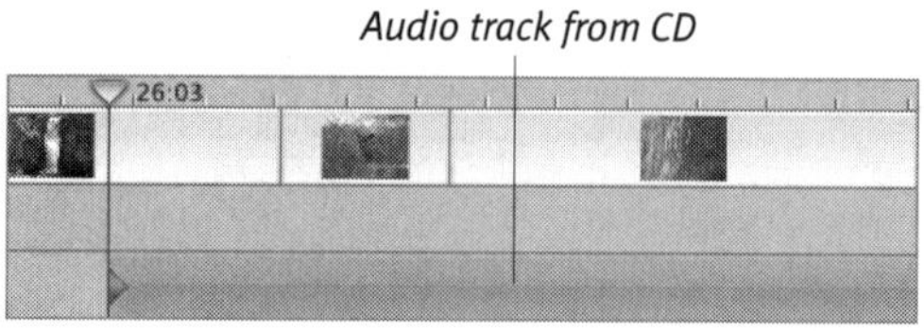

Figure 10.22 Tracks added from a CD show up as orange audio clips.

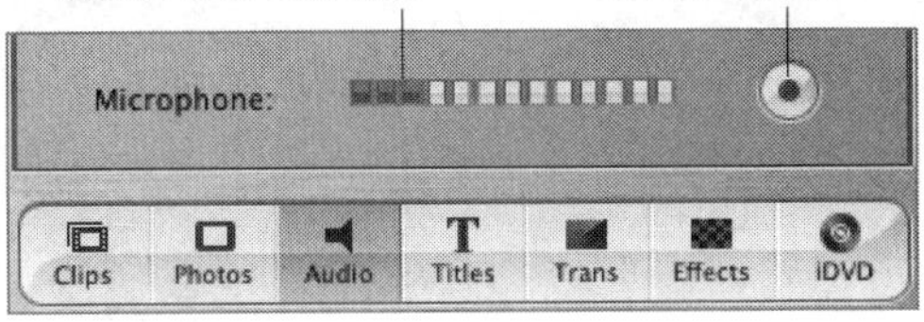

Figure 10.23 As you're recording a voice-over, the Record button becomes the Stop button.

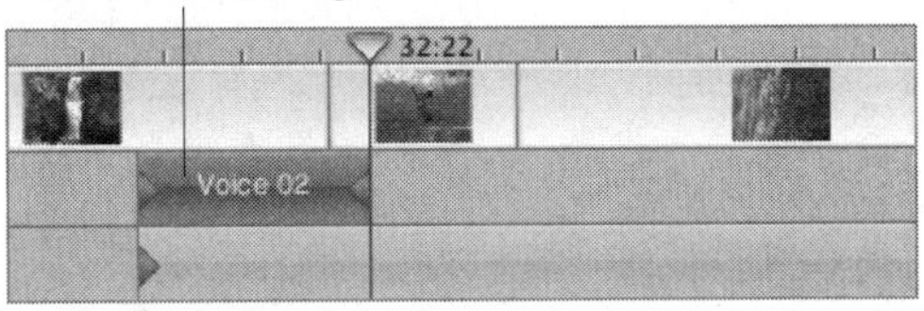

Figure 10.24 The recorded voice-over appears in the Timeline Viewer as a regular audio clip, named "Voice 01" (or whichever number applies).

Recording Voice-overs

I read that while shooting *Crouching Tiger, Hidden Dragon*, actor Chow Yun Fat (who doesn't speak Mandarin Chinese natively) didn't put much work into pronouncing his dialogue correctly while shooting. Instead, he fine-tuned his accent when re-recording the dialogue in post production. Most likely you won't be doing much re-recording (also called *looping*), but iMovie's narration capability lets you add voice-overs or other sounds directly to your movie.

To record a voice-over:

1. Connect a microphone to your Mac, if necessary.
2. Click the Audio button in iMovie to display the Audio pane.
3. Position the Playhead in the Timeline where you want to begin recording.
4. Click the round Record button to begin recording (**Figure 10.23**). The indicator above the button lights up according to the sound level.
5. Click the Record button again to end. A new audio clip, which can be edited just like other audio clips, is now in the Timeline (**Figure 10.24**).

✔ Tips

- iMovie automatically stops recording after 5 minutes.
- You can record multiple takes, then delete the ones you don't end up using.
- Some of Apple's current computers don't include a microphone port, unfortunately. Instead, consider buying a USB audio device such as Griffin Technology's iMic (`www.griffintechnology.com`).

Adding Sound Effects

You can't capture *every* sound when you're shooting—the laser blasts in *Star Wars* weren't real, for example (they were actually recordings of wrenches striking power cables). Sometimes you need ready-made sound effects (many are included with iMovie), or you can even create your own.

To add a sound effect to your movie:

1. Switch to iMovie's Audio pane.
2. From the popup menu, choose iMovie Sound Effects (**Figure 10.25**).
3. Double-click an effect's name to preview it, or select an effect and click the Play button.
4. Drag the effect you want to the Timeline Viewer and drop it into one of the audio tracks (**Figure 10.26**).

   You can edit sound effects just as you can with any other audio clip in iMovie.

✔ Tips

- Kudos to Apple's engineers: iMovie automatically displays the Timeline Viewer when you start dragging a sound effect.
- A broad assortment of audio clips are available. Apple lists some you can download (`www.apple.com/imovie`), and there are many companies that sell or license audio libraries.

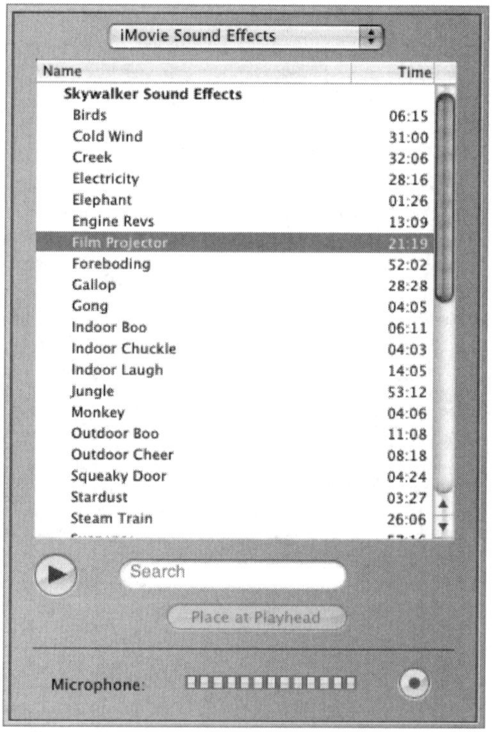

Figure 10.25 iMovie includes a number of common sound effects that you can add to your movie.

Sound effect added

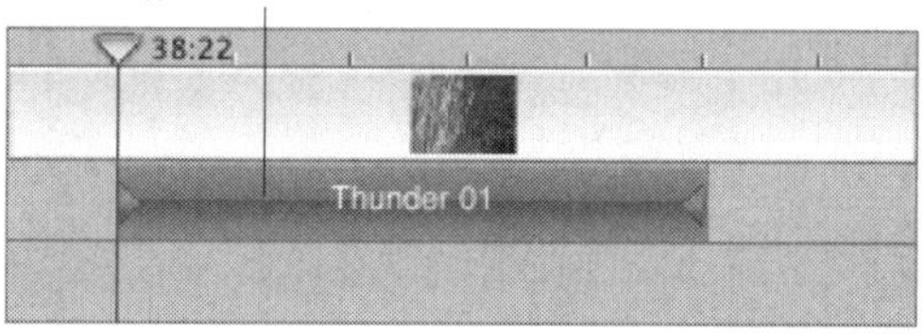

Figure 10.26 A sound effect appears in the Timeline like any other audio clip.

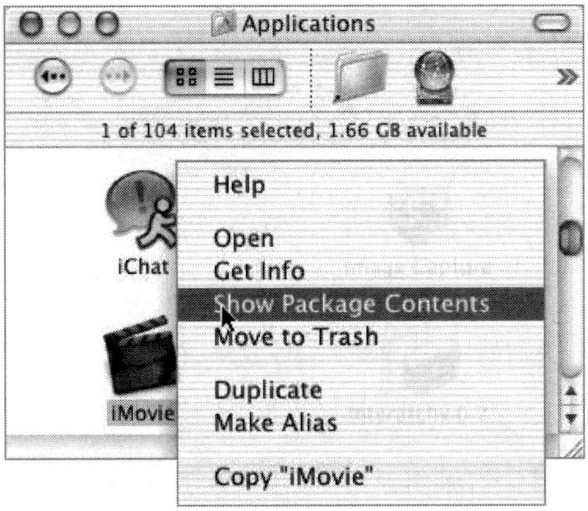

Figure 10.27 Control-click the iMovie application icon to display the contextual menu above.

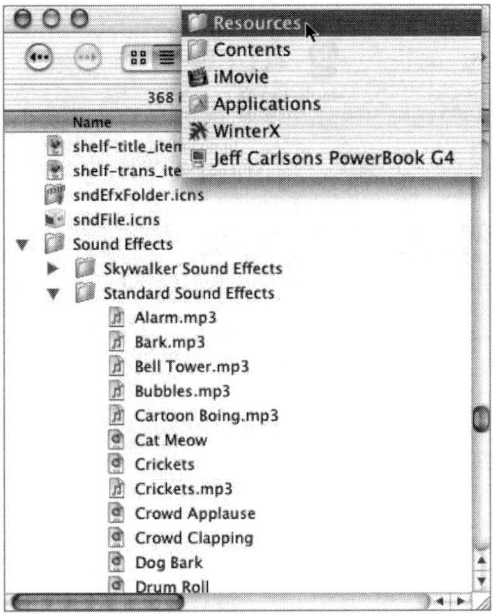

Figure 10.28 Copy your sound effect file to the Standard Sound Effects folder.

To add new sound effects to iMovie:

1. Quit iMovie.
2. Make sure the sound file is in the AIFF or MP3 format. A number of utilities, such as Apple's QuickTime Pro Player, can convert sound formats.
3. Locate iMovie in your Applications folder in the Finder. Adding sound effects entails opening up the iMovie application's package file—in essence, you're changing the iMovie application itself, so it's not a bad idea to make a copy of it.
4. Control-click the iMovie application icon and select Show Package Contents (**Figure 10.27**).
5. Open the Contents folder, then the Resources folder, and locate the Sound Effects folder (**Figure 10.28**).
6. Copy your sound effect file to the Standard Sound Effects folder.
7. Close the window and launch iMovie. The sound is now listed in the iMovie Sound Effects list.

✔ Tips

- Many iMovie 2 sound effects appear in the Sound Effects folder, but not in iMovie 3. Move them to the Standard Sound Effects folder to use them in the latest version.
- Don't go overboard with adding sound effects to iMovie's library: the more items, the longer it takes iMovie to launch.
- A cheap and easy way to create your own sound effects is to record them in iMovie using the narration feature (see "Recording Voice-overs" earlier in this chapter).

Importing Audio Files

As I mentioned earlier when talking about sound effects, there are many companies that provide royalty-free music and audio clips. iMovie can import any audio files that are supported by QuickTime.

To import an audio file:

1. Position the Playhead in the Timeline Viewer where you want the imported file to begin.
2. Choose Import from the File menu, or press Command-Shift-I.
3. In the dialog box that appears, navigate to the audio file (**Figure 10.29**). Click Import.
4. Wait several seconds for the file to be imported, then be amazed when it shows up as an editable audio clip in the Timeline's track 2 (**Figure 10.30**).

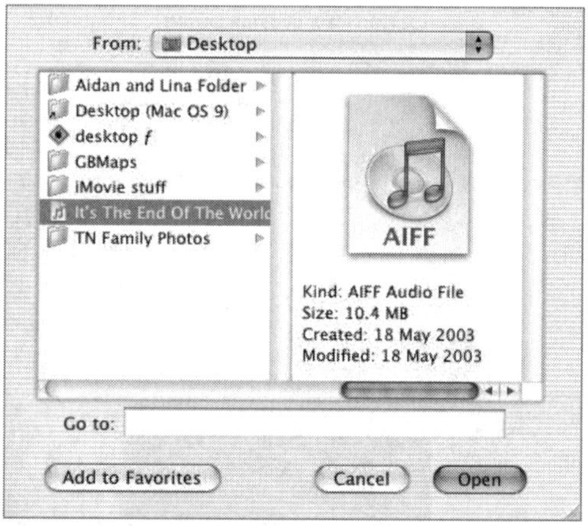

Figure 10.29 Locate an audio file. iMovie reads any formats supported by QuickTime.

AIFF file added at Playhead

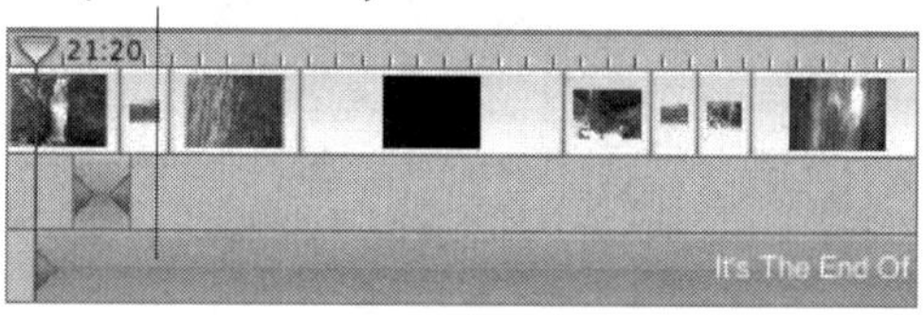

Figure 10.30 iMovie automatically places imported audio files into track 2 in the Timeline Viewer.

11

TRANSITIONS

Transitions can be equally wonderful and terrible things. They can move you from one scene to another without the abruptness of a straightforward cut, or help define a movie's pace by easing you gently into or out of a scene.

But transitions can also become a distraction, because you're introducing motion or visuals that weren't recorded by the camera. Too many transitions can be like using too many fonts in a word processing application: pretty soon, all you see is the style, not the content.

My best advice is to let the content determine the transition, if one is even needed: most of the time, a jump cut (moving from one clip to another without a transition) is all that's required. I'm not saying you should skip this chapter—rather, using fewer, *better* transitions is almost always the better route.

What's really pertinent at this stage is that iMovie creates professional transitions without breaking a sweat, enabling you to concentrate on how your movie plays instead of trying to jump over technical hurdles.

This chapter covers how to apply and modify transitions.

Editing Transition Settings

Clicking the Trans button below the Clips pane displays the Transitions pane, where you can preview different effects and adjust their durations.

To preview a transition:

- Click a transition name. The preview window automatically plays a rough version of the transition (**Figure 11.1**).
- Click the Preview button to view the rough transition in the Monitor (**Figure 11.2**). Note that it will play slower than normal.

To change a transition's duration:

1. Select a transition, either in the Transitions pane's list or one that you've already added to the movie.
2. Drag the Speed slider. The duration appears in the lower-right corner of the preview window. Transitions can be as short as 10 frames or as long as 4 seconds.

✔ Tips

- To stop a preview, simply click elsewhere on the screen.
- To watch the transition again in the preview window, click the transition name again or click an empty area of the list of transitions.
- iMovie creates a preview based on the location of the Playhead. If it's near the beginning of the clip, iMovie transitions the previous clip into the current one; if the Playhead is near the end of a clip, it transitions the current clip to the next one.

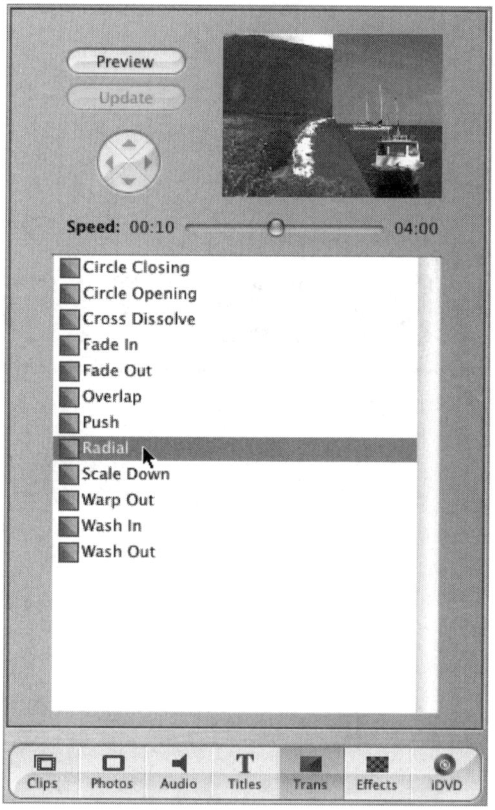

Figure 11.1 Clicking a transition name previews its effect in the Transition pane's preview window.

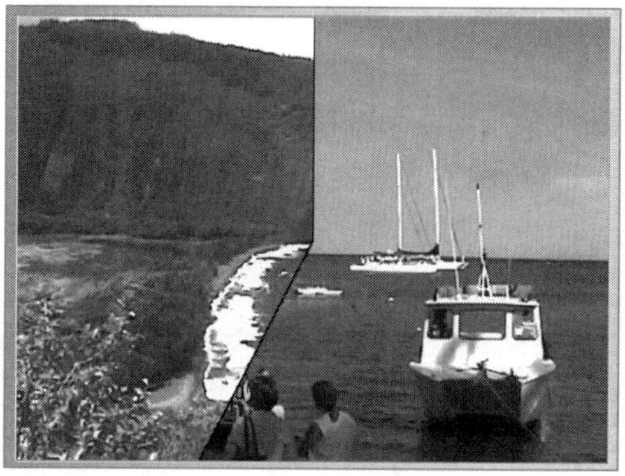

Figure 11.2 You can view a full-size, though rough, version of a transition in the Monitor.

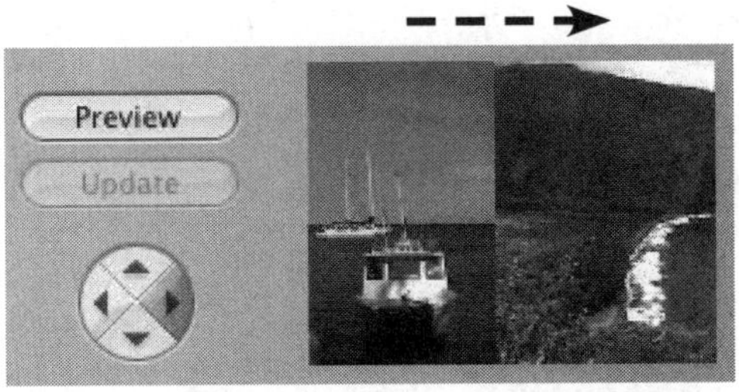

Figure 11.3 The Push transition is Apple's only one that features a directional arrow.

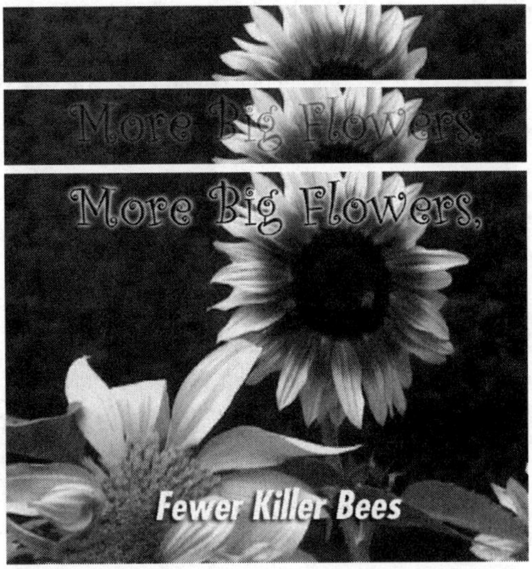

Figure 11.4 Use Overlap to slowly dissolve from a clip to a modified still image.

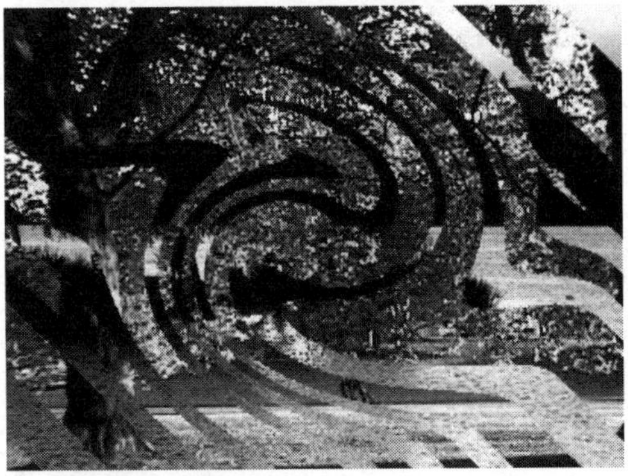

Figure 11.5 Several third-party companies offer transitions you can add to iMovie, such as this one from GeeThree.

To set an effect's direction:

1. Select the Push transition for an example of this type of setting. Although Push is the only transition from Apple to use a directional control, other developers use it, too.
2. Click a button on the directional controller to specify how the effect plays (**Figure 11.3**). Using Push, the control indicates where the old clip exits the frame and the new clip enters (by default, the new clip "pushes" the old clip from left to right).

✔ Tips

- If you click the *name* of the Push transition, it reverts back to the default left-to-right push, even if you specified a different direction.
- Transitions can also blend between movie footage and still clips. For example, you're editing an interview and you want to dissolve to an embarrassing high school photo of the interviewee. You can also achieve some low-tech special effects: suppose you want to end your video with a still image overlaid with styled text. Save one frame as a still image (explained in Chapter 8), and add the text in Photoshop or a similar program. Then, import the changed still image, and add a Cross Dissolve or Overlap transition before it (**Figure 11.4**).
- Apple has built into iMovie the most commonly used types of transitions, but you may be looking for a different kind of effect. If so, check out transitions and plug-ins offered by third-party developers. Although I can't honestly say I'll ever use a transition that draws video within a heart shape, for example, other transitions range from the beautifully subtle to truly psychedelic (**Figure 11.5**). See Appendix B for a list of iMovie plug-in developers.

Adding Transitions

Like so many things in iMovie, adding a transition to your movie is as easy as dragging and dropping an icon. The trickery (and I use the term loosely) is in configuring how it appears in the movie. Don't worry about nailing it the first time, though: you can always change a transition's settings, even after you've added it to your movie.

To add a transition:

Drag the transition to the intersection of two clips in the Clip Viewer or Timeline Viewer. (Transitions can be added to the beginning and end of the movie as well.) A transition icon appears, containing a red line moving from left to right (**Figure 11.6**).

That line indicates iMovie's progress of rendering the transitions. To build a transition, iMovie recreates the affected frames of the clip with the transition applied. For example, if we add a Fade In transition that's one second (30 frames) in duration, iMovie redraws each frame with a different brightness setting (**Figure 11.7**). This ensures that in the final movie, the transition appears at its best resolution and plays smoothly.

✔ Tips

- Leave enough padding in your clips to accommodate transitions. Otherwise, iMovie displays an error that one or both of the clips is too short (**Figure 11.8**).
- To cancel a transition while it's rendering, choose Undo from the Edit menu or press Command-period (.).
- Go ahead and continue working while a transition is rendering, or even add other transitions, which are rendered concurrently. You can also play your movie before the rendering finishes, though the unrendered clips will appear jumpy and rough until they're fully rendered.

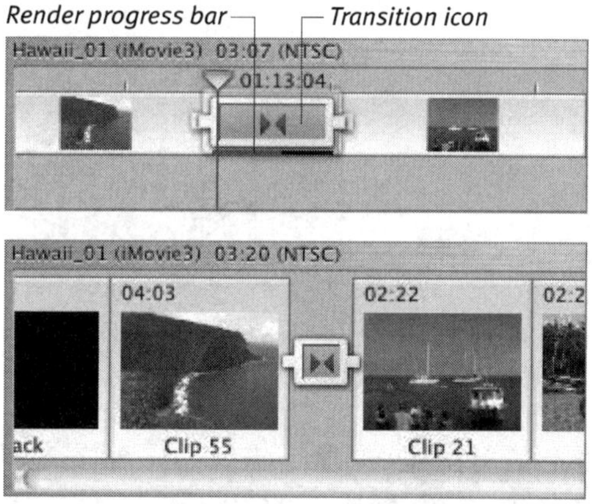

Figure 11.6 Transitions need to render before they can play back smoothly in the Monitor (top). The transition icon is similar in the Clip Viewer (bottom).

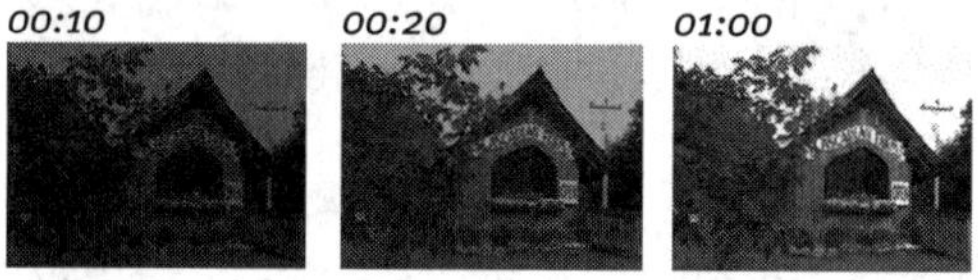

Figure 11.7 An iMovie transition recreates your footage with the transition's effect applied. Here are three frames from a Fade In transition.

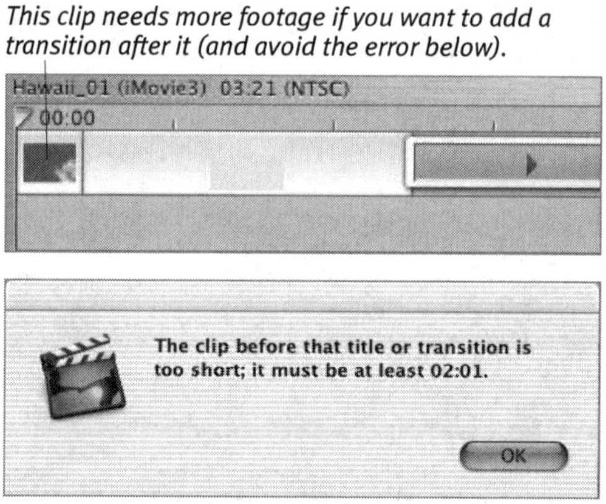

Figure 11.8 iMovie needs a certain amount of source material to work with. It will tell you how much footage is needed, based on your Speed slider setting.

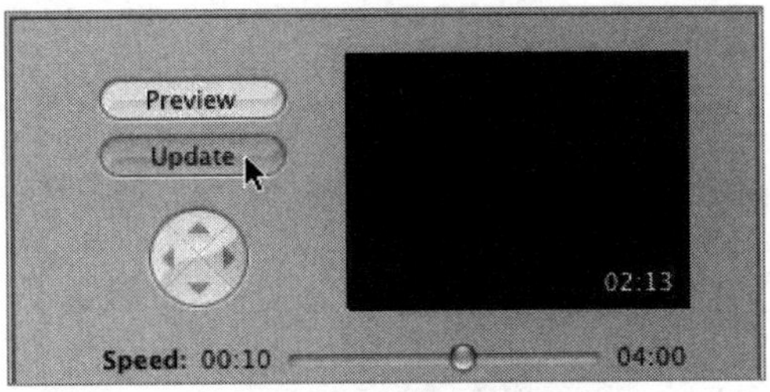

Figure 11.9 If you change a transition's settings, click the Update button to re-render it in the Timeline.

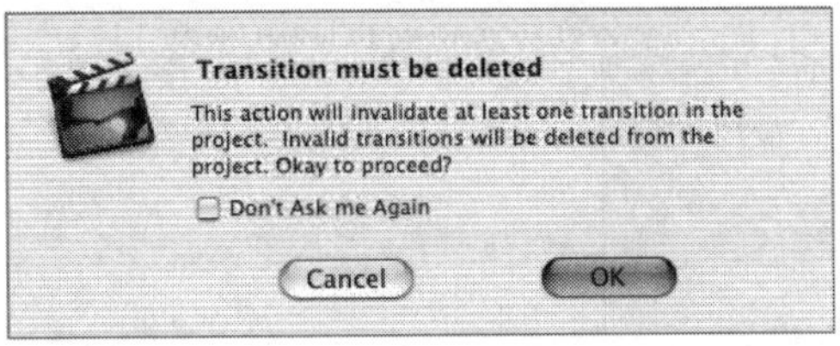

Figure 11.10 Don't say you weren't warned about moving a transition out of place. Then again, if you click the Don't Ask Me Again checkbox, you can say you weren't warned—but you won't get any sympathy from me. Well, all right, maybe a little sympathy. But just this one time, got it? Okay? Good.

To modify existing transitions:

1. Select the transition in the Clip Viewer or Timeline Viewer.
2. Adjust the transition's settings in the Transitions pane.
3. Click the Update button to re-render the transition (**Figure 11.9**).

✔ Tips

- Since transitions become their own clips, you can edit their volume levels, including fading sound in and out. The Fade In and Fade Out transitions automatically apply audio fades, which you can edit (see Chapter 10).
- When you update a transition, most of the time you're adjusting the clip's duration. However, you can also change the type of transition entirely: just click your transition clip, select a new transition from the list, and click Update.
- In the Clip Viewer, you might think you can pick up a transition and move it to another clip because the surrounding clips move aside when you drag the icon. However, all you really get is an error warning you that your foolhardy action will delete the transition (**Figure 11.10**).

iMovie's Habit of Stealing Time

As you add transitions, you may notice something odd happening: your movie is getting *shorter*. Is it possible to add things to a movie and still end up with less than when you started? (And if so, does it apply to eating ice cream?)

Yes. (But no to the ice cream.) Here's how iMovie steals time using transitions (**Figure 11.11**):

1. For the sake of not straining my math abilities, let's assume we want to add a Cross Dissolve transition between two 10-second clips. The clips contain outside shots of a lake and some trees, so in order to maintain a comfortable pace, we decide to make our transition 2 seconds long.
2. We drag the transition into place between the clips, and notice that each clip has become 8 seconds in length, not 9 seconds (to split a 2-second transition between two clips leaves 1 second for each clip: 10 – 1 = 9).
3. The mystery is solved when we look at how iMovie is building the transition. It needs to start dissolving one clip into the other clip at the very beginning of the transition, so iMovie merges 2 seconds of each clip, removing 4 seconds total. The transition is still 2 seconds in duration, but required 4 seconds to perform the blends. Think of it as tightening a belt: you still have the same amount of material, but the overlap where the buckle rests allows you to encompass a smaller area.

Watching iMovie grab and modify clips is also the best motivation for locking any audio clips you've extracted (see Chapter 10). It only takes one transition to throw the rest of your movie out of sync.

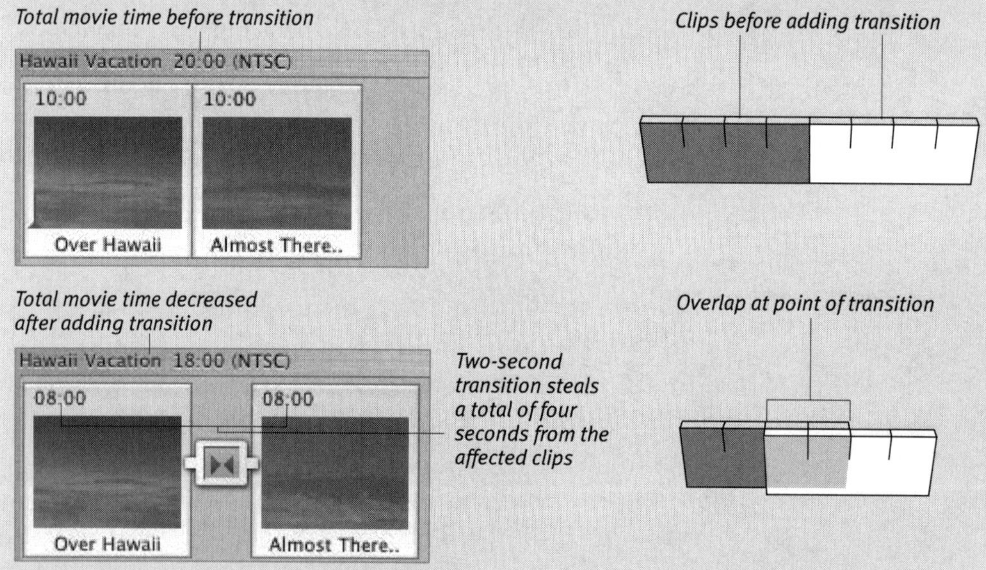

Figure 11.11 Some transitions, such as Cross Dissolve, need to overlap two clips in order to merge the number of frames needed for the effect. This creates a shorter overall movie.

Before

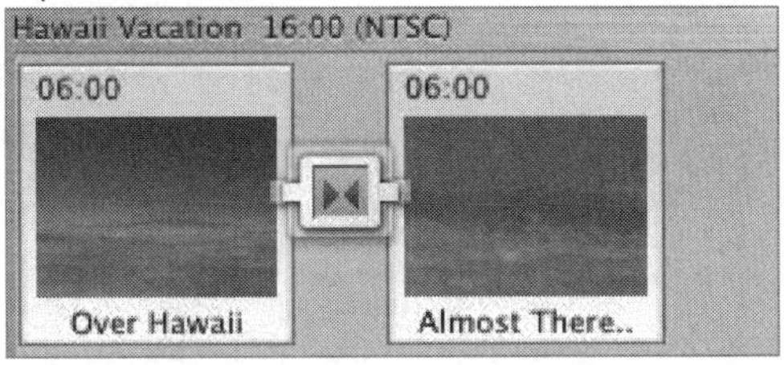

After

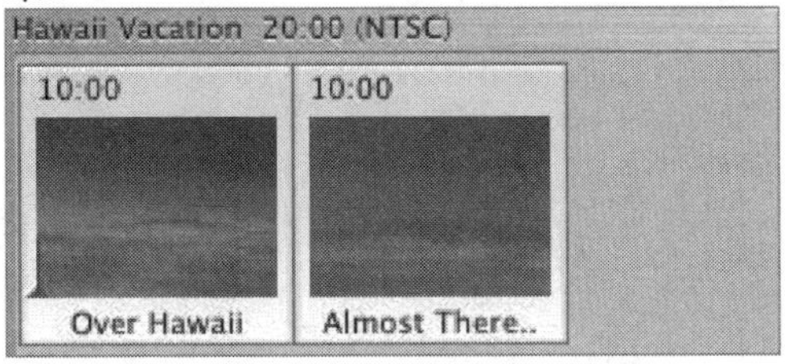

Figure 11.12 A transition acts like a regular clip most of the time, but when you delete it, the pieces of footage it used are returned to the nearby clips.

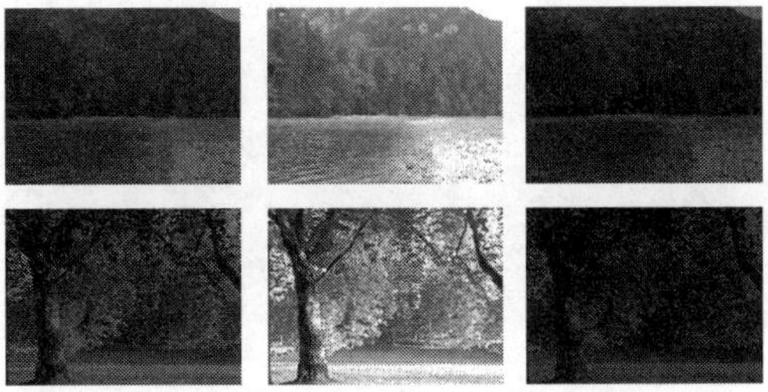

Figure 11.13 Using several Fade In and Fade Out transitions, these two images appear, then disappear quickly and smoothly (the QuickTime version is a better representation, believe me).

Removing Transitions

Think of transitions as clips that are placed on top of the video track, rather than wedged between the other clips. This enables you to delete them without worrying that you're destroying any underlying footage.

To delete a transition:

1. Select the transition in the Clip Viewer or Timeline Viewer.
2. Press the Delete key, or choose Cut or Clear from the Edit menu. The sections of clips that were used by the transition are restored (**Figure 11.12**).

Most Valuable Transitions

In most situations, you'll find yourself using only a handful of transitions: Fade In, Fade Out, Cross Dissolve, and Overlap. I'm also partial to Wash In and Wash Out, in the right context. The others, to me, are usually too flashy for regular use.

One of the best uses of the subtle Fade In and Fade Out transitions is to pair them back to back to intercut a series of short scenes or still images: the picture goes from black to full strength (Fade In), runs for a second or two (or even shorter), then dissolves to black again (Fade Out), only to start again with a different scene (**Figure 11.13**). I've created an example and posted it at `www.necoffee.com/imovievqs/`.

12

TITLES

In Hollywood, movie titles aren't mere words that flash up on the screen. Actors, agents, and studio executives negotiate for the length of time a person's name appears, how large or small the typeface is, whether the name comes before or after the movie title, and all sorts of other conditions that inflame my natural aversion to fine print. Hopefully, you won't deal with any of that, because the other aspects of movie titles—i.e., actually *creating* them—are made extraordinarily easy in iMovie.

The program's title capabilities are more robust than one would think, though I'll admit I'd like to see more typographic control in future versions. In the meantime, use the titling features with the knowledge that, as with a lot of iMovie capabilities, you're creating elements quickly and cheaply that used to cost a fortune for studios and filmmakers.

Editing the Text

Obviously, you'll need some text in your title. iMovie offers three types of text fields, depending on the type of title used. To begin editing titles, click the Titles button beneath the Shelf (**Figure 12.1**). As with transitions and effects, a rough example of each title plays in the preview window when clicked, and you can view a larger approximation in the Monitor by clicking the Preview button.

Text fields

Most of the title options use a set of two text fields. The top field typically acts as the primary title and appears larger in some titles than the bottom field.

To add text to title fields:

1. Click once within a field to select its contents. Click again to position the pointer.
2. Type new title text, then press Return or click outside the field (**Figure 12.2**).

Multiple text fields

If a two-line title isn't long enough, some titles offer multiple text fields, which are one or more field pairs. Usually, the extra fields are used for animating the text—for example, the Centered Multiple title displays the first field pair, clears the title, then displays the next field pair. Multiple fields are also used to set up titles, such as Rolling Credits, which face each other across the screen (**Figure 12.3**). You can add more text pairs and change their order, if you like.

To add text fields:

1. With a title selected that offers multiple text field pairs, click the plus-sign button. A new pair is created (**Figure 12.4**).
2. Type your text into the fields and press Return or click outside the field.

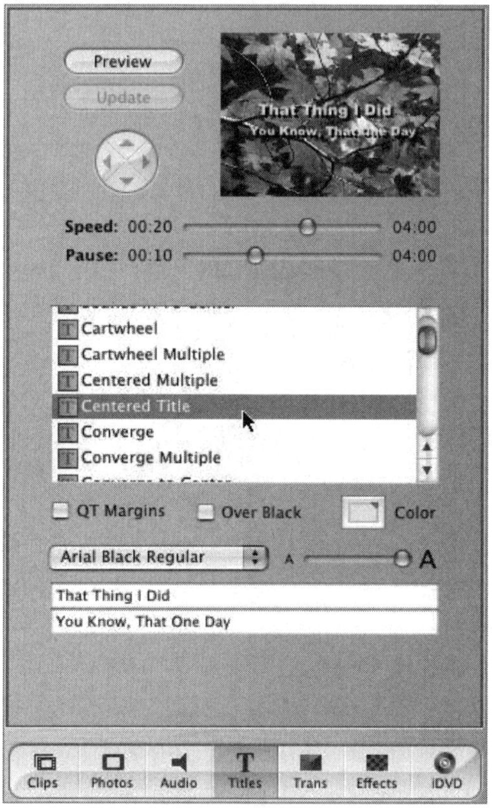

Figure 12.1 The Titles pane contains more controls than anything else in iMovie—and it's still easy.

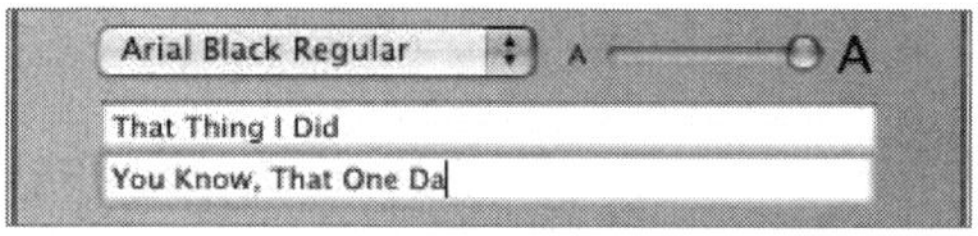

Figure 12.2 Once you type your title into the text fields, you don't need to type it again when switching between title styles.

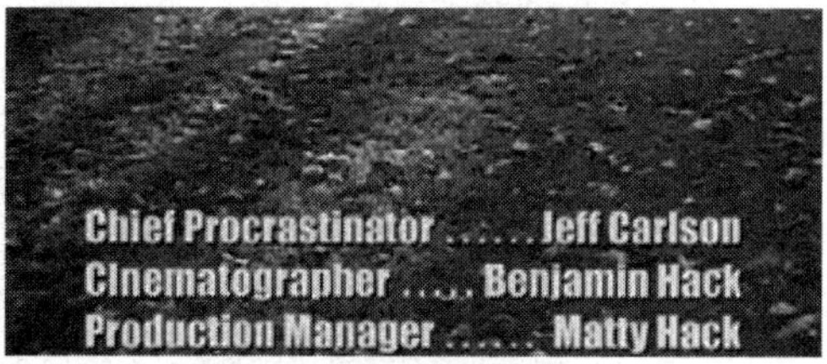

Figure 12.3 Multiple text fields enable you to create titles with opposing elements, such as Rolling Credits.

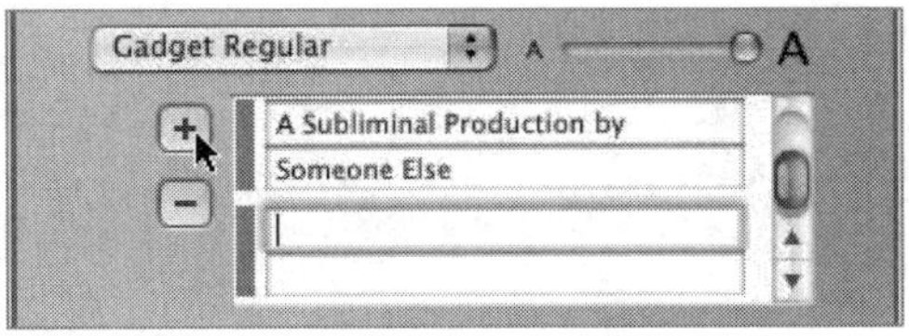

Figure 12.4 In title styles with multiple text fields, use the plus-sign button to add more fields.

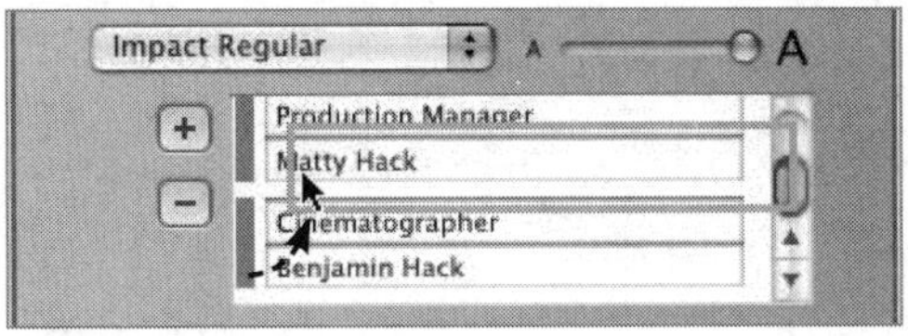

Figure 12.5 Think your name needs to appear sooner in the credits? Click and drag the text field into place.

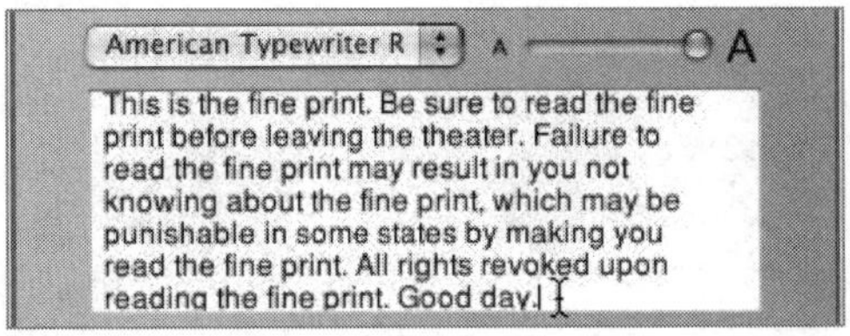

Figure 12.6 Text blocks let you enter more text than is allowed in other text fields.

Titles Don't Look Good Onscreen

One of the most common questions I get from readers is, "Why don't my titles look good when I play them in iMovie?" Text appears jagged, or sometimes there's a lot of visual noise surrounding the letters.

Don't worry, this is actually normal. The picture you're viewing in the Monitor has been optimized to fit into a normal television aspect ratio—in reality, the video dimensions are wider than what appears in iMovie (see Chapter 15 for more info). To view your titles properly, export your movie to tape and play it back on a television (see Chapter 14), or connect a monitor to your computer (see Chapter 6).

To remove text fields:

1. Click a text pair to select it.
2. Click the minus-sign button. The pair is deleted.

To rearrange text fields:

1. Click a text pair to select it.
2. Drag the selection up or down the list to change its position, then drop it in place (**Figure 12.5**).

Text blocks

If you still need more text in your title, use a style with a text block field, such as Music Video. It accommodates more text and can wrap your words (i.e., move them to the next line) as space allows.

To add text to block fields:

1. Type your text into the field.

   or

   Paste some text you've copied elsewhere, such as from a word processing application (**Figure 12.6**).
2. Click the name of the text style to apply the text. (Unlike the other text fields in iMovie, pressing the Return or Enter key in a text block creates a line break instead of applying the edit.)

✔ Tips

- You can select (and therefore delete or move) only one text pair at a time.
- iMovie remembers the last text you entered, so you don't need to type it again if you click another title effect—or even if you create a new project.
- iMovie 3 can help with your spelling. Select some text and choose Check Spelling from the Edit menu, or choose it from the contextual menu.

Editing Text Style

Now that you've entered some text, it's time to give it style: select a color and a font, change the type size, and optionally view the title on a black background. The title controls are also particularly important if you're planning to export the movie into QuickTime format.

To select text color:

1. Click the square Color field below the titles list in the Titles pane. The Colors palette appears (**Figure 12.7**).
2. Click within the color wheel to select a color, or click one of the buttons at the top to change selectors (such as sliders or even Crayon colors). You can try as many colors as you like while the palette is visible, and see them applied to text in the preview window.
3. Click the palette's red close button to accept the last color you applied.

To specify font and size:

1. Choose a font from the Title Font popup menu.
2. Drag the Title Text Size slider to increase or decrease the type size (**Figure 12.8**).

✔ Tips

- The color control affects the color of the text itself, except in the case of Stripe Subtitle, where the color setting applies to the text's background stripe.
- To ensure that fonts appear smooth in titles, use Adobe PostScript, TrueType, or OpenType fonts. These include the fonts included with the Mac OS. Don't use bitmap fonts, which contain only enough data to draw their letters onscreen in a few specific sizes.

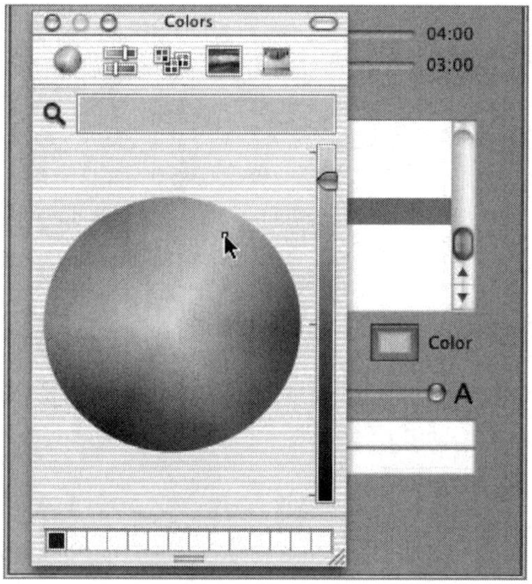

Figure 12.7 Click the Color field to bring up the Colors palette, giving you access to a full range of color.

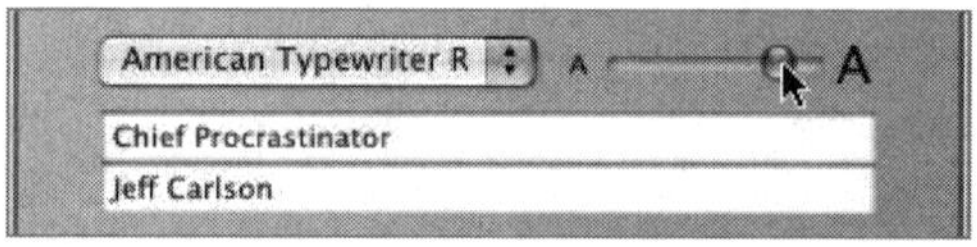

Figure 12.8 I'd really prefer a more specific way of setting the font size, but the method used by the Title Text Size slider is easy to comprehend.

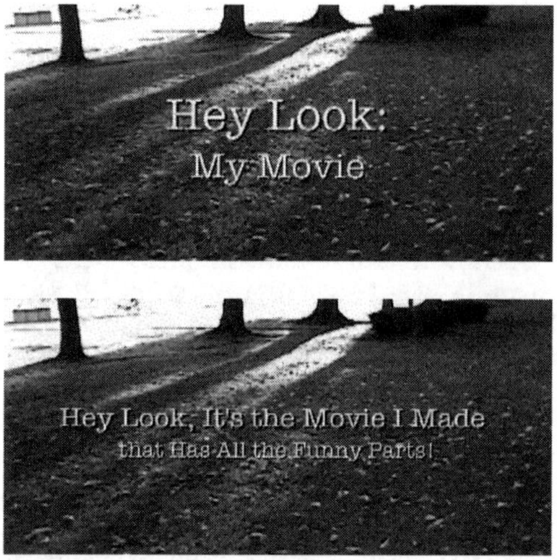

Figure 12.9 Both of these titles were made using the same font at the largest setting.

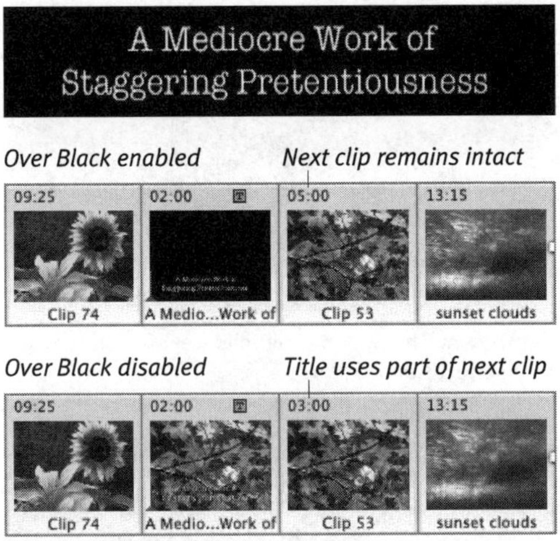

Figure 12.10 When the Over Black option is enabled (top), the text clip that's created doesn't incorporate the next clip's footage (middle). When Over Black is turned off, the text clip uses the next clip's footage (bottom) as background for the title.

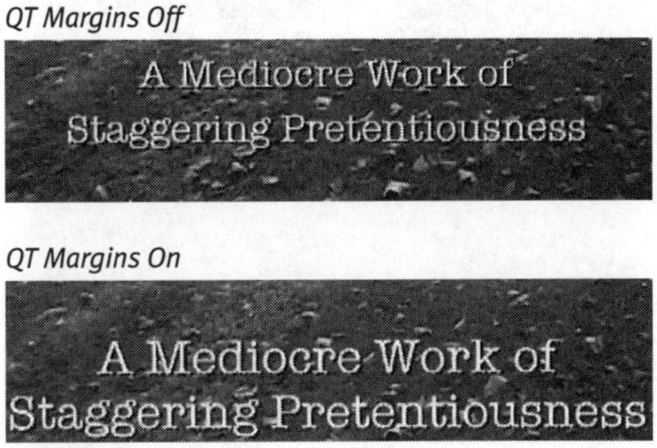

Figure 12.11 QT Margins uses every available bit of space to render titles, running the risk of the words getting cut off when viewed on a TV.

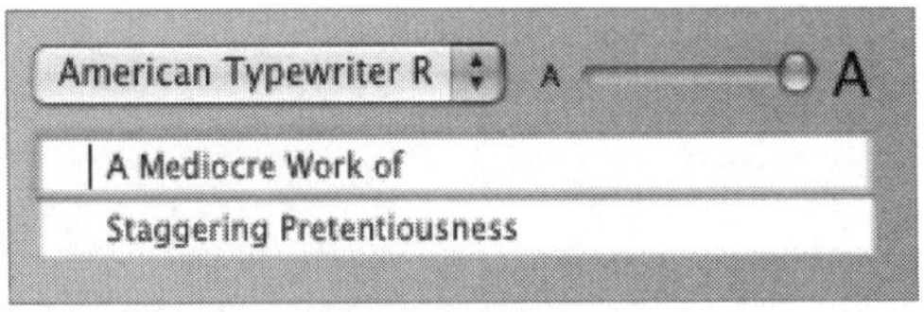

Figure 12.12 Using iMovie 3.0.3, I've had to add spaces before the title lines to make them appear properly centered. Hopefully, this bug will be fixed by the time you read this.

- The longer your title, the smaller it appears, regardless of the font size you've specified (**Figure 12.9**).

To display text against a black background:

Click the Over Black checkbox. When you apply this style to your movie, it pushes aside the clip that follows the title and displays the text on a black background, rather than overlaying it on clip footage. (**Figure 12.10**). Make sure any extracted audio clips are locked in place before you add a title with Over Black enabled.

Setting QuickTime margins

Remember toward the beginning of the book when I advised you to know in what format your movie will end up? Here's a chance to put that advice to the test. If you know the movie will only appear in QuickTime format, enable QT Margins, which uses more of the video area for titles (**Figure 12.11**). If you're exporting your movie back to tape to play it on a television, turn QT Margins off or your text might run outside the screen's edges.

✔ Tips

- If you don't use the Over Black option, your title appears over your footage. What if you want a different look? Consider importing images that can be used as backdrops for your titles.
- At the time of this writing, iMovie 3 has a bug that causes some titles to not be properly centered, such as Subtitle. To compensate, add spaces before your text to center it on the screen (**Figure 12.12**).
- The text style settings apply to every title effect listed in the Title pane. When I'm creating a title, I'll play with five or six options before settling on one, so it's nice that I don't need to enter the settings each time I click a title.

Setting Title Duration

If we were dealing with still images, our work here would be done. But video is about movement, so don't expect titles to just flash onscreen and then disappear. Almost every iMovie title is animated in some way, which means you need to control how it moves. iMovie has two methods of doing this: the speed of the effect, and the length of the pause following the effect.

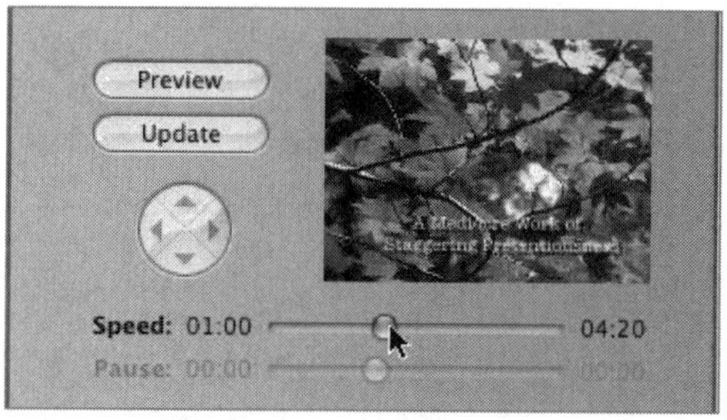

Figure 12.13 The Speed slider dictates the duration of a title effect's animation.

To set a title's duration:

1. Drag the Speed slider to specify how long it takes to complete the title's effect. The times vary between titles (**Figure 12.13**).
2. Drag the Pause slider to specify how long the titles remain onscreen after the title animation has finished. Some effects, such as Subtitle, don't offer a pause option. The combined times are shown in the preview window, indicating the total time of the title clip (**Figure 12.14**).

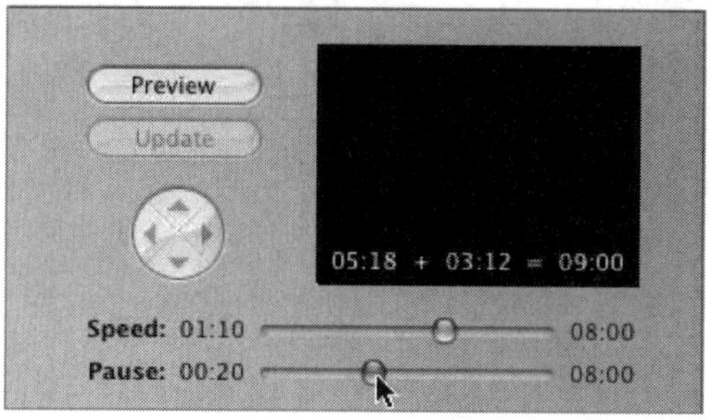

Figure 12.14 The Pause slider controls how long the title remains onscreen once the effect is finished. Dragging the slider updates the total time of the effect, as shown in the preview window.

✔ Tips

- Some titles' speeds vary depending on what you've typed into the text fields. The Flying Letters title, for example, needs more time if there are more letters, which is why the maximum Speed setting changes for long titles (after typing your title, click another title, then click Flying Letters again to see the difference).
- Remember that not everyone may be able to read as fast as you. Give your viewers plenty of time to read your title—without boring them, of course.

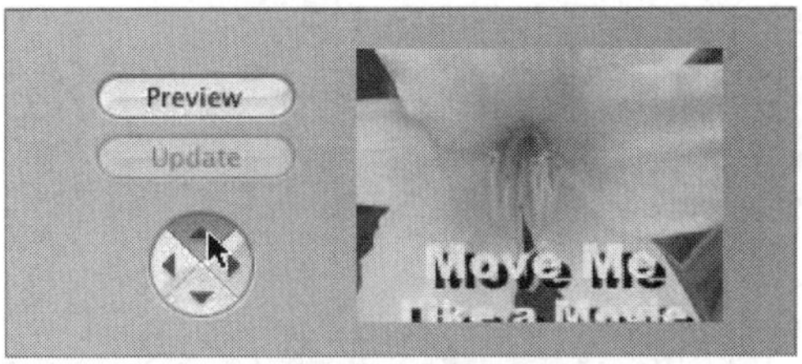

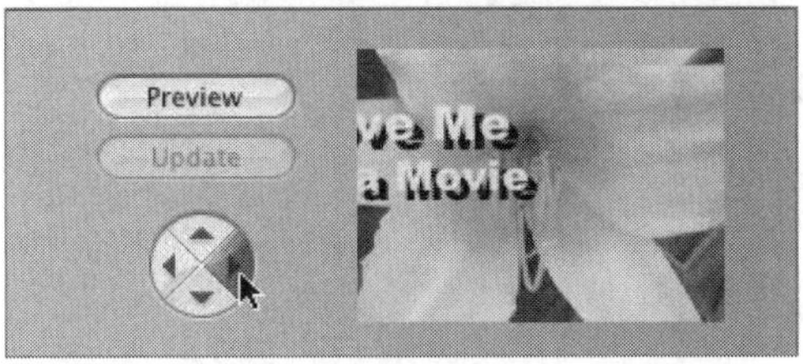

Figure 12.15 The directional controller on some title effects determines which way the words move onto the screen.

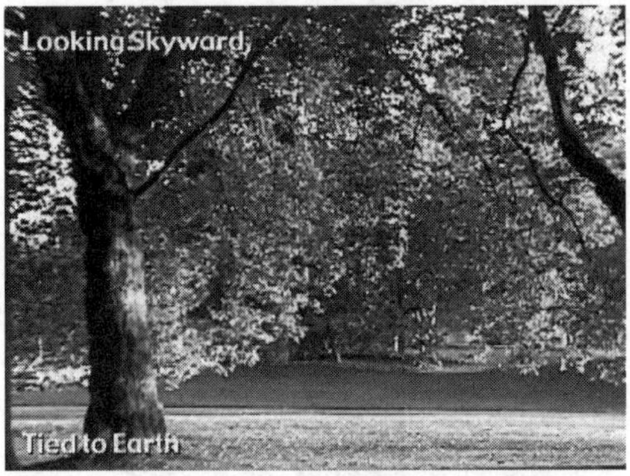

Figure 12.16 Music Video gives you a little more control over text positioning because it's a block title.

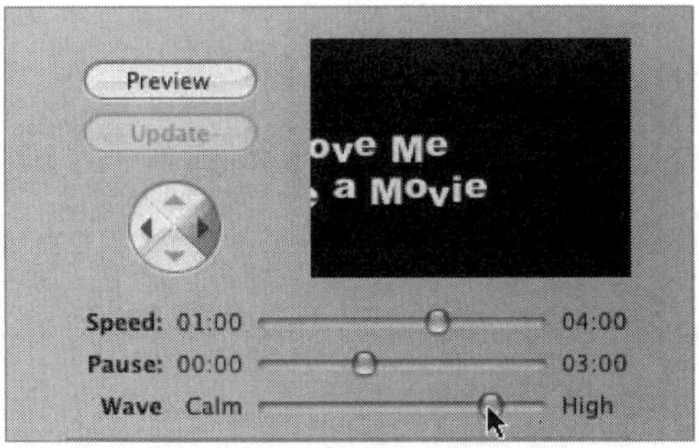

Figure 12.17 A few titles include other controls for effects, such as this Wave setting in Bounce Across.

Setting Title Position

Some effects, such as Bounce In To Center, feature a control for placing text on the screen or specifying the direction in which the text animates.

To set title position:

1. Click the title you wish to use.
2. Click an arrow on the directional controller to the left of the title list (**Figure 12.15**).

✔ Tips

- The Music Video title gives you the option of running text along the left or right sides of the screen. But it's also a text block title, which means you can type line breaks (using Return or Enter). If you put the two features together, you can position text in the upper-left or upper-right corners of the screen (**Figure 12.16**).
- All sorts of controls can appear in the Titles pane, as you'll discover if you install third-party plug-ins. The Bounce Across title, new in iMovie 3, adds a control for setting the amount of "waviness" applied to the text (**Figure 12.17**).

Adding Titles

Once you've decided how your title will look, you're ready to add it to your movie.

To add a title:

Drag and drop the title's name or icon to the left of the clip onto which it will appear in the Timeline (**Figure 12.18**). iMovie begins rendering the title in a new clip and names it with the start of the title's text.

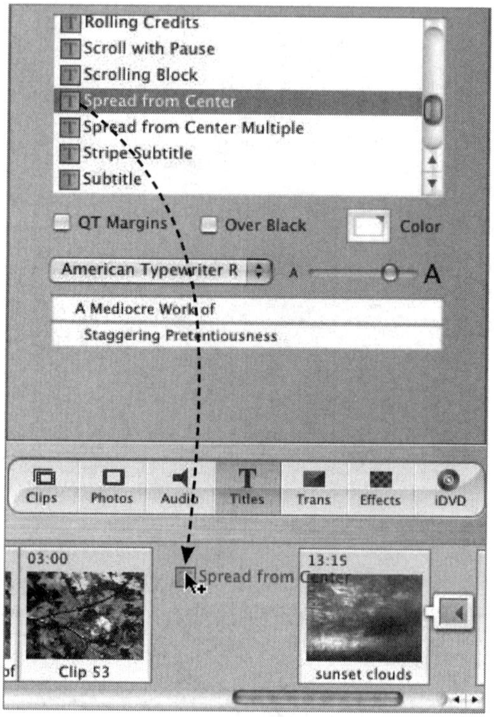

Figure 12.18 Once you've specified how your title will appear, drag and drop it onto the Clip Viewer or Timeline Viewer.

Title clip rendering

When a title is rendered, iMovie actually writes the pixels to your footage, rather than generating them on the fly (such as when you preview a title's style). And like transitions and effects, titles render as their own clips. You can continue to work or play your movie while the title is rendering, though the playback won't be as smooth.

If a title clip is longer than the clip it's being applied to, the title clip runs on into the next clip (**Figure 12.19**).

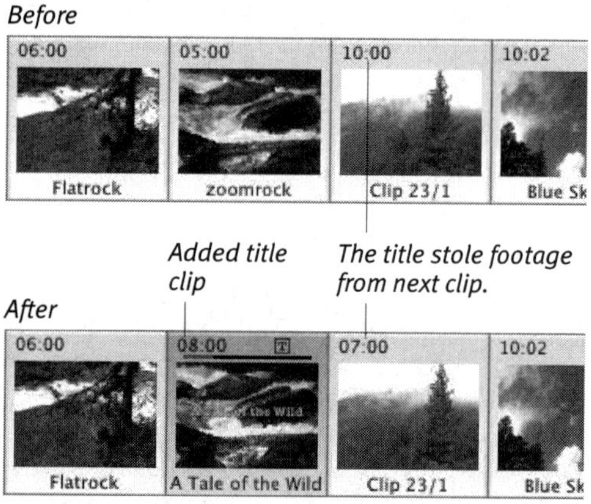

Figure 12.19 The title is 08:00 in length, so putting it in front of a clip that's 05:00 ("zoomrock") causes the title to render over all of "zoomrock" and grab footage from the next clip.

✔ Tips

- Hold down the Command or Control key to prevent Clip Viewer icons from sliding around before you drop the clip.
- Add multiple titles to the same section of footage by applying titles to a section of footage that already contains a title. For example, I've used Centered Title to gradually display a scene's name, and added a Music Video title in the middle of the Drifting clip that shows day and time (**Figure 12.20**).
- iMovie creates a new file on your hard disk called "Subtitle 01" (or similar) that contains the rendered footage—the original untitled clip is still intact. Be aware that using many titles can increase the hard disk space used by your project.

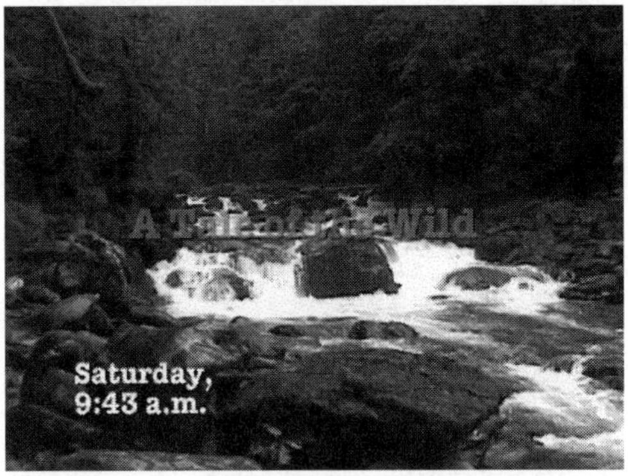

Figure 12.20 Combine multiple titles by applying a new title effect to an existing one.

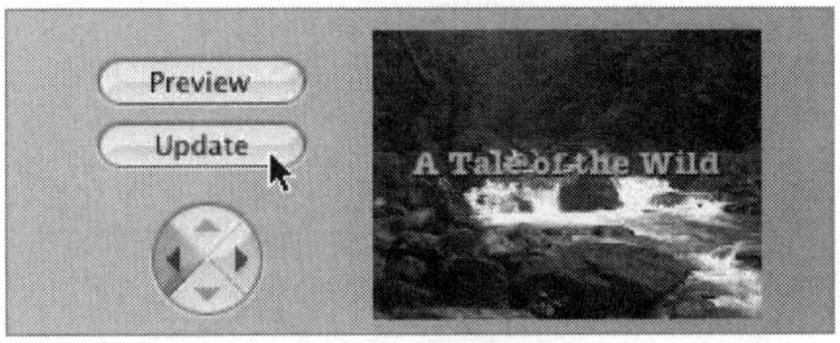

Figure 12.21 The Update button becomes active if you select a clip with a title applied. Change its settings and click Update to re-render the clip.

Modifying and Deleting Existing Titles

When you add a title clip, it actually exists on top of your footage. If you don't like the way it turned out, you can easily change its properties, or get rid of it altogether.

To modify an existing title:

1. Select the title clip.
2. Make any changes you wish in the Titles pane.
3. Click the Update button to apply your changes (**Figure 12.21**).

To remove a title:

1. Select the offending title clip.
2. Press the Delete key. You can also drag the clip to the Trash if you're in the Clip Viewer. Or, you can choose Cut or Clear from the Edit menu.

13

Effects

By now, you're probably sold on the notion of working with digital footage, but just in case there are any lingering doubts, consider iMovie's effects capabilities. Because you're manipulating pixels instead of strips of film, you can apply several types of changes to your footage, ranging from color correction to special effects.

When I first heard that iMovie offered effects, I admit I feared the worst. What better way to destroy footage you worked so hard to shoot than to apply a bunch of filters to mangle those pixels?

I'm happy to report that my fears were unfounded. Instead of garish methods of swirling video into a toilet bowl of colors, iMovie gives you genuinely useful and powerful tools to adjust color, sharpen blurry images, and easily turn your multi-hued images into classic-looking black-and-white footage.

Editing Effect Settings

Like transitions and titles (see the previous two chapters), iMovie effects are accessed from their own Effects pane (**Figure 13.1**). Clicking an effect's name displays the effect in the preview window; clicking the Preview button shows a rough version of the effect in the Monitor.

Some effects, such as Black & White, don't contain any additional controls; others, such as Adjust Colors, involve several sliders that determine the effect's end result. All of them, however, let you apply or remove the effect gradually.

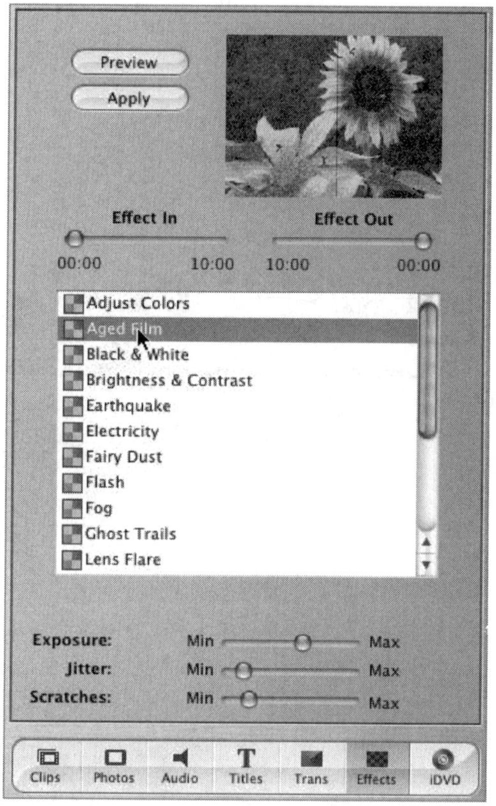

Figure 13.1 The Effects pane is a similar layout to the Transitions and Titles panes.

To control how an effect begins and ends:

1. Select an effect's name in the list.
2. Move the Effect In and Effect Out sliders to control the time it takes for the effect to start and end (**Figure 13.2**). You can, of course, leave them set at 00:00 to apply the effect throughout the entire clip, but changing these values lets you ease into and out of the effect. (For example, suppose you want someone's flashback to appear in black and white, then blend back into color as the flashback merges into the present day.) The Effect In point and Effect Out point times are shown at the bottom of the preview window as you make adjustments.

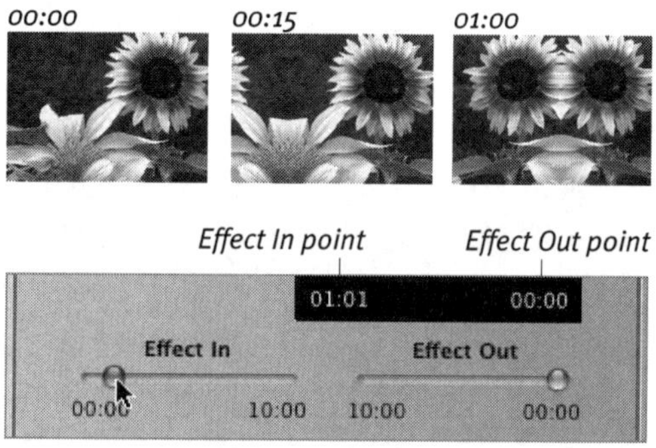

Figure 13.2 Setting Effect In to 01:00 causes the effect to gradually apply, instead of starting at the beginning of the clip. In this case, the Mirror effect pushes the mirror image into the scene from the left. If we kept the Effect In slider set to 00:00, the first frame would look like the 01:00 frame, above.

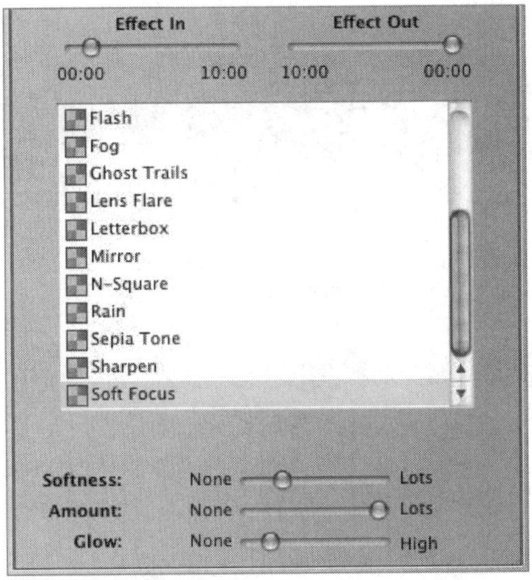

Figure 13.3 Effect-specific controls appear below the list of effects. Changing them updates the preview window dynamically.

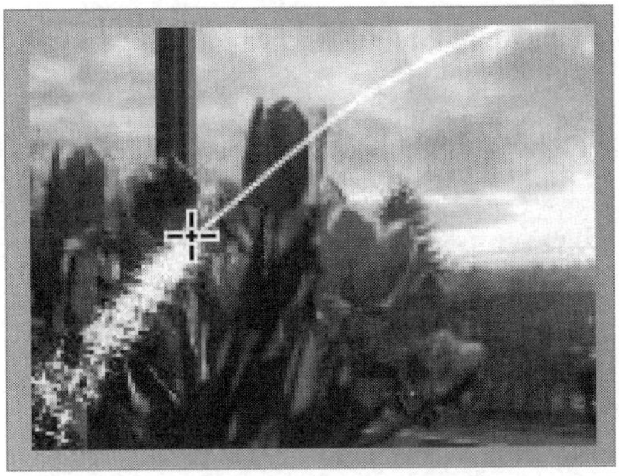

Figure 13.4 Some effects feature controls within the preview window. For example, clicking in the preview window with Fairy Dust sets the sparkles' arc.

To adjust an effect's settings:

1. Select an effect's name in the list. If it features additional controls, they appear below the list (**Figure 13.3**).
2. Move the sliders to adjust the effect's settings. The preview shows your changes immediately, so feel free to experiment.

To adjust an effect's settings in the preview window:

◆ If an effect includes controls in the preview window (such as Fairy Dust or Lens Flare), click within the window to specify a focus point (**Figure 13.4**). There's no obvious indication that such controls exist for any given effect, though, so you need to click the window to see if a control is available.

✔ Tips

- To reset the sliders to their original positions, click another effect, then switch back to the one you're adjusting. The defaults return when you do, saving you the trouble of trying to approximate the controls' original positions.

  This doesn't apply to the Effect In and Effect Out sliders, however. They stay put when you click other effects in the list.

- Third-party iMovie plug-in developers have gone wild with effects. In addition to adding "painterly" looks, you can create picture-within-picture effects (as seen on TV newscasts), and even perform some rudimentary greenscreen matting effects (for when you want to make your cat look like she's rampaging through downtown Tokyo!). See Appendix B for a list of plug-in vendors.

Applying Effects

Editing effects is similar to editing transitions and titles, but the way effects are added to your movie is slightly different. Instead of dragging the effect's name to the Timeline, you use the Effects pane's Apply button.

To apply an effect:

1. Select the clip you want to modify.
2. Select the effect you want to apply, and adjust its settings to your liking.
3. Click the Apply button in the Effects pane. The clip begins rendering with the effect applied. In the Clip Viewer, clips with effects are marked with a checkerboard icon (**Figure 13.5**).

✔ Tips

- You can reverse steps 1 and 2. Sometimes I select a clip first, sometimes I tinker with effects settings without any clip selected.
- Effects cannot be applied to clips on the Shelf. However, you can add an effect to a clip in the Timeline and then drag it to the Shelf for use later.
- To cancel rendering, press Command-period (.) or choose Undo from the Edit menu.
- If you apply some types of effects to a still image, the image needs to be converted to a regular clip. Don't worry, iMovie warns you if this is the case, and gives you the option to cancel (**Figure 13.6**). (See Chapter 9 for more on using still images.)
- After you've applied an effect, you can still add transitions or titles to that clip.
- If you apply multiple effects to a clip, a number next to the effects icon tells you how many there are (**Figure 13.7**).

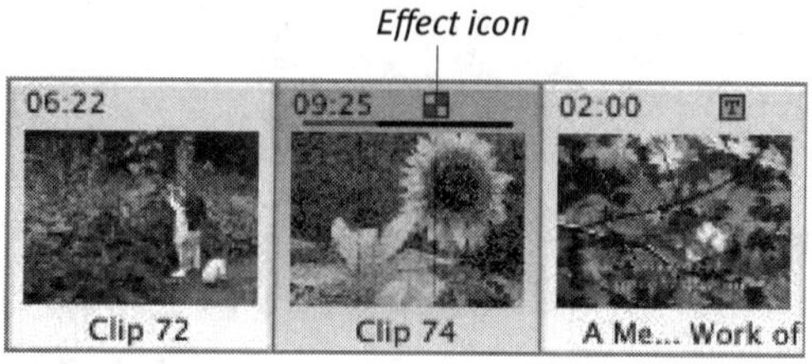

Figure 13.5 Clips with effects applied show up in the Clip Viewer with a checkerboard icon.

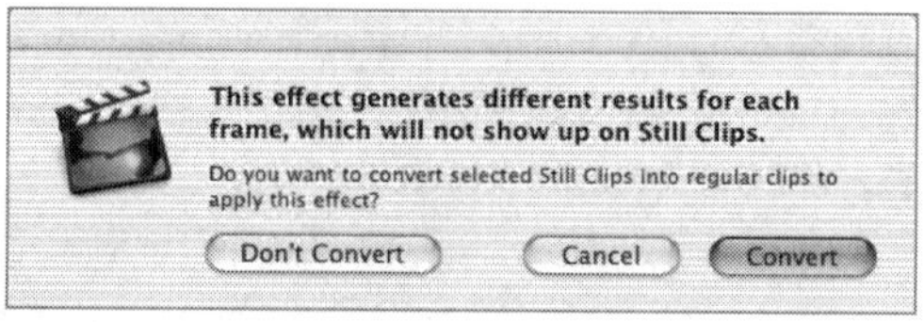

Figure 13.6 Some effects require that still images be converted to regular clips.

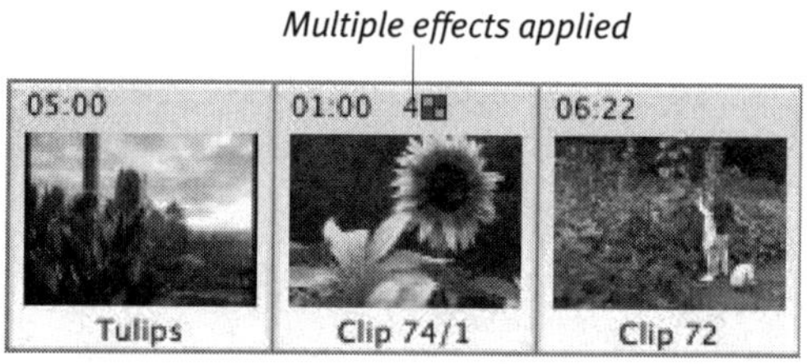

Figure 13.7 The number next to the effects icon indicates how many effects have been applied to the clip.

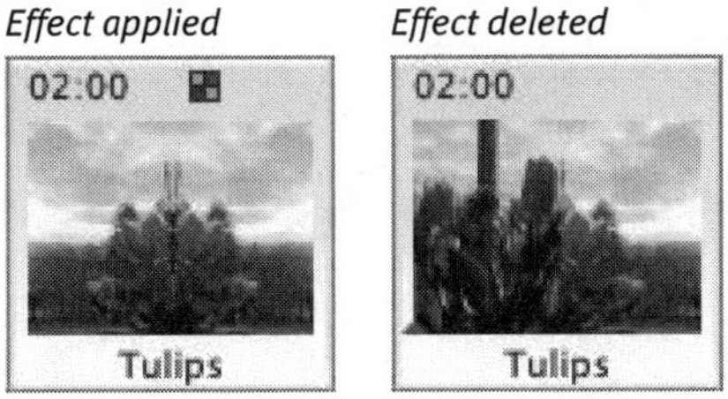

Figure 13.8 Deleting an effect doesn't delete the entire clip.

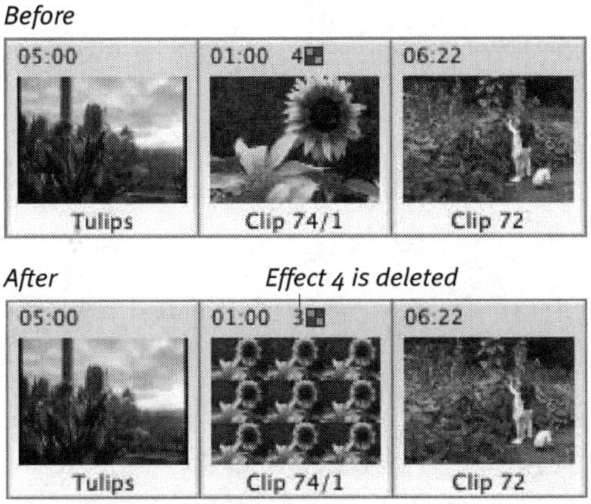

Figure 13.9 Deleting multiple effects from a clip is like peeling paint in an old house—sooner or later you get to the original.

Modifying Existing Effects

In iMovie 2, you could tweak an effect's settings after you had applied it to a clip, then click the Update button to apply the new settings. However, if you wanted to use multiple effects, you first needed to *commit* the clip, rendering it so that iMovie no longer recognized it as an effects-laden clip. iMovie 3 no longer requires the commit step, but you cannot modify settings in effects that have already been applied. You must delete the effect and start over. I recommend making a copy of the clip before deleting its effect (Option-drag it to the Shelf) so you have a backup of the first version of the effect.

Removing Effects

On the off chance that you applied several effects in your sleep, waking up in horror to discover that everyone on your spouse's side of the family has been mirrored, there's an easy way to restore those clips: simply delete the effect, as you would with a title or transition.

To remove an effect:

1. Select the clip in your movie to which the effect has been applied.
2. Press the Delete key or choose Clear from the Edit menu. The effect is deleted, leaving the original clip intact (**Figure 13.8**).

✔ Tips

- When multiple effects are applied to a clip, you must remove each one in turn (**Figure 13.9**). To save time, you *could* use the Restore Media command (from the Advanced menu), but then you get the clip's entire original footage—overkill.
- If you move a clip with effects applied to the Shelf and select it there, pressing Delete or choosing Clear from the Edit menu deletes the clip entirely.

Part 3 Exporting

14

Moving Back to Tape

Your movie is finished! Now what?

While it's feasible that you could transport your Mac (especially if it's an iBook or PowerBook) to every location where someone might see your movie, that plan runs into a few snags when you want to share your masterpiece with grandparents in Humboldt or your sister in South Africa. Fortunately, getting completed footage out of iMovie is almost as simple as bringing raw footage in.

Exporting to the Camera

There are two main advantages to exporting your footage back to your camcorder's DV tape. The camera stores the footage in digital format, so you'll have a copy saved off your computer that retains the same level of quality as what you edited. This is handy in case you need to make a backup of your work so far, or for when you want to hook your camcorder up to a television to show the movie. You can also export your completed movie—which up until now existed as a collection of edited clips—then re-import it into iMovie as one long unbroken clip (depending on length; see Chapter 7) to reclaim some disk space or merge the movie with new footage.

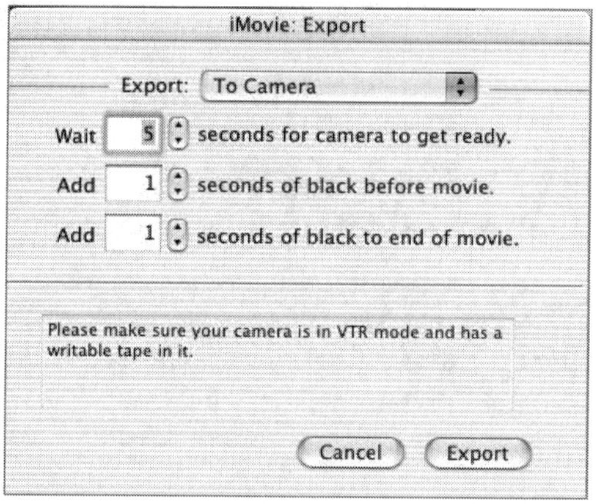

Figure 14.1 The iMovie: Export dialog box includes controls for setting up the camcorder and adding black frames.

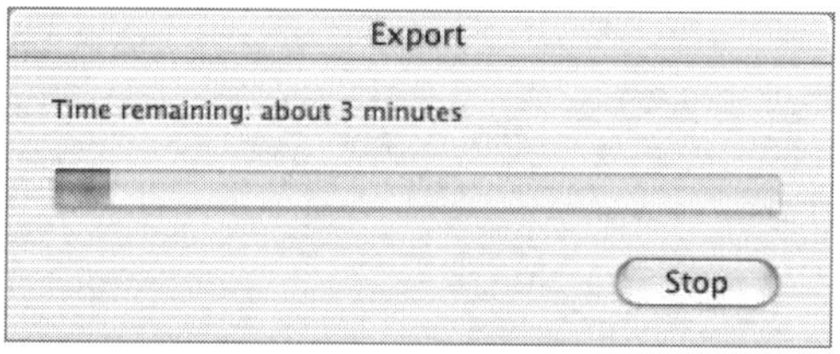

Figure 14.2 Exporting to camera requires the same amount of time as your movie's length.

To export to the camera:

1. Switch your camcorder to Play/VCR/VTR mode.
2. Choose Export from iMovie's File menu, or press Command-Shift-E. iMovie displays the iMovie: Export dialog box, with To Camera selected in the Export popup menu (**Figure 14.1**).
3. Enter a number in the field marked Wait [number] seconds for camera to get ready. Your camcorder needs to spin up and get into position before recording, so iMovie will wait for this length of time. If your movies on tape are getting cut off at the beginning, increase this number.

   If you want some black frames before or after your movie, enter numbers in the two remaining fields. This gives you some extra time on the tape and tends to look more professional than just launching into the movie from the beginning.
4. Click the Export button to begin exporting (**Figure 14.2**). When it's finished, iMovie automatically stops the camera.

Tape Backup

Exporting your footage to tape serves another important function: providing a backup of your work. Even a modest iMovie project will swamp most backup capacities (such as DAT tape systems) due to the sheer number of gigabytes needing to be backed up. Instead, export your movie to DV tape. In the event that you suffer a hard disk crash (trust me, it's not a fun experience), you won't have your iMovie project, but you'll be able to re-import the edited footage and not lose all of your work.

Exporting to Camera

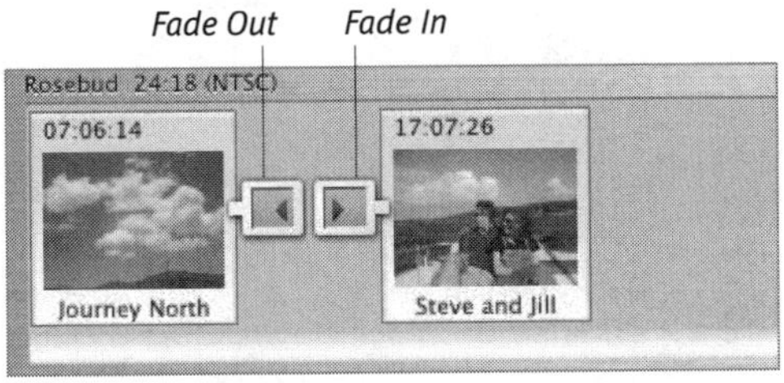

Figure 14.3 Combining a Fade Out and a Fade In transition elegantly bridges these two long segments.

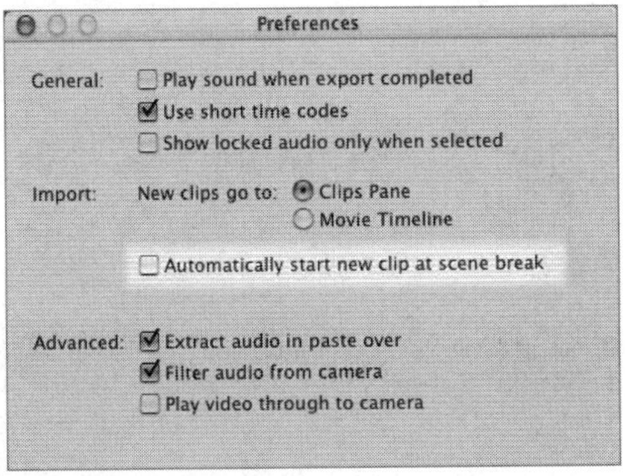

Figure 14.4 To import your segment as one long clip, turn off the option labeled Automatically start new clip at scene break.

Are You Really Ready?

The downside to this approach is that you need to make sure your movie segments are finished (or close enough to being done), because when you re-import them into iMovie, you won't have the clips of unused footage from the individual projects at your disposal.

However, you can always bring in selected media footage using the Import File command under the File menu.

Combining Movie Segments

It's often a good idea to break up a longer movie into smaller segments, working on 10- or 20-minute chunks at a time. But when 10 minutes of footage takes up nearly 2 GB, you simply may not have enough storage space, even with today's bigger hard drives.

To combine movie segments:

1. Export each segment to DV tape using the steps on the previous pages. It's helpful to add a few seconds of black frames to the end of each segment, then rewind the tape a bit so the next segment plays right on the heels of the previous one.
2. Create a new iMovie project by choosing New Project from the File menu. Make sure you have enough hard disk space to accommodate the segments you wish to combine.
3. Switch to Camera Mode and import the segments. Depending on how you've split the segments, you may only have to add a simple transition between them to create a unified whole (**Figure 14.3**).

✔ Tip

- If you're confident that you've finished editing the segments individually, consider importing them as long clips instead of letting iMovie try to split out each scene. In iMovie's preferences, turn off Automatically start new clip at scene break (**Figure 14.4**).

Transferring to Videotape

Until everyone has a DVD player, and until Macs with DVD burners are cheap, the best way to share your movies is still videotape. You can record from your camcorder, or transfer directly from iMovie.

To transfer from your camcorder:

1. Export your movie from iMovie to your camcorder's tape as discussed on the previous pages.
2. Connect your camcorder to a VCR using the AV cables that came with the camcorder (**Figure 14.5**).
3. Switch the camcorder to Play/VCR/VTR mode if it's not already on.
4. Put a blank videotape in the VCR, and rewind the camcorder's tape to the beginning of your movie.
5. Push Record on the VCR.
6. Push Play on the camcorder.
7. When the movie is finished, push Stop on both machines.

To transfer directly from iMovie:

1. Connect your camcorder and VCR as described above.
2. Connect the camcorder to your Mac via FireWire, if it's not already connected.
3. In iMovie's preferences, turn on the Play Video Through to Camera option.
4. Remove the tape from the camcorder, then choose Export from the File menu. A dialog box notifies you that there's no tape (**Figure 14.6**).
5. Press Record on your VCR, and click the Export button in iMovie.
6. When the movie is finished, push Stop on the VCR.

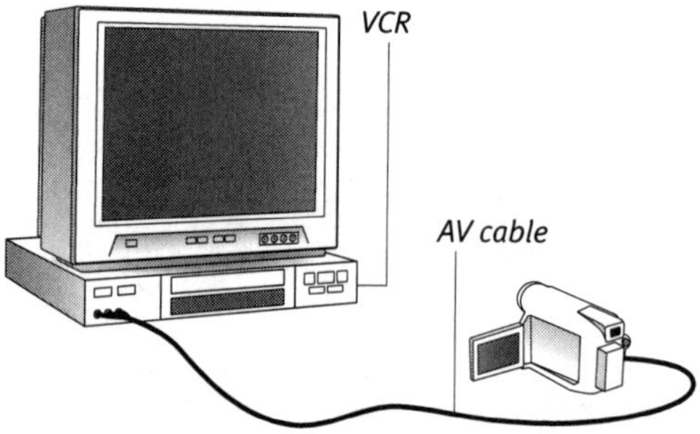

Figure 14.5 Connect your camcorder to a VCR using the AV cable included with the camcorder.

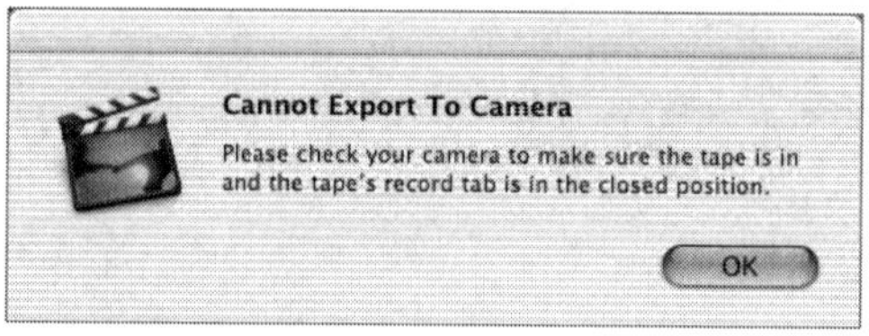

Figure 14.6 iMovie notifies you if you try to export a movie with no tape in the camcorder.

15 QuickTime and the Web

On the surface, QuickTime is a great little utility for playing movies on your Mac. I often visit `www.apple.com/trailers/` to see which new movie trailer is ready for download—I click a link, and in a couple of minutes the clip is playing. (It's amazing what you can learn about filmmaking from trailers; they're some of the best sources for how to present ideas and images in a short time span.) Sometimes the movie appears in a window in your Web browser, while other times the QuickTime Player plays the movie.

Now, you have the opportunity to export your movies to the QuickTime format. In so doing, you gain a number of advantages: your file sizes become much smaller (a 1-minute clip can easily shrink from around 200 MB to 2 MB without destroying its quality); your movies can be played on any Macintosh sold within the last four or five years; and you can upload them to the Web, where anyone with a Web browser and the QuickTime software (that includes Windows users, too) can download and view the movie.

You can choose one of iMovie's recommended settings or configure the details yourself to tweak performance. And when it comes time to put the file on the Web, several methods are available, from building a `mac.com` Web page to hand-coding the HTML yourself.

Exporting to QuickTime

Exporting your movie to QuickTime can be as straightforward or as complicated as you want it to be. Understanding that most users won't wade into the complexities of what the QuickTime format can offer, iMovie gives you five pre-configured settings. Following are the basic steps for creating a QuickTime movie from your footage; the intricacies of what QuickTime can do are on the next page.

To export as a QuickTime movie:

1. Choose Export from the File menu, or press Command-Shift-E.
2. In the iMovie: Export dialog box, select a format from the Formats popup menu (**Figure 15.1**). These are some common settings for various types of distribution (such as Web versus CD-ROM). See "Choosing a QuickTime format" below for explanations and examples of each.
3. Click the Export button to begin creating the QuickTime movie.

Choosing a QuickTime format

When you're exporting to QuickTime, remember to keep your audience in mind. You may create a cinematic masterpiece, but if it's several hundred megabytes in size, it likely won't be downloaded over the Web or fit onto a CD-ROM easily. iMovie offers five preset export configurations (**Figures 15.2** and **15.3**); the specifications for each are shown in **Table 15.1**.

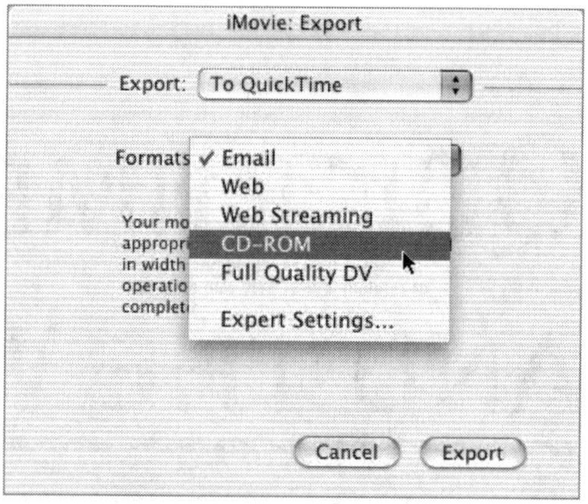

Figure 15.1 iMovie includes five presets for exporting movies in the QuickTime format.

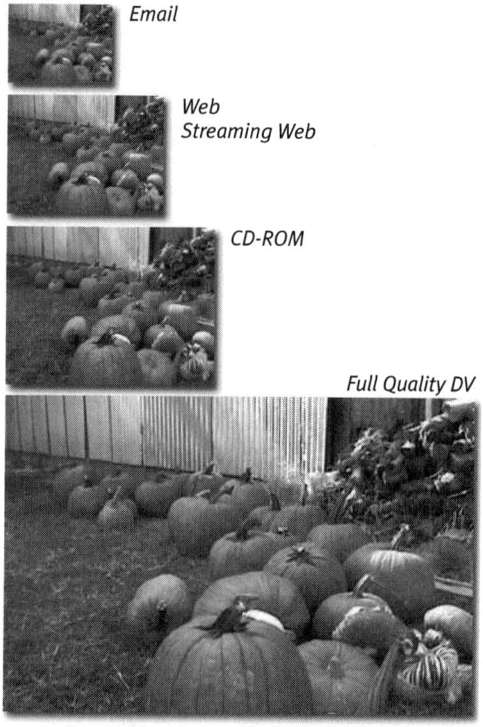

Figure 15.2 This should give you an idea of how the QuickTime export settings compare in iMovie. These images are roughly 25 percent of actual size.

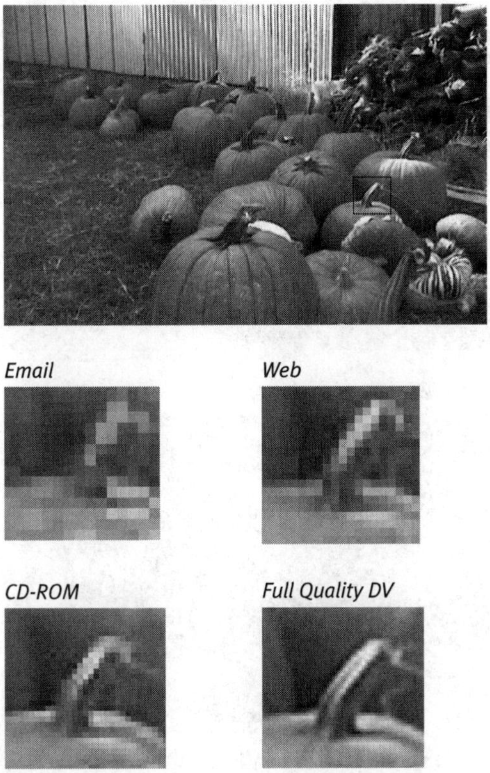

Figure 15.3 The different QuickTime export formats vary in visual quality too, based on how much compression is applied with the Image Settings options.

- **Web.** At first glance, it looks as if iMovie lists the formats from smallest to largest, but this format is the second-smallest one. Web is a good compromise between file size and video quality.
- **Email.** This is the smallest format available from the presets, and represents quite a sacrifice of quality in favor of small file sizes. Don't expect titles to be read easily, but do expect speed: this movie can be half the size of a Web movie.
- **Streaming Web.** A movie that's streamed is played as it downloads, so you don't have to wait for the entire movie to arrive before viewing it. Slightly larger in file size than the Web movie above, this format includes data that enables the movie to be streamed from a dedicated streaming server (versus downloaded as a file, then played back).
- **CD-ROM.** The CD-ROM format increases the file size quite a bit from the Web movie, but the quality differences are immediately apparent. Note that the "CD-ROM" designation refers to file size, not a requirement that it can only be used on CD-ROMs.

continues on next page

Table 15.1

iMovie's Stock Compression Settings

iMovie Format	Video Compression	Size (pixels)	Frame Rate	Audio Compression	Stereo/ Mono	Sample Rate	Sample File Size*
Web	H.263	240 x 180	12.00 fps	QDesign Music 2	Stereo	22050.00 Hz	2.0 MB
Email	H.263	160 x 120	10.00 fps	QDesign Music 2	Mono	22050.00 Hz	1.0 MB
Streaming Web	H.263	240 x 180	12.00 fps	QDesign Music 2	Stereo	22050.00 Hz	2.2 MB
CD-ROM	H.263	320 x 240	15.00 fps	IMA 4:1	Stereo	44100.00 Hz	5.8 MB
Full Quality DV	DV - NTSC	720 x 480	29.97 fps	No compression	Stereo	48000.00 Hz	216.8 MB

* File size is based on exporting the sample one-minute movie found on the previous page.

◆ **Full Quality DV.** This format should be titled "Full Quality HUGE" due to its massive file size. What makes it so big? It's the same format as what your camera produces (DV), so you're looking at essentially uncompressed footage. It's big and beautiful, but you take a serious hard disk hit (about 200 MB per minute of video).

✔ Tips

- If you want to export your movie to the hard disk instead of to tape (see Chapter 14), use Full Quality DV to create a new DV file. This is also what you'd do to create footage for import into more advanced programs such as Apple's Final Cut Pro. Make sure you have plenty of disk space, though!
- Why is the video size for Full Quality DV set to 720 x 480, instead of the Monitor's size of 640 x 480? You know that each frame is composed of pixels, but what's not obvious is that the pixels in digital video are rectangular (taller than they are wide, as shown in **Figure 15.4**).

  Similarly, the NTSC frame rate of 29.97 fps isn't rounded up to 30 fps. Way back when the first color televisions were introduced, the frame rate needed to be adjusted slightly to avoid audio distortion—and the setting stuck.

Full Quality DV (720 x 480 pixels)

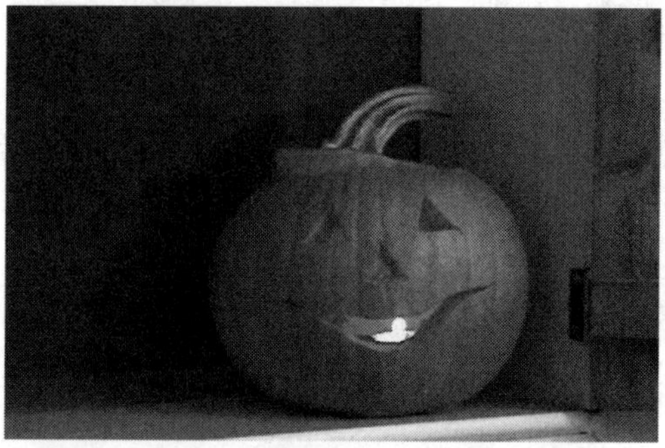

Full Quality DV (640 x 480 pixels)

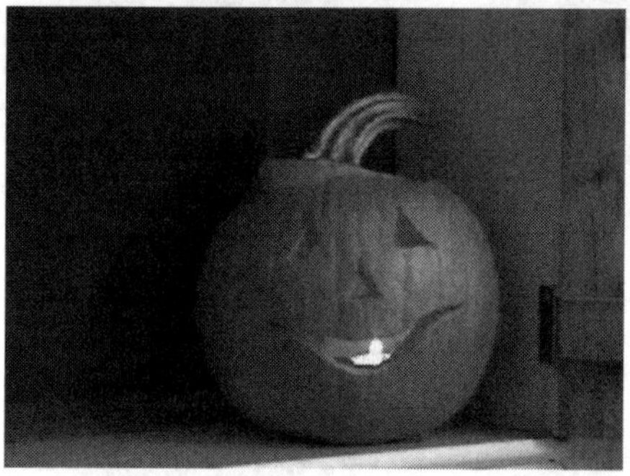

Figure 15.4 The Full Quality DV format exports video measuring 720 x 480 pixels, compared to the 640 x 480 pixel size you're accustomed to. If you were to import it into another video-editing application, it would appear as 640 x 480 (just like in iMovie).

Video Compression Terms You Should Know

Codec: Short for compression/decompression; another name for a compressor.

Compression: The method used to reduce the size of the movie file while still retaining image quality. Video and audio compression are a tricky business: you have to weigh the benefits of smaller file sizes (and therefore potentially faster downloads) against the desire to have the best-looking movies possible. There are many methods of compression available, each with its own strengths. **Table 15.2** on the next page provides an overview of the compressors available when exporting from iMovie. There are more available if you export files from QuickTime Player Pro, and still more offered by professional editing packages such as Cleaner (`www.discreet.com`).

Data Rate: The amount of data sent from one point to another during a given time, such as the number of kilobytes delivered during a Web download.

Frame Rate: The number of frames displayed during 1 second. As more frames are included, the movie will play smoother—but adding frames increases the size of the file. Uncompressed DV video runs at 30 frames per second (fps) for NTSC, or 25 fps for PAL; a typical QuickTime movie can contain 15 or 12 frames per second.

Key Frame: A complete movie frame that acts as the image base for successive frames. Unlike film, which displays 24 full frames per second on a reel of celluloid, QuickTime compares most of the frames in a movie with its key frames and notes the differences. Although this sounds like more work than just displaying each frame in its entirety, it actually means the movie player is drawing less data.

For example, consider a clip where the camera is stationary, filming a person talking. Every pixel of the first frame, the key frame, is drawn; in the next frame, the only change is that the person's lips have moved. Instead of redrawing the background and everything else, QuickTime holds onto the first frame and only changes the pixels around the person's mouth. So, the second frame (and third, fourth, and so on) contain only a few pixels' worth of information, dramatically reducing the total amount of data required and creating a smaller file. Of course, the entire movie likely won't be composed of just the person talking, so QuickTime creates several key frames along the way, allowing the player to regroup and start over. The more key frames that appear in your movie, the larger the file size will be.

Sample Rate: The quality of audio, measured in hertz (Hz). The higher the number, the more audio data is present, and therefore the better the quality of sound.

Exporting to QuickTime Using Expert Settings

iMovie's stock QuickTime format settings are good for most situations, but you can also use other compression formats and options by way of the Expert option under the Formats popup menu (**Table 15.2**).

Table 15.2

Video Compressors Included with QuickTime*

Compressor Name	Comments
Animation	Works best on computer-generated animations with broad areas of flat color. Doesn't work well for scenes with lots of color changes.
BMP	Used for still images to be exported in BMP format. Does minimal compression. Inappropriate for video-based movie playback.
Cinepak	Commonly used for video movies that require CD-ROM playback. Compresses very slowly.
Component Video	High-quality compressor. Good for capture on Macs with built-in video capture capabilities and for use as an intermediate storage format. Low compression ratios (larger files).
DV-PAL, DV/DVCPRO-NTSC, DVCPRO-PAL	Used with digital video cameras.
Graphics	Good for 8-bit graphics files. Usually better than the Animation compressor in 8 bits. Slower to decompress than Animation.
H.261	Originally designed for videoconferencing. Extremely high compression ratios.
H.263	Originally designed for videoconferencing. Very high compression ratios. Sometimes good for Web video.
JPEG 2000	High image quality and resolution for still images, using wavelet compression.
Motion JPEG A, Motion JPEG B	Used to decompress files made with certain Motion-JPEG cards when the card isn't available or to compress in a format that can be played by certain hardware Motion-JPEG cards.
MPEG-4 Video	High quality compressed video based on QuickTime.
None	Good for capture only. Does almost no compression.
Photo-JPEG	Ideal for high-quality compressed still images. Also useful as an intermediate storage format for movies and QuickTime VR panoramas. Decompresses too slowly for video-based playback.
Planar RGB	For images with an alpha channel.
PNG	Typically used for still-image compression. Can get high compression ratios.
Sorenson Video	Very high compression ratios and high quality. Excellent for Web and CD-ROM.
Sorenson Video 3	Very high compression ratios and very high quality (better than Sorenson Video). Currently the best choice for Web and CD-ROM.
Targa	Typically used for still-image compression. Does minimal compression.
TIFF	Typically used for still-image compression. Does minimal compression.
Video	Very fast video compression and decompression. Decent compression ratios. Good for real-time capture of video, particularly when hard disk space is at a premium. Good for testing clips. OK for hard disk playback. Image quality is poor when compressing enough for CD-ROM playback.

Note: The Minimum Install of QuickTime (which many users will choose) doesn't install all these compressors. If the computer being used to play a movie that requires one of these compressors has an Internet connection, QuickTime downloads the necessary compressor when it is needed for decompression.

* This table has been adapted from one that originally appeared in *QuickTime 5 for Macintosh and Windows: Visual QuickStart Guide*, by Judith Stern and Robert Lettieri, and is used here with their permission. `www.judyandrobert.com/quicktime/`

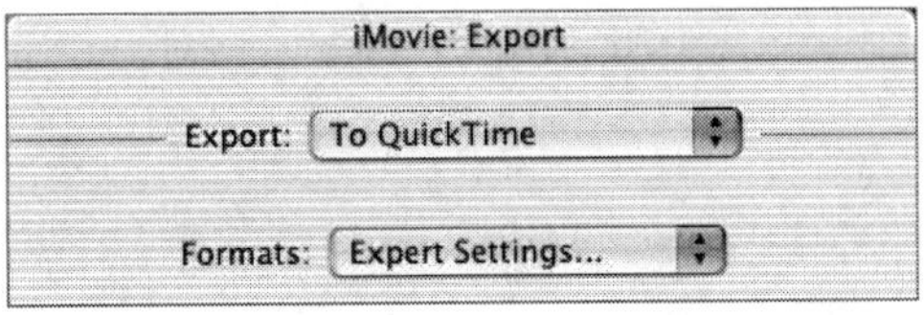

Figure 15.5 The Expert QuickTime Settings provide many more options for controlling the compression.

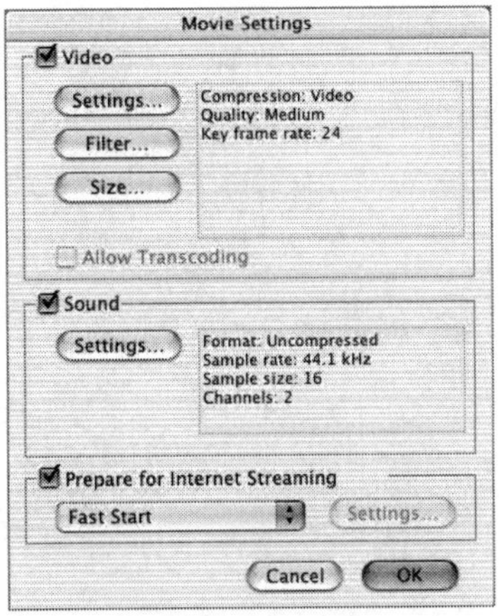

Figure 15.6 The Movie Settings dialog box presents an overview of the current export settings.

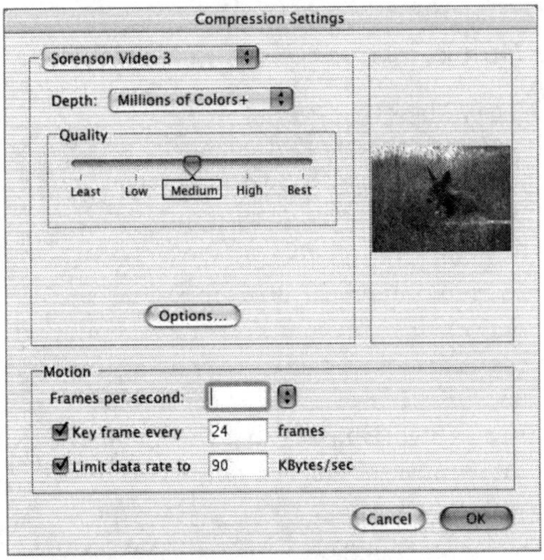

Figure 15.7 After that long progression of dialog boxes, you finally reach Compression Settings, where you can adjust the type and amount of compression used for exporting.

To change image settings:

1. Choose Export from the File menu, or press Command-Shift-E.
2. In the iMove: Export dialog box, choose Expert Settings from the Formats popup menu (**Figure 15.5**). Click Export.
3. In the Save Exported File As dialog, make sure Movie to QuickTime Movie is selected in the Export popup menu, and click the Options button.
4. The Movie Settings dialog box displays the current video and sound settings (**Figure 15.6**). To fine-tune the type and amount of video compression applied, click the Settings button under Video.
5. In the top area of the Compression Settings dialog box, choose a compression method from the first popup menu (**Figure 15.7**). The Depth popup menu specifies how many colors to use when exporting the file (fewer colors equal more compression, but lower image quality).
6. Move the Quality slider to the lowest level you can that maintains good image quality; the thumbnail in the upper-right corner of the dialog box shows you how much compression is being applied.
7. In the Motion area, select the number of frames per second from the popup menu beside the field, or just enter a value.
8. Enter a number in the Key frame every [number] frames field to set how often a key frame is generated. If you don't want iMovie to generate key frames (i.e., every frame is a full frame), deselect this option.

continues on next page

9. To target a specific data rate, enter a value in the field labeled Limit data rate to [number] KBytes/sec.

10. Click OK to return to the Expert QuickTime Settings dialog box.

✔ Tips

- To get a sense for how the compressors compare, create a short movie (30 seconds or so) that's representative of your footage and export it using the various formats, and then compare the results.
- The Sorenson Video codecs are highly regarded for having high video quality with good compression. For some suggested Sorenson settings, select iMovie Help from the Help menu and search for "Sorenson Codec".

QuickTime versus QuickTime Pro

Every Mac comes with QuickTime, including the free QuickTime Player, which allows you to play back QuickTime movies and a host of other file formats (ranging from MPEG-formatted movies to MP3 audio files). If you're serious about optimizing your QuickTime movies for the Web, however, consider paying the $30 for a QuickTime Pro license, which turns QuickTime Player into a sophisticated movie editor. Not only does it give you an easy way to resize or recompress QuickTime movies, it also lets you save your movies into other formats, such as AVI, which Windows users can view if they don't have QuickTime installed.

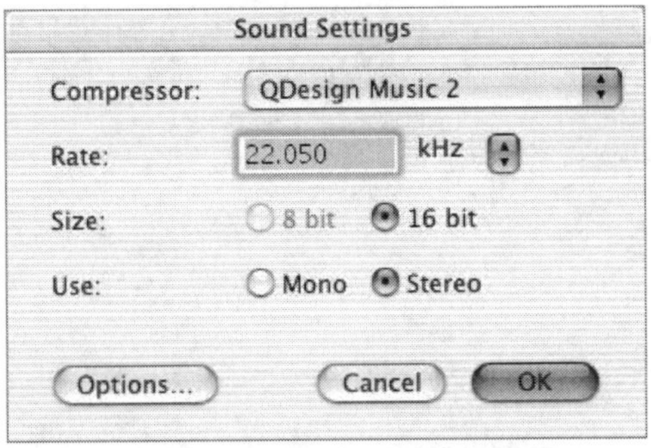

Figure 15.8 Choose an audio compressor to fine-tune how your movie's audio sounds after exporting.

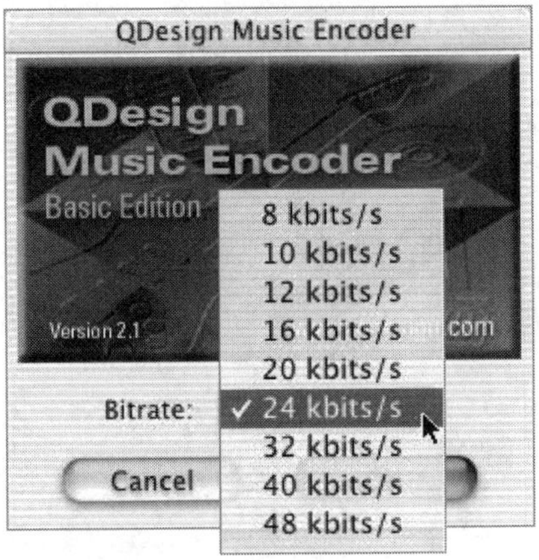

Figure 15.9 Some compressors include other settings to help reduce your movie's file size without sacrificing too much quality.

To change audio settings:

1. Choose Export from the File menu, or press Command-Shift-E.
2. In the iMove: Export dialog box, choose Expert Settings from the Formats popup menu. Click Export.
3. In the Save Exported File As dialog, make sure Movie to QuickTime Movie is selected in the Export popup menu, and click the Options button.
4. In the Sound portion of the Movie Settings dialog box, click the Settings button to display the Sound Settings dialog box (**Figure 15.8**).
5. Choose a format from the Compressor popup menu. Some of the compressors include further settings, which are accessed by clicking the Options button. These usually determine how the data is encoded or specify a data rate (or bit rate) (**Figure 15.9**).
6. In the Rate field, type a kHz value or select one from the popup menu to the right. Lower kHz settings will degrade the sound quality.
7. Click either the 8 bit or 16 bit button to determine how much audio data is included in the file. The higher number provides for better sound quality, but at the expense of a larger file size.
8. Decide whether the audio will play back in stereo or mono by checking a button next to the Use option. Stereo sounds better, but Mono offers a smaller file size.
9. Click OK to return to the Movie Settings dialog box.

To prepare a movie for Internet streaming:

1. Choose Export from the File menu, or press Command-Shift-E.
2. In the iMovie: Export dialog box, choose Expert Settings from the Formats popup menu. Click Export.
3. In the Save Exported File As dialog, make sure Movie to QuickTime Movie is selected in the Export popup menu, and click the Options button.
4. In the Movie Settings dialog box, click the Prepare for Internet Streaming box in the lower-right corner (**Figure 15.10**).
5. From the popup menu, select a streaming method:
   - ▲ **Fast Start.** The movie file is downloaded like any other media file, and begins playing once enough data has been transferred.
   - ▲ **Fast Start - Compressed Header.** Like Fast Start, the movie is downloaded as one file, but the header information is compressed to save disk space.
   - ▲ **Hinted Streaming.** Use this option if the movie will be hosted by a QuickTime Streaming Server. Hinting the data breaks it up into more manageable chunks for streaming. With Hinted Streaming selected, you can click the Options button to further tweak the settings (**Figure 15.11**). For more information, see Apple's article: `http://docs.info.apple.com/article.html?artnum=36640`.

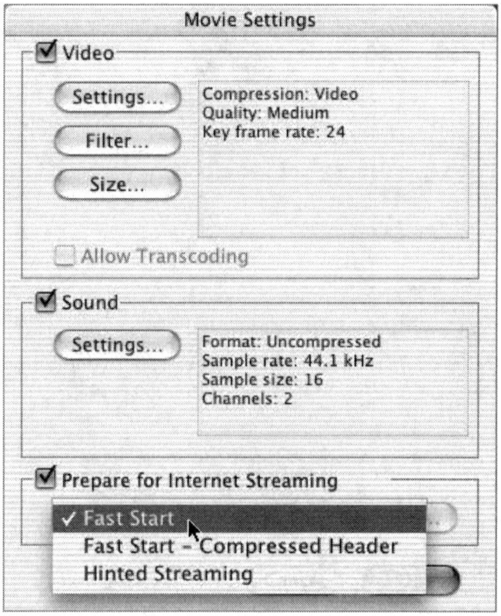

Figure 15.10 To enable Web streaming, click the Prepare for Internet Streaming box and choose a streaming method.

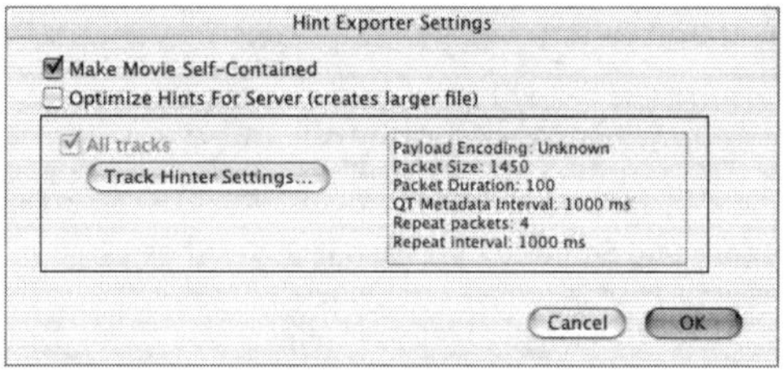

Figure 15.11 Preparing a QuickTime movie for streaming can get into a lot of geeky detail, but if you know what you're doing, you can improve streaming quality.

QuickTime Geekery

Trust me: everything described so far in this chapter is really just the tip of a very large iceberg. If you're willing to shell out the bucks, software such as Discreet's Cleaner can encode and compress your movies into nearly any possible movie format, with more control than can be found in iMovie's or QuickTime Player's export features.

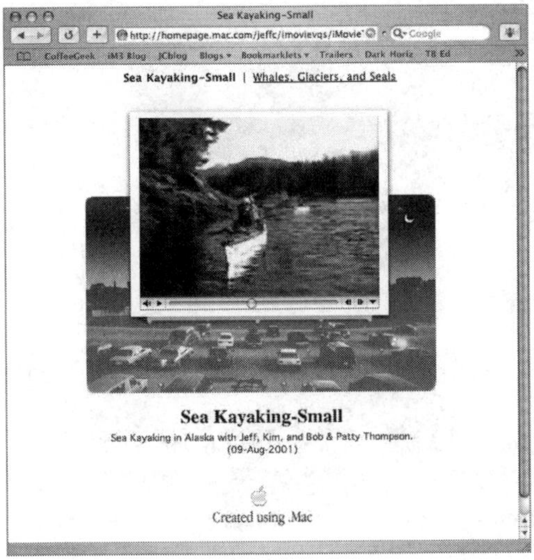

Figure 15.12 You spent all that time editing—put your movies on the Web where others can see (for example, `homepage.mac.com/jeffc/imovievqs/`).

Getting Your Movie on the Web

You may be creating movies that will live only on your hard disk, for your eyes only, never to be seen by anyone. More likely, though, your movies are meant to be viewed. As I've covered already, you can export the movie to a videotape and mail it to your relatives—if you don't mind purchasing the tape, filling it with movies (or just using a few minutes of it for one movie), then paying to mail it across the country or around the world. Where's the instant gratification in that? Instead (or in addition), post your movie to the Web (**Figure 15.12**), where anyone can download and view your creation within minutes of its completion (and which is also available 24 hours a day, perfect for your uncle who likes to work online at 2 a.m.).

When putting movies online, keep your audience in mind: do they have fast broadband connections like DSL or cable, or are they connecting with dialup modems? That will affect which format you export the movie to. The Web setting provides a decent trade-off between quality and compression, but it may be easier for some folks to handle the Email format instead. (Or, if you have the storage space on your server, consider making multiple versions so your audience can decide which size is best for them.)

If you use a Web design program such as Adobe GoLive or Macromedia Dreamweaver, follow the instructions for adding QuickTime movies to your pages. For our purposes here, I'm going to assume that you don't own a Web design application and instead want to either post a movie on the Web using Apple's simple .Mac ("dot-Mac") service, or hand-code the HTML (HyperText Markup Language) necessary to make the movie appear on a Web page of your own coding.

Using .Mac

These days, the easiest method for putting your movies on the Web is to use Apple's .Mac service (`www.mac.com`). When you sign up for a membership (which costs $100 per year), you gain access to an iDisk, which is essentially a networked 100 MB hard drive that lives at Apple. You also get to use the online Homepage tools to create a site, and a mac.com email thrown into the mix, too. Once you've created an account, you simply copy your movie to a folder in your iDisk, then use it to build a Web page.

To mount your iDisk:

- In the Finder, choose iDisk from the Go menu (**Figure 15.13**).

  or

- Click the iDisk icon in the Toolbar (**Figure 15.14**). (If you don't see an iDisk icon, choose Customize Toolbar from the View menu, and drag the iDisk icon to the Toolbar area. Press Done to accept the change.)

  or

1. In the Finder, choose Connect to Server from the Go menu (or press Command-K).
2. Type `afp://idisk.mac.com` in the Address field, and click the Connect button.
3. Enter your user name and password. The iDisk appears on the Desktop.

To copy a movie to your iDisk:

1. Double-click your iDisk to open it. Inside, you'll see a folder titled Movies.
2. Drag and drop your QuickTime movie file on the Movies folder (**Figure 15.15**). After the file copies to your iDisk, it will be available to the Homepage module of iTools.

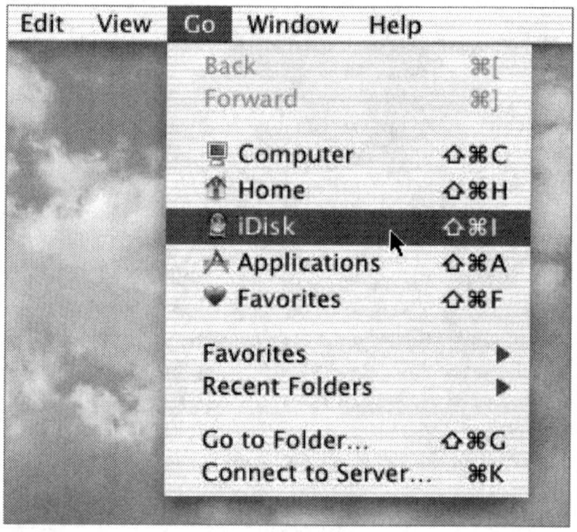

Figure 15.13 Your iDisk is always available under the Finder's Go menu.

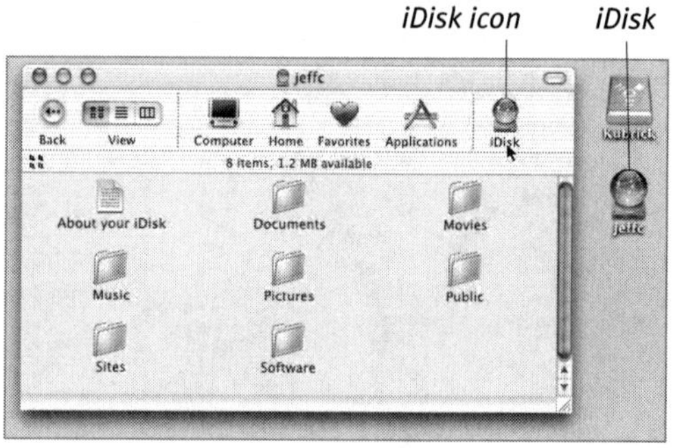

Figure 15.14 Putting the iDisk icon in your Toolbar makes your iDisk available from any Finder window.

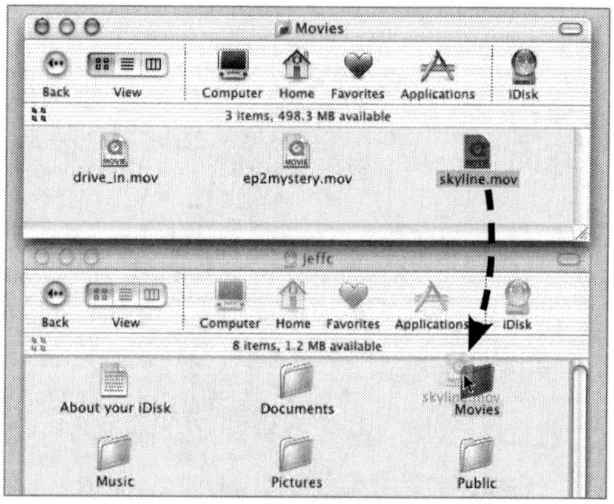

Figure 15.15 Copy movie files to the Movies folder of your iDisk to make them available at .Mac.

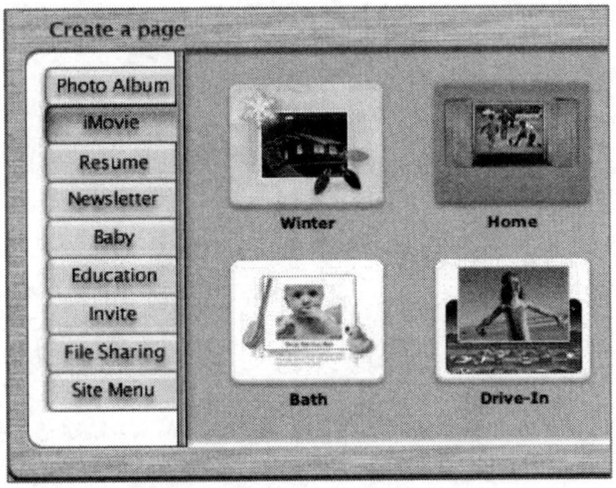

Figure 15.16 .Mac includes several pre-designed templates for Web pages, such as for iMovies.

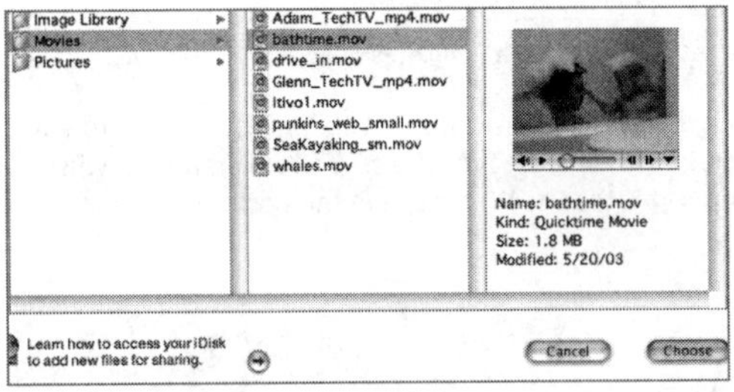

Figure 15.17 Select a movie from the list to view a preview in the right-hand pane.

To build a Web page using .Mac:

1. Launch a Web browser and enter `www.mac.com` in the Address field to connect to Apple's .Mac page (if you're not already connected).
2. Click the Homepage icon.
3. Log in with your .Mac user name and password (if required).
4. In the area marked Create a Page, click the iMovie tab (**Figure 15.16**).
5. Click a theme that will surround the movie, such as a drive-in theater or retro-TV. A preview of the page appears.
6. Click the Edit button at the top of the page, which loads the same page but with editable text fields.
7. Type the page title, movie title, and page description text in the fields provided.
8. Click the Choose button below the movie placeholder to select your movie. You will be redirected to a new page listing the movie files located in your iDisk's Movies folder (**Figure 15.17**).
9. Click the name of the movie file you want to use, then click the Choose button. You will be taken back to the editing page.
10. Click the Preview button to see what it will look like, or click the Publish button to create the new page. The site will then display the URL of the page that you can send to other people.

✔ Tip

- iTools automatically prepares your movie for Web streaming after you copy it to your iDisk.

Writing HTML

This, of course, isn't a book about HTML, so I'm going to assume that you know the basics about coding Web pages, and that you have an application (such as Bare Bones Software's BBEdit, or even TextEdit) that you use to build pages. If that's not the case, check out Elizabeth Castro's book *HTML for the World Wide Web: Visual QuickStart Guide*, which remains the best HTML guide I've read (I said so even before I got involved with Peachpit Press).

That said, there are still some important things to know about adding a movie to a Web page using HTML. There are two ways of going about it: you can copy the file to your Web directory (provided by your Internet service provider) then link directly to it; or you can embed the movie on a Web page so that it's part of the page's layout.

To link to a QuickTime movie file:

1. In your HTML editing application, enter the following code where you want your movie link to appear. The user will see only the linked text; clicking it will download the movie.

```
<a href="http://www.youraddress.com/
sample.mov">Click here</a>
```

2. Insert the real names of your Web address and movie filename in place of *youraddress.com* and *sample.mov* (**Figure 15.18**). For example, a movie on my Web site would look like this (go ahead and put the URL below into your Web browser to view the movie).

```
<a href="http://www.necoffee.com/
imovievqs/secretmovie.mov">Is it
really a secret?</a>
```

HTML text that creates link

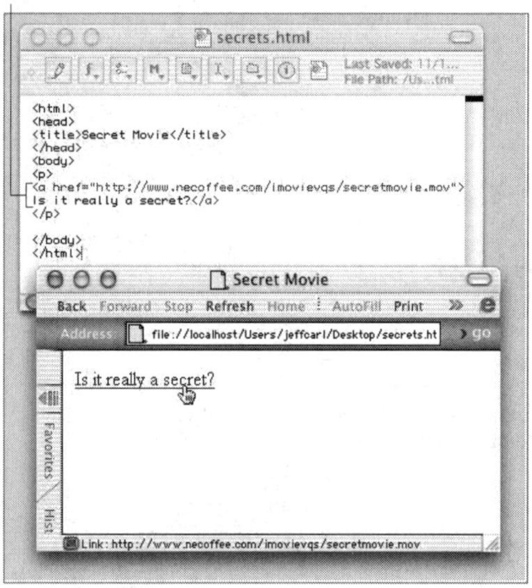

Figure 15.18 Add a simple Web link that points to your QuickTime movie file. The HTML text in the top window creates the Web page in the bottom window.

Embed a Headache

If you know how to embed an object already, you may be wondering why the example on the next page contains so much other information. In late 2001, Microsoft stopped supporting the plug-in architecture used by Web browsers since long before Microsoft even got into the browser business (when a QuickTime movie appears on a page, a QuickTime plug-in—not the browser by itself—is doing the work of playing it back correctly). Instead, Microsoft switched to its own ActiveX architecture—but only under Internet Explorer 5.5 and later for Windows. So although movies added using the regular method of embedding objects still work on your Mac, anyone with a recent version of Windows likely won't be able to see it. Find more information at `developer.apple.com/quicktime/compatibility.html`.

Deciphering HTML Attributes

So what is all that junk I threw in there? Here's a breakdown of the tag attributes:

OBJECT CLASSID: To work properly under Windows, a QuickTime movie must be defined as an object. The CLASSID value identifies the content as a QuickTime movie.

WIDTH and **HEIGHT:** These values tell the browser the width and height of your movie in pixels.

CODEBASE: This URL gives Internet Explorer for Windows some necessary information about the QuickTime format.

PARAM: This is a parameter of the object, which consists of a name and a value. SRC is the URL that points to your movie file; AUTOPLAY tells the browser whether to automatically play the movie when it loads (in this case "true" means yes); CONTROLLER tells the browser whether to display the QuickTime controller beneath the movie (in this case "false" means no).

EMBED: This is the tag that actually puts your QuickTime movie on the page. It includes the same attributes as PARAM, though in a slightly more compact fashion. A Web page that contains only this tag will display the movie correctly in all Web browsers except Internet Explorer 5.5 and later for Windows.

PLUGINSPAGE: This tells the browser where to go in the event that the QuickTime plug-in is not installed.

</EMBED> and **</OBJECT>:** These are closing tags, indicating the end of the commands.

To embed the movie on a page:

- In your HTML editing application, enter the following code where you want the movie to appear. Be sure to change the two instances of `sample.mov` to your actual filename, plus the two instances where the width and height are defined.

```
<OBJECT CLASSID="clsid:02BF25D5-8C17-
4B23-BC80-D3488ABDDC6B" WIDTH="160"
HEIGHT="144"
CODEBASE="http://www.apple.com/
qtactivex/qtplugin.cab">
<PARAM name="SRC" VALUE="sample.mov">
<PARAM name="AUTOPLAY" VALUE="true">
<PARAM name="CONTROLLER"
VALUE="false">
<EMBED SRC="sample.mov" WIDTH="160"
HEIGHT="144" AUTOPLAY="true"
CONTROLLER="false" PLUGINSPAGE=
"http://www.apple.com/quicktime/
download/">
</EMBED>
</OBJECT>
```

Note that the unintelligible gobbledygook following "CLASSID=" must be entered exactly as shown; it's required for viewing the page properly in Microsoft Internet Explorer 5.5 and later under Windows (see the sidebar on the previous page).

Creating a Poster Movie

Accessing a QuickTime movie on the Web introduces one big problem: whether you link to it directly or embed it onto a page, the entire movie begins downloading. Depending on the size of the movie, this could slow your browser or other Internet applications while the movie is being fetched.

As an alternative, create a poster movie, which displays a one-frame movie that your visitors can click to initiate the download. (Sometimes this can be frustrating: I've clicked on links expecting the movie to load in the background while I'm working on something else, only to realize that I needed to then click the poster movie to get the download started. Still, at least this route gives the visitor the option to start the movie at her convenience.) The poster movie has the added benefit of preloading the Quick-Time plug-in before the movie starts.

Creating a poster movie involves two steps: creating the one-frame movie using Quick-Time Player (the Pro version), then adjusting the EMBED tag in the HTML to properly handle it.

To create the poster movie:

1. Open your movie in QuickTime Player.
2. Use the movie control buttons or the location indicator to find a frame you'd like to use as the poster movie's image (**Figure 15.19**).
3. Choose Copy from the Edit menu, or press Command-C. This copies the selected frame.
4. Create a new movie by choosing New (Command-N) from the File menu.

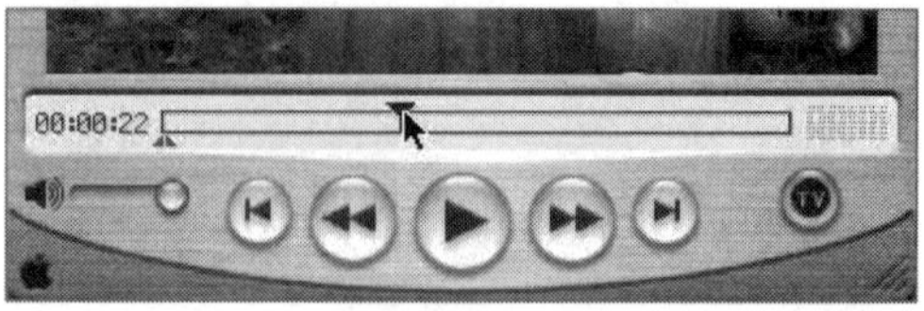

Figure 15.19 Use the Playhead in QuickTime Player to locate the frame you'd like to use for the poster movie.

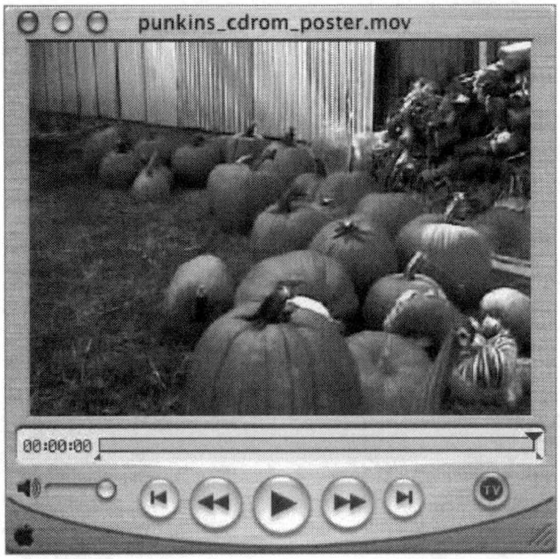

Figure 15.20 To make the poster movie work, your one frame needs to be saved as a QuickTime movie, not an individual image format like TIFF or JPEG.

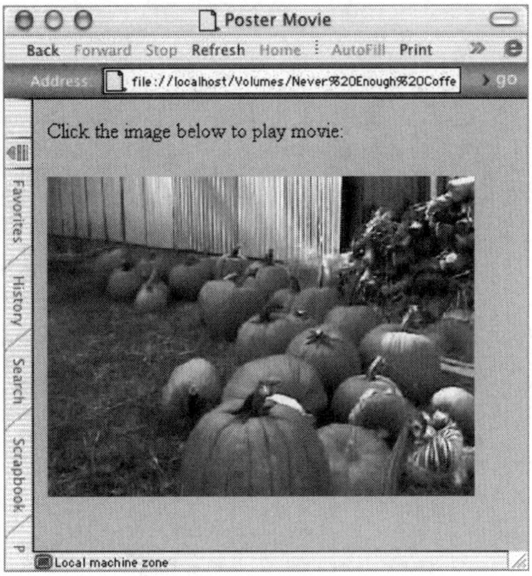

Figure 15.21 The end result is a single image that shows up in place of the movie, but one you can click to immediately begin playing the movie.

5. Choose Paste (Command-V) from the Edit menu. Your copied frame appears as its own one-frame movie (**Figure 15.20**).
6. Save the movie with a distinctive name, such as "punkins_cdrom_poster.mov" (to use my example).

To embed the poster movie:

1. In your HTML editor, type the code you used to embed the movie (shown two pages back).
2. In the EMBED tag, add the HREF and TARGET attributes (underlined):

```
<EMBED SRC="sample_poster.mov"
WIDTH="160" HEIGHT="144"
AUTOPLAY="true"
CONTROLLER="false" HREF="sample.mov"
TARGET="myself" PLUGINSPAGE=
"http://www.apple.com/quicktime/
download/">
```

   The HREF tag tells the browser to first load the poster movie, while the TARGET tag instructs it to play the real movie in the same space as the poster movie when clicked.
3. Save and upload your files. When you view them in a Web browser, the poster image shows up first (**Figure 15.21**).

✔ Tips

- If you're seeing only half of the movie controller, add 15 to the height values in the OBJECT and EMBED tags.
- Be sure the controller attributes are set to "false," or else you'll see a controller in the poster movie, which can be confusing. Viewers might click the controller to play the movie, which works—but only plays the one frame.
- It's a good idea to include instructions near the poster movie that say something like, "Click to play movie."

16

Exporting to DVD

My father has amassed a fairly large videotape collection over the past several years. So you can imagine that he's done a fair bit of eye-rolling as DVD discs have quickly gained in popularity, because now he has to decide whether he wants to begin building a DVD collection, too.

It's going to be a hard sell to hold on to old VHS tapes. The single advantage videotape holds is that VHS players are still much more common than DVD players. But that won't be the case for long.

DVD has several key advantages over VHS. The discs are smaller than videotapes, their image and sound quality are much better, and discs don't degrade over time (at least, not remotely as fast as tape, a fact you're no doubt aware of if you have an aging wedding or graduation video sitting on a shelf). And DVDs are interactive: jump to your favorite scene in a movie; play a director's commentary while watching a movie; or, in the case of making and playing iMovie videos, store several movies on one disc that can be accessed without fast-forwarding (and rewinding, then fast-forwarding again as you try to find selected clips on a tape).

This chapter explains how you can easily export your footage from iMovie and bring it into the equally easy-to-use iDVD software.

Creating Chapter Markers

When you watch a feature movie on DVD, you usually have the option of skipping to specific scenes, or chapters. If you're going to export your movie to iDVD, you can set up chapter markers in iMovie that iDVD imports as chapters, saving you time when you build your DVD project.

To create a chapter marker:

1. Place the Playhead at the point that you'd like to set as a marker.
2. Switch to iMovie's iDVD pane.
3. Click the Add Chapter button; a thumbnail of the current frame appears in the iDVD Chapter Markers list (**Figure 16.1**), and a yellow diamond appears in the Timeline Viewer (**Figure 16.2**).
4. iMovie inserts the name of the current clip as the chapter name. If you want to call it something else, type a new name into the highlighted field.

✔ Tips

- With a chapter highlighted in the iDVD pane, hit Return, Enter, or Tab to select the next chapter in the list.
- You can't move a chapter marker to a new time location. Instead, simply create a new marker at the new location and delete the old marker.
- Highlighting chapters in the iDVD pane is a fast way to reposition the Playhead in long movie projects.

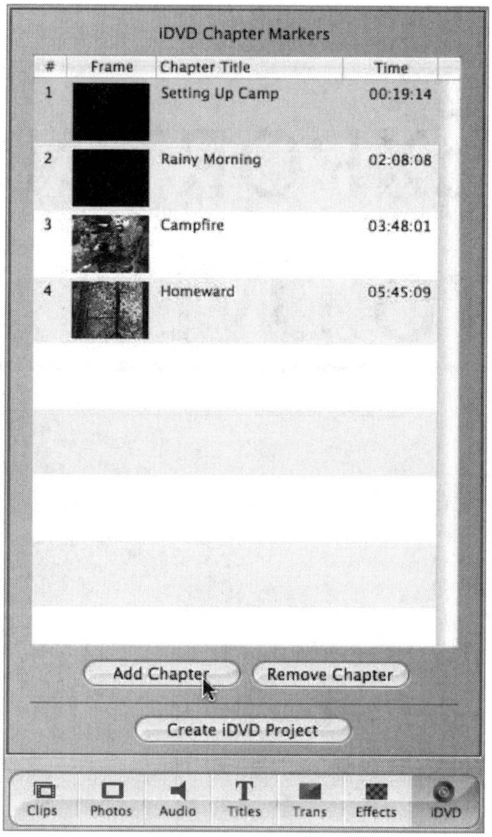

Figure 16.1 Click the Add Chapter button to create a new iDVD chapter marker.

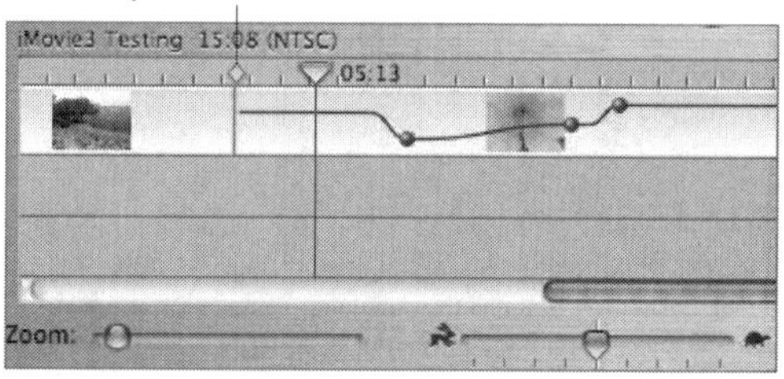

Figure 16.2 iDVD chapter markers appear in the Timeline as yellow diamonds.

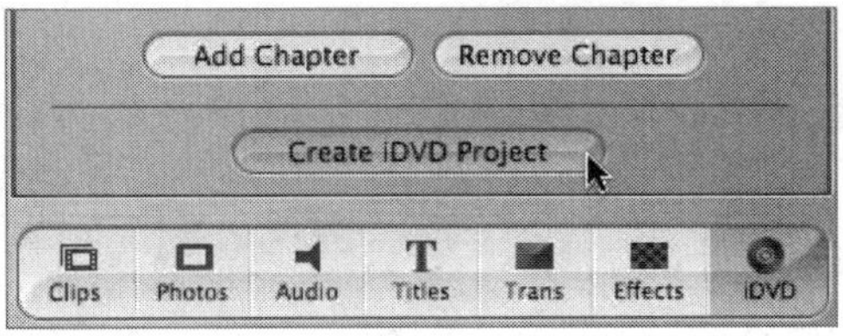

Figure 16.3 Click the Create iDVD Project button to send your movie to iDVD 3.

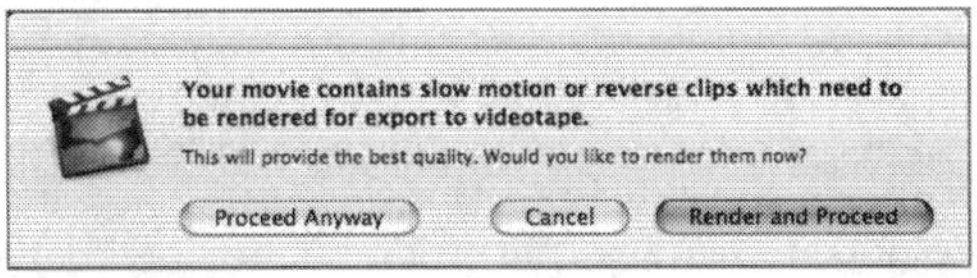

Figure 16.4 iMovie gives you the option of rendering clips that need it before sending the movie to iDVD 3.

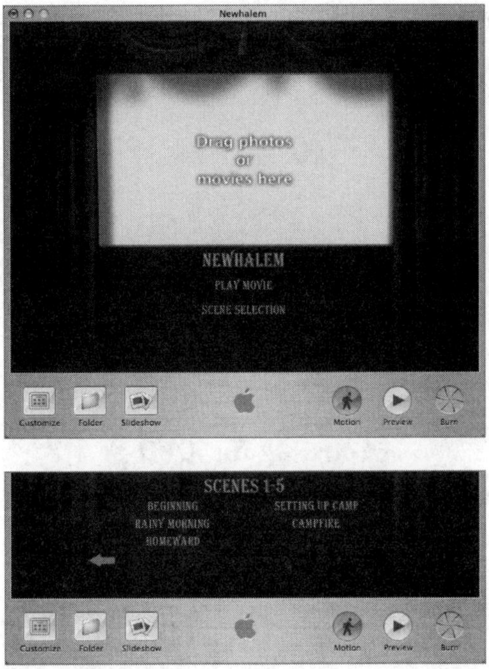

Figure 16.5 The new iDVD project includes an option to play your entire movie (top), or you can access the chapters you created by double-clicking the Scene Selection option (bottom).

Creating an iDVD 3 Project

Apple expects that at some point everyone will have a Mac equipped with a DVD-R drive (DVD-Recordable, which Apple calls a SuperDrive). If you do own one of these machines, you can use iDVD.

However, iDVD 3 will only run on a Super-Drive-equipped Mac running Mac OS X 10.2 or later—that excludes comparable systems without SuperDrives, even if you own a third-party DVD burner.

To create an iDVD 3 project:

1. Click the iDVD button under the Shelf to switch to the iDVD pane.
2. Click the Create iDVD Project button (**Figure 16.3**).

   If any clips in your movie are sped up, slowed down, or reversed, iMovie displays a dialog with the option to render the clips (**Figure 16.4**), which redraws them at a higher quality than the preview you see during normal playback. If you choose the Proceed Anyway option, those clips may flicker or otherwise look bad when you play back the DVD. Similarly, if the project isn't saved, iMovie gives you that option, too.

   When those steps are completed, iMovie launches iDVD 3 (if it's not already running), and switches to it (**Figure 16.5**).

✔ Tip

- iMovie 3's DVD integration works only with iDVD 3. If you don't own iDVD 3, or don't have a system that will support it, iMovie displays a warning dialog. You will need to export your movie first; see "Exporting for iDVD 2" on the next page.

Exporting Movies for DVD

Using the Create iDVD Project button is the easiest method of turning your movie into a DVD project, but it's not the only option. You can export QuickTime files that can be added to an iDVD project.

To export for DVD:

1. Choose Export from iMovie's File menu.
2. In the iMovie: Export dialog box, choose To QuickTime from the Export popup menu (**Figure 16.6**). Choosing To iDVD gives you no options.
3. From the Formats popup menu, choose Full Quality DV.
4. Click the Export button to export the movie.
5. Name the movie file and choose a location, then click the Save button. iMovie saves it as a DV-formatted QuickTime movie.

✔ Tip

- The file created by this operation is a self-contained QuickTime file, which means all the video and audio is present in the single file. That's the best method to use if you need to transport the movie file to another computer. However, if you're using iDVD on your own machine, it's easier to grab the QuickTime movie that's created in your project's folder in the Finder. Although that file is a reference movie, which points to the content in your Media folder, you can drag it into iDVD just as if it were a self-contained QuickTime movie.

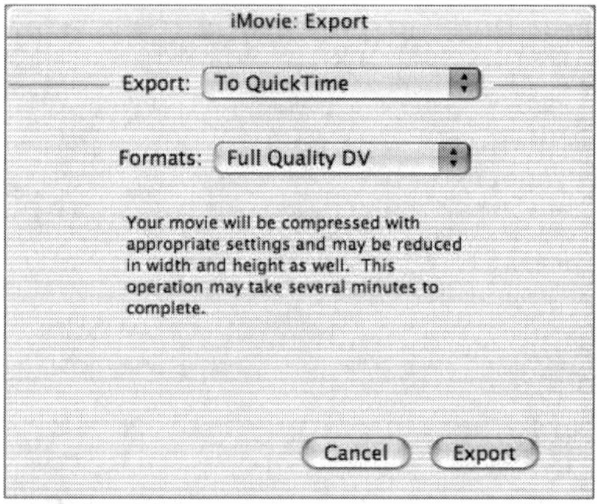

Figure 16.6 Choose the Full Quality DV option to export a movie that can be used with iDVD 2.

Exporting for iDVD 2

My original PowerBook G4 had no SuperDrive, so I couldn't install iDVD on that machine. Instead, I exported my iMovie projects as QuickTime files using the steps on this page, then used the files to build a DVD on a friend's SuperDrive-equipped Mac. This technique also applies to SuperDrive owners using iDVD 2 who choose not to upgrade to iDVD 3. You lose the capability to set chapter markers, but it's cheaper than buying a new Mac or iDVD 3.

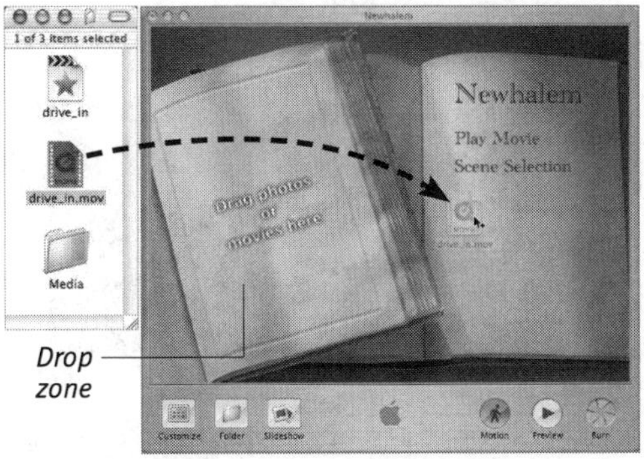

Figure 16.7 Simply drag a project's reference movie to iDVD to add it to an iDVD project. Avoid the drop zone unless your movie is meant as an interface addition.

How to Add Chapters to an Existing iDVD Project

My wife and I worked on a vacation video using two different Macs, which meant that we had multiple iMovie projects—one for each day of the vacation. When it came time to create a DVD, I hit a stumbling block: once you've created an iDVD project, any new movies you import aren't included when you select the Play Movie option. So, our multi-part movie could only be accessed one day at a time. Ick.

The solution is to combine the separate iMovie projects into one, then use the combo movie as the basis for the iDVD project. Unfortunately, you'll have to redefine any iDVD chapter markers that were set up separately.

Open a new iMovie project, then drag the other projects' reference movies to the Clips pane or directly to the Timeline. Set up chapter markers, switch to the iDVD pane, and click the Create iDVD Project button.

Adding Movies to an Existing iDVD Project

With your movie exported as a DV-format QuickTime file, you have two ways to add it to an existing iDVD project.

To add a movie to an existing iDVD project (option 1):

1. Choose Import from iDVD's File menu, then select Video from the submenu that appears.
2. Locate the QuickTime file you exported from iMovie and click Open. The new movie appears in the iDVD window.

To add a movie to an existing iDVD project (option 2):

- Drag and drop the QuickTime file from iDVD's Movies pane or from the Finder onto the iDVD window. Make sure you don't drag the file onto a drop zone (marked with the words "Drag photos or movies here"), or else the movie will appear only as an interface element (**Figure 16.7**).

✔ Tip

- Here's another reason to use an iMovie project's reference movie (see tip on previous page) instead of exporting a self-contained QuickTime movie: dragging a reference movie to iDVD creates a new folder for that movie, including any chapter markers that have been defined. But more important, this is the only way to be able to include a Play Movie option that can play through the entire movie, in addition to keeping the chapters intact.

Editing and Burning in iDVD

If you think iMovie is easy to master, wait until you spend five minutes with iDVD. Since this isn't an iDVD book, I won't go into too many specifics, but this should get you started.

To edit a project in iDVD:

1. In iMovie, switch to the iDVD pane and click Create iDVD Project.
2. Select a theme by clicking the Customize button and choosing one from the Themes pane that pops out from the left side of the main window (**Figure 16.8**).
3. Click the title in the main screen and retype a new one if you want.
4. If you want to add other movies to your project, switch to iDVD's Movies pane or position the iDVD window so that you can see the movie files you wish to add in the Finder.
5. Drag and drop a movie file to the iDVD window (**Figure 16.9**).
6. Click the name of your imported movie and type a new name if you want (which is better than having movies named "movie.mov").
7. If you want to add a movie preview or still images to themes that support them, drag a movie or image file to the theme's drop zone.
8. (This is my favorite feature.) If the theme includes movie thumbnails (such as Portfolio Color, for example), click one and drag the Playhead that appears above it to choose a frame to be used as the movie's thumbnail (**Figure 16.10**). If you want the movie to play in the preview, click the Movie button. You're not stuck

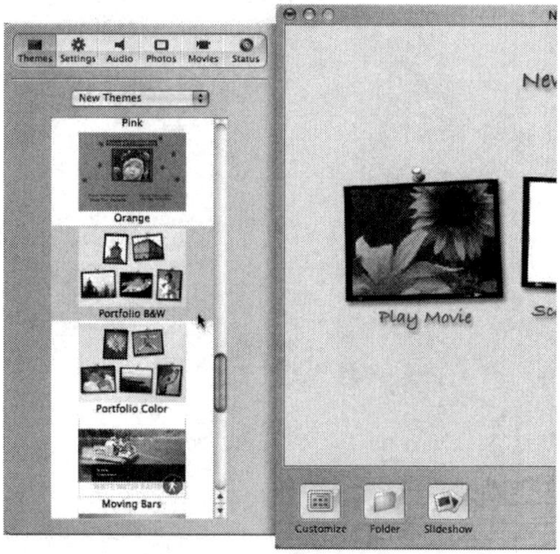

Figure 16.8 Click the Customize button to display iDVD's panes. The Themes pane includes a number of professionally designed templates to use.

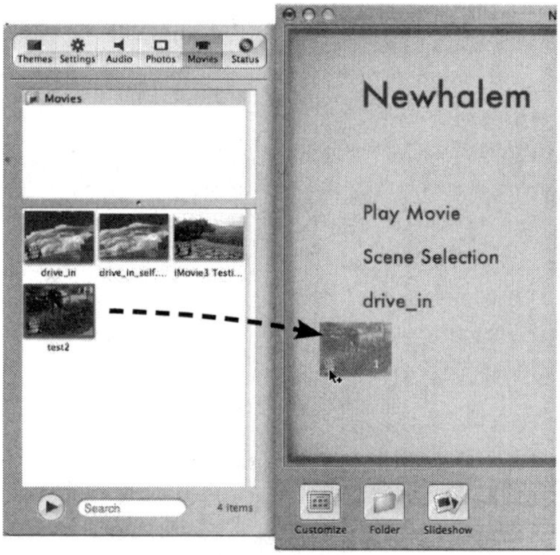

Figure 16.9 Additional movies can be dragged from the Movies pane in iDVD.

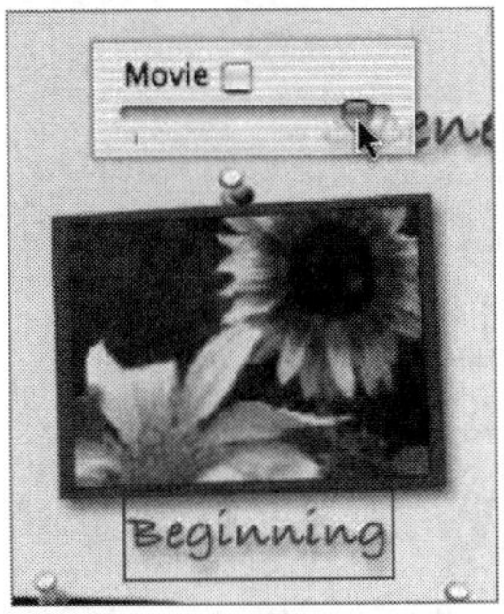

Figure 16.10 When you click a movie, you can set its thumbnail image by dragging the Playhead to the frame you want to use.

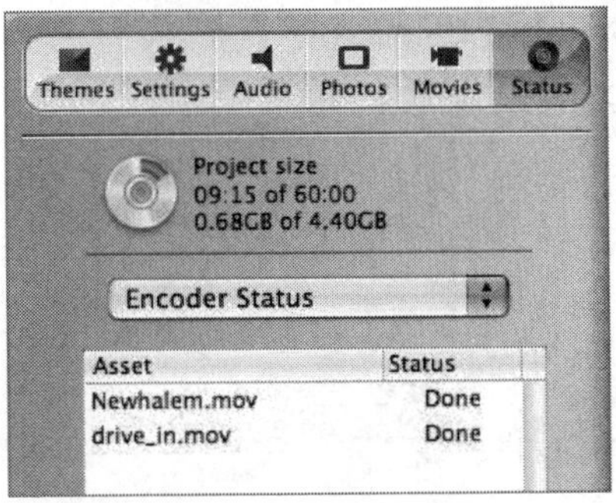

Figure 16.11 The Status pane shows how much space will be used on the disc, and which files are used by the project.

DVD Data Burn

This chapter focuses on using iDVD to put together a project of your movies, but iDVD isn't required if you want to simply store your movies on a DVD disc. The Mac OS features the capability to drag QuickTime movies (and any other type of file) to a DVD disc for high-capacity storage. When you insert the disc into your Mac, you can play the movies in the QuickTime Player. If you take this route, however, you can't view the movies in a consumer DVD player.

with the first frame of your movie (which is often just an empty frame)—and best of all, you don't have to export a frame from iMovie, modify it in an image editing application, and bring it back in to use as a still image.

iDVD keeps track of how much time your project is occupying via iDVD's Status pane (**Figure 16.11**).

To burn the DVD disc:

1. When your project is ready to go, be sure to save it, then choose Burn DVD from the File menu, or click the Burn button.
2. Insert a blank DVD disc in your Mac's SuperDrive. The burning process takes approximately twice as long as the combined length of your movies.

✔ Tips

- Click the Preview button to see how the DVD will appear in a DVD player. This step is a must before you irreversibly burn a DVD disc.
- Although you'll get better image quality by importing DV-formatted QuickTime movies into iDVD, you can drag any QuickTime movie into your project. Just remember that movies with more compression won't appear as sharp—but at the same time, if you're willing to sacrifice a little quality, you can store more movies on a single DVD disc.
- iDVD can also create slideshows of photos and still images (such as artwork), using the same drag-and-drop approach, or in conjunction with iPhoto 2.
- Be sure you use *DVD-R* discs, not DVD-RW or DVD+R when burning discs that will be played on consumer DVD players.

Playing the DVD

With your DVD created, your work is done and it's time to enjoy the project.

To play the DVD disc in a consumer DVD player:

Insert the disc into your DVD player and push the Play button. Use the remote control to select which movies to play.

To play the DVD disc on your Mac:

1. Insert the DVD disc in your DVD-ROM drive or SuperDrive-equipped Mac.
2. Depending on how your computer is configured, the DVD Player software may load automatically when the disc is inserted. If it doesn't, locate and launch DVD Player (**Figure 16.12**).
3. Click the Play button on the DVD Player's floating Controller, or choose Play from the Controls menu (**Figure 16.13**).

✔ Tips

- To turn off your Mac's preference to automatically launch DVD Player when a DVD disc is inserted, go to the CDs & DVDs pane of System Preferences. Choose a different behavior from the popup menu labeled "When You Insert a Video DVD."
- You can play the DVD on PCs running Windows, too. The steps for launching the player software and viewing a disc should be similar.

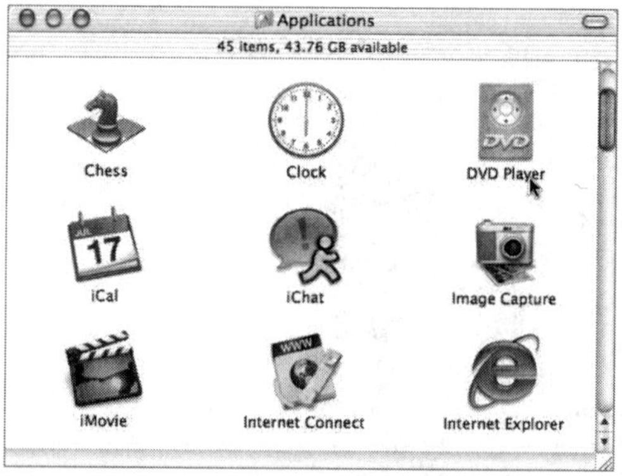

Figure 16.12 If DVD Player doesn't start up when you insert a DVD disc, locate the program in your Applications folder. Double-click its icon to launch it.

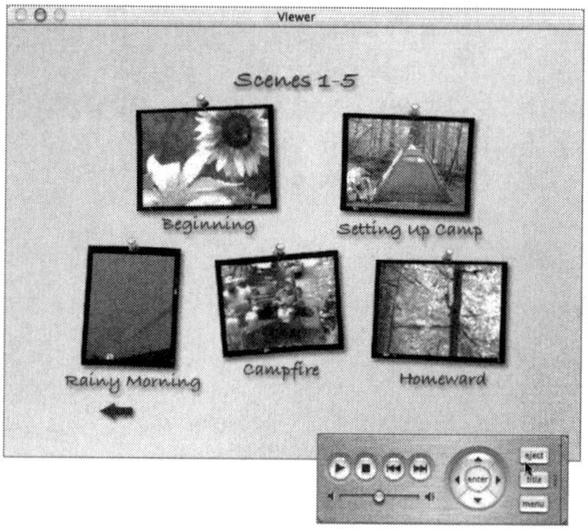

Figure 16.13 Use the floating controller to begin playing your DVD. You can then navigate the interface with your mouse to click on specific movies.

A

Troubleshooting

No software is ever perfect, and unfortunately iMovie 3 has more than its fair share of "challenges," as an optimistic friend of mine likes to say. It would be easy to say that Apple released it too early, or just didn't perform the type of quality control that one would expect—but some iMovie 3 users report none of the problems that other people are running into.

As of this writing, Apple has released three updates since the introduction of iMovie 3.0, which have made strides toward improving performance and fixing bugs. So, my first bit of troubleshooting advice is to make sure you're running the latest version of iMovie; check the iMovie page at Apple's Web site (`www.apple.com/imovie/`) or run Software Update (in your System Preferences).

Also, check Apple's online support discussion forums (`http://discussions.info.apple.com/webx/iMovie`) to see if other users have found solutions or workarounds to a problem you may be experiencing. iMovie users make up a dedicated community, and I owe a great debt to many folks online who have prodded the program to find answers.

Finally, and perhaps most important—give Apple feedback (`http://www.apple.com/feedback/imovie.html`). It's the best way to communicate what needs fixing.

Troubleshooting Performance

iMovie 3 seems to prefer lots of memory and fast processors, but even on powerful Macs it can be sluggish. Try the following suggestions to improve performance.

Make iMovie Window Smaller

Use the resize handle on the bottom-right corner of the iMovie window to make it as small as it will go.

Quit Other Running Applications

This frees up more memory for iMovie to use. Although Mac OS X manages memory better, I've seen iMovie gain some pep if it's not competing with other processes.

Remove Third-Party Plug-ins

Try paring iMovie down to its essentials. Remove any third-party plug-ins, such as those from a version of iMovie 2 that you upgraded to iMovie 3, from `[Home]/Library/iMovie/` (they may also be in a `Plug-ins` folder in that iMovie folder, too).

Trash iMovie Preferences

If the iMovie preferences have become corrupted, it places a load on the program's operation. iMovie re-creates the files it needs the next time you launch the program.

To trash iMovie preferences:

1. Quit iMovie. (You may want to quit all running applications, too.)
2. Go to your preferences folder at `Users/[YourUserName]/Library/Preferences/iMovie/`, and delete the following files (you may not have all three):
   - iMovie Preferences
   - com.apple.imovie.plist
   - com.apple.iMovie3.plist

Common Problems and Hope for the Future

Some people have run into problems in iMovie 3 when working with projects that were created in iMovie 2. Try creating a new iMovie 3 project from scratch, then import any footage from tape or from the old project's Media folder to see if performance improves.

Others have reported stability and slowness issues with long projects, typically 30 minutes or longer. If you're seeing the same things, try breaking up your movie into smaller projects when editing. (See Chapter 14 for steps on how to combine movie segments.)

Realize, too, that iMovie 3 has problems that aren't fixed by clever workarounds. I see dropped frames, stuttery playback, and audio popping that will most certainly require work by Apple to correct. Given that iMovie is one of the crowning components of iLife, it's just a matter of time before we see improvement.

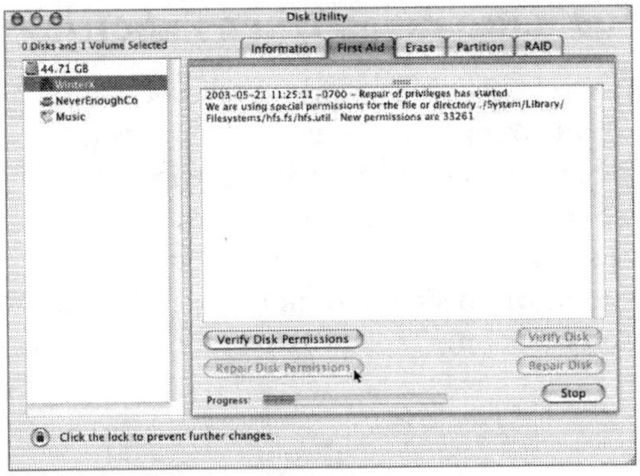

Figure A.1 Repair disk permissions using the Disk Utility tool to help improve performance.

Launch iApps in Order

Some people have reported success by launching the iLife applications in the following order: iTunes, iPhoto, iMovie, iDVD. I haven't noticed a difference on my system, but it's worth a try.

Repair Mac OS X Permissions

For whatever reason, some of the thousands of files that Mac OS X relies on wind up with improper permissions. I've found that fixing permissions is often a good general cure-all for when my Mac starts getting flaky.

To repair Mac OS X permissions:

1. Open Disk Utility, which is located within the Utilities folder of your Applications folder.
2. Select your main hard disk (your "boot drive") from the list at left.
3. Switch to the First Aid tab.
4. Click the Repair Disk Permissions button (**Figure A.1**). The process can take several minutes.

Fix Mac OS X Prebindings

Mac OS X employs a system of "prebindings" to help speed up tasks like application launching. As a last resort, try the following.

To fix Mac OS X Prebindings:

1. Launch Terminal (located in the Utilities folder).
2. Type `sudo update_prebinding -root /`, and press Return.
3. Enter your administrator password, then press Return. The task can take between 10 and 20 minutes.

Troubleshooting Video

The following are some video-related issues that have cropped up.

Frames Saved as JPEG Are Cropped

When you save a frame to disk as a JPEG file, the right side of the image is cropped. To get around this (using an admittedly lengthy and wonky process), export your video to QuickTime using the Full Quality DV setting, then open the QuickTime movie in the QuickTime Player application. Locate the frame you want using the scrubber bar and choose Export from the File menu. At the bottom of the Save Exported File As dialog box, set the Export popup menu to Movie to Picture, and set the Use popup menu to Photo-JPEG, then click the Save button.

Imported Image Files Turn White

If pictures are turning white, try cropping them in iPhoto, then using the Pictures pane in iMovie to bring them into your project.

Also, the PICT format isn't supported well in iMovie 3. Convert your PICT image files to JPEG in an image editing program before importing them into iMovie.

Troubleshooting Audio

Unfortunately, iMovie 3's audio seems to experience the most—or just most frustrating—problems.

Video and Audio Out of Sync

If your audio and video are out of sync in a video clip, try extracting the clip's audio track, which locks the audio to the video (see Chapter 10).

Audio Problems When Exporting

Are audio fades not working after you export your movie? Or perhaps clips you had marked as silent are still playing after export? The fix seems to be to have one clip selected in the Timeline when you export your movie, believe it or not. Hopefully, this (and other bugs) will be fixed soon.

B

RESOURCES

Essential Information

Apple iMovie

http://www.apple.com/imovie/

iMovie 3 for Mac OS X: Visual QuickStart Guide companion Web site

http://www.necoffee.com/imovievqs/

Canon Digital Camcorders

http://www.canondv.com/

Sony Digital Camcorders

http://www.sonystyle.com/digitalimaging/H_Camcorders.shtml

JVC Digital Camcorders

http://www.jvc.com/

Panasonic Digital Camcorders

http://www.panasonic.com/consumer_electronics/camcorder/

Recommended Books

The Computer Videomaker Handbook, by the editors of *Computer Videomaker Magazine* (Focal Press, 2001)

http://www.videomaker.com/

continues next page

***FireWire Filmmaking*, Scott Smith (Peachpit Press, 2002)**

***The Little Digital Video Book*, Michael Rubin (Peachpit Press, 2001)**

***Real World Digital Video*, Pete Shaner and Gerald Everett Jones (Peachpit Press, 2003)**

***The Macintosh iLife*, Jim Heid (Peachpit Press, 2003)**

`http://www.peachpit.com/`

Online Tutorials and Reference

Cyber Film School

`http://www.cyberfilmschool.com/`

DVcreators.net

`http://www.dvcreators.net/`

2-pop.com

`http://www.2-pop.com/`

Post Forum

`http://www.postforum.com/`

The "Unofficial" iMovie FAQ

`http://www.danslagle.com/mac/imovie/iMovieFAQ.html`

Audio Editing Applications

SmartSound Movie Maestro

`http://www.smartsound.com/`

Coaster

`http://www.visualclick.de/products/coaster/index.html`

SoundApp

`http://www.spies.com/~franke/SoundApp/`

SndSampler

`http://www.sndsampler.com/`

Other iMovie-Related Software

Still Life

http://www.grantedsw.com/still-life/

Moving Picture

http://www.smartsound.com/

Royalty-Free Audio Clips

Freeplay Music

http://www.freeplaymusic.com/

Killer Sound, Inc.

http://www.killersound.com/

Sound Dogs

http://www.sounddogs.com/

iMovie Plug-ins

eZedia

http://www.ezedia.com/

GeeThree

http://www.geethree.com/

Virtix

http://www.virtix.com/

Stupendous Software

http://www.stupendous-software.com/

INDEX

D

INDEX

INDEX

INDEX

K

L

M

INDEX

Q

R

S

U

V

W

Y

Z